Defending Qualitative Research

Focussing on the phases of qualitative research which precede and follow fieldwork – design, analysis, and textualization – this book offers new theoretical tools to tackle one of the most common criticisms advanced against qualitative research: its presumed lack of rigour. Rejecting the notion of "rigour" as formulated in quantitative research and based on the theory of probability, it proposes a theoretical frame that allows combining the goals of rigour and that of creativity through the reference to theory of argumentation. As such, it will appeal to scholars and students across the social sciences with interests in qualitative research methods.

Mario Cardano is Full Professor of the Qualitative Methods for Social Research and the Sociology of Health at the Department of Cultures, Politics and Society, University of Turin, Italy.

Routledge Advances in Research Methods

Dialectics, Power, and Knowledge Construction in Qualitative Research
Beyond Dichotomy
Adital Ben-Ari and Guy Enosh

Researching Social Problems
Edited by Amir Marvasti and A. Javier Treviño

Action Research in a Relational Perspective
Dialogue, Reflexivity, Power and Ethics
Edited by Lone Hersted, Ottar Ness and Søren Frimann

Situated Writing as Theory and Method
The Untimely Academic Novella
Mona Livholts

Foundations and Practice of Research
Adventures with Dooyeweerd's Philosophy
Andrew Basden

Gambling, Losses and Self-Esteem
An Interactionist Approach to the Betting Shop
Cormac Mc Namara

Institutional Ethnography in the Nordic Region
Edited by Rebecca W. B. Lund and Ann Christin E. Nilsen

Freedom of Information and Social Science Research Design
Edited by Kevin Walby and Alex Luscombe

Defending Qualitative Research
Design, Analysis and Textualization
Mario Cardano

For more information about this series, please visit: www.routledge.com/Routledge-Advances-in-Research-Methods/book-series/RARM

Defending Qualitative Research
Design, Analysis, and Textualization

Mario Cardano

LONDON AND NEW YORK

First published 2020
by Routledge
2 Park Square, Milton Park, Abingdon, Oxon OX14 4RN

and by Routledge
52 Vanderbilt Avenue, New York, NY 10017

Routledge is an imprint of the Taylor & Francis Group, an informa business

© 2020 Mario Cardano

The right of Mario Cardano to be identified as author of this work has been asserted by him in accordance with sections 77 and 78 of the Copyright, Designs and Patents Act 1988.

All rights reserved. No part of this book may be reprinted or reproduced or utilised in any form or by any electronic, mechanical, or other means, now known or hereafter invented, including photocopying and recording, or in any information storage or retrieval system, without permission in writing from the publishers.

Trademark notice: Product or corporate names may be trademarks or registered trademarks, and are used only for identification and explanation without intent to infringe.

British Library Cataloguing-in-Publication Data
A catalogue record for this book is available from the British Library

Library of Congress Cataloging-in-Publication Data
Names: Cardano, Mario, author.
Title: Defending qualitative research : design, analysis and textualization / Mario Cardano.
Description: Abingdon, Oxon ; New York, NY : Routledge, 2020. | Series: Routledge advances in research methods | Includes bibliographical references and index.
Identifiers: LCCN 2019049351 (print) | LCCN 2019049352 (ebook) | ISBN 9781138614055 (hbk) | ISBN 9780429464232 (ebk)
Subjects: LCSH: Research—Methodology. | Qualitative research.
Classification: LCC H62 .C34132 2020 (print) | LCC H62 (ebook) | DDC 001.4/2—dc23
LC record available at https://lccn.loc.gov/2019049351
LC ebook record available at https://lccn.loc.gov/2019049352

ISBN: 978-1-138-61405-5 (hbk)
ISBN: 978-0-429-46423-2 (ebk)

Typeset in Times New Roman
by Apex CoVantage, LLC

Printed and bound in Great Britain by
TJ International Ltd, Padstow, Cornwall

To my sons, Andrea and Emilio

Contents

List of figures	viii
Acknowledgements	ix
Introduction	1
1 A premise about two crucial issues: invisibility and method	7
2 Qualitative research: a portrait	26
3 The theory-of-argumentation survival kit	45
4 The qualitative research design	64
5 On qualitative data analysis	112
6 The textualization	143
Index	161

Figures

1.1	Membership of the set of adults in bimodal logic	18
1.2	Membership of the set of adults in multimodal or fuzzy logic	18
2.1	Islands in the archipelago: a map of qualitative methods	33
4.1	Relevance of a research question for sociology and society	68
4.2	Reciprocal adaptations among research question, empirical context, and method	70
4.3	Partition of the property space of nurses working in an acute psychiatric ward	73
4.4	Four strategies to obtain information-rich cases	76
4.5	Assumption of linearity in the most different systems design	85
4.6	Profile of the three cases compared in the Kuhn study on Ethnic Mobilization against Resource Extraction	91
4.7	Sample design for study of deconversion from Italian New Religious Movements: an example of proleptic argumentation application	99
4.8	Sample design for a study of deconversion from Italian New Religious Movements	100
5.1	Comparison between two stylized versions of asking questions relates to three properties, in quantitative and qualitative research	115
5.2	Researcher agency impact on the action observed and on its portrayal	119
5.3	Hypothetical matrix on Doctor Venice's psychiatric clinical interviews	133
6.1	Double description through the geometrical representation of the binomial square	150

Acknowledgements

In writing this book, I have contracted numerous intellectual debts that I cannot repay even with these words of acknowledgement. Many of the ideas proposed in this book germinated during my teaching activity in the classes of Qualitative Methods in the master's degree in sociology of my university and in the seminars I hold with the students of the PhD school in Sociology and Methodology of Social Research (SOMET), held jointly by the University of Turin and the University of Milan. With these students, I tested many of the ideas presented here, receiving important advice on how to define them better. Among my students, the ones who have recently obtained their master's degree or their PhD were particularly helpful in defining my points. So, I would like to thank Michele Cioffi, Eleni Koutsogeorgou, Martina Panzarasa, Valeria Quaglia, Eleonora Rossero, and Alice Scavarda. In recent years, I have discussed my obsession with the marriage between qualitative research and the theory of argumentation with the colleagues who, together with me, are part of the Qualitative Research Lab, based in my university. Thank you to Claudio Baraldi, Marinella Belluati, Sonia Bertolini, Rita Bichi, Elisa Bignante, Nicoletta Bosco, Roberta Bosisio, Carlo Capello, Cristopher Cepernich, Enzo Colombo, Raffaella Ferrero Camoletto, Annalisa Frisina, Luigi Gariglio, Carlo Genova, Rossella Ghigi, Giampietro Gobo, Antonella Meo, Manuela Naldini, Manuela Olagnero, Domenico Perrotta, Barbara Poggio, Paola Sacchi, Roberta Sassatelli, and Giovanni Semi. During my stay, as a visiting scholar, at the Brasilian University of Pelotas, I had the opportunity to discuss many points of my methodological research, receiving valuable comments and suggestions. So I am happy to thank my colleague Luciane Prado Kantorski, her colleagues, and her students for their attention to my work. Just in the middle of my last writing effort, I was invited by the Faculty for Social Wellbeing of Malta University for a three-day workshop on ethnography and qualitative research. The workshop gave me the chance to discuss my work in progress, so thank you to Ann-Marie Callus for inviting me, and thank you to her colleagues and students for the rich dialectical exchange. I have written this book during this sabbatical year. Thank you to the head of my department, Franca Roncarolo, and to my colleagues for allowing me to use this time to the greatest possible advantages. Before and during my writing, I reached out to a couple of colleagues to read my work, receiving relevant comments and suggestions. Thank you to Mariano

x   *Acknowledgements*

Longo and Martyn Hammersley. I asked some colleagues to read the first draft of some chapters, getting precious suggestions. I am not sure that I was able to valorize all their comments, but I would like to thank Fabrizio Macagno, Iddo Tavory, and Luigi Gariglio. I am specially indebted to Luigi Gariglio, who besides being the only one who has so far read all the chapters of the book and giving me valuable advice, has always generously supported my efforts, encouraging my desire to be on the straight and narrow path. Thank you also to my wife, Carla Nanni, for her patience during the writing of this book and her attentive reading of the parts of the book whose clarity I doubted. Two kind, experienced Routledge editors, Neil Jordan and Alice Salt, helped greatly. Thank you both. Finally, thank you to Eunan Sheridan for his competent and painstaking revision of my English. The usual disclaimers apply.

Introduction

Qualitative research is one of the most widespread approaches in social research, particularly among the youngest generation of scholars. However, this way of doing research still receives pungent criticisms of the soundness of its results and, even more bitter, of the possibility of their generalization (Gobo 2008). All these reprimands are frequently framed within a more general criticism that refers to qualitative research's lack of rigour, moving from the tacit idea that the only possible form of rigour is that of quantitative research based, according to John Goldthorpe, on the "logic of inference" (Goldthorpe 2000: 67, 88).

The gist of this book is quite simple: qualitative research must be rigorous, but pursuing an idea of rigour different from the one that inspires quantitative research, an idea of rigour that promotes the intrinsic creativity of the "experience experiment" (Piasere 2002: 27) to which we commit ourselves in doing qualitative research. The logical frame that was proposed for this purpose is that of the theory of argumentation, mainly in the Canadian School version, inspired by the work of Douglas Walton. The general idea is that the theory of argumentation can perform, in qualitative research, the same function as the theory of probability does in quantitative research. The reference to the frame of argumentation theory allows – by the way – refining the meaning of the volume's title, *Defending Qualitative Research*. According to the theoretical sensitivity of this philosophical field, defending is meant more as the production of arguments to guarantee the soundness of our claims than as the practice of martial arts to be applied against the enemies of Qualitative Research. The book is focussed on what happens before and after the fieldwork. On fieldwork and data collection there are so many good handbooks that it is arduous to write something new. Attention is paid to qualitative research design, to the logical structure of data analysis and the process of textualization. All these phases are framed in the general process of producing a persuasive argument about the robustness of our research results and the conditions in which their scope can be extended. For this last aspect, the book proposes the notion of "conditional plausibility", thought of as the analogical equivalent, in the area of argumentative reasoning, of the conditional probability proper of statistical inference.

To mount a defence of qualitative research, I combine different analytical frames, with the theory of argumentation, the "evidential paradigm" (Ginzburg

2   Introduction

1978), the fuzzy set theory (Zadeh 1965), the Gregory Bateson notion of "double description" (Bateson 1979), with some elements of the theoretical reflections of my favourite contemporary philosophers Charles Sanders Pierce, Ludwig Wittgenstein, and Hans Gadamer. I hope that this assorted dish is palatable to the reader.

The book is organized in six chapters, all written combining analytical discussion with some research examples. The first chapter introduces some general premises for the main argument of the book – the defence of the soundness of qualitative research results – focussing on an aspect of our work hidden, like Poe's purloined letter, in the surface of our practices. The chapter tackles the issue of invisibility, the paradoxical situation that imposes upon us to observe the unobservable, to read, through the evidential paradigm the visible signs of, for example, values, beliefs, representations, and attitudes. This challenge commits both quantitative and qualitative research, but this last way of doing social research can count on a specific competitive advantage. To read people's minds, we need their cooperation, and qualitative research offers scholars the richest information about the degree of participants' cooperation, and so the richest information about the validity – borrowing the quantitative jargon – of our information.[1] Moving from this comparison between qualitative and quantitative research, Chapter 1 continues with a kind of synoptic reading of the communalities and differences between what I have called the two Muses of social research. The first chapter closes with a reflection on the notion of method that seems more appropriate to a postwar juxtaposition between qualitative and quantitative research. The notion proposed is borrowed from Gary Brent Madison's reflections. Madison offers a definition of method as a *set of principles* that receive a different interpretation according to the context in which they are applied, instead of a *collection of rules* that act as orders (Madison 1988: 28–29). These principles, guiding the method, are more like the ethical or juridical norms of jurisprudence than the laws of physics; principles for which there is no single correct application, but more than one, depending on context; principles whose application, not unlike a sentence handed down in court, must be defended with appropriate arguments.

The second chapter presents a concise portrait of qualitative research, recognizing three "family resemblances" (Wittgenstein 1953, English translation 1958 § 66–67), that crosses this heterogeneous archipelago. These common traits are three: i) the context-sensitivity of data collection procedures; ii) details-focalization; iii) the multivocality of the writing. The chapter goes on to outlining a map of this territory, taking into account Jorge Luis Borges's assertion (originally formulated by Alfred Korzybski) that the map is not the territory. The chapter closes with a critical presentation of the strength and the alleged weakness of qualitative research.

The third chapter offers, so to speak, a theory-of-argumentation survival kit. The chapter introduces the essential notions of the theory of argumentation requested to recognize its value for qualitative research. It gives an overview of this multidisciplinary field, then introduces the argumentative schemes approach elaborated by Douglas Walton, Chris Reed and Fabrizio Macagno (2008). Among the

Introduction   3

rich collection of schemes proposed by Walton and colleagues, a set was selected and adapted for the methodological purposes of the book. Thus, the reader will meet the argument from analogy, from signs, from position to know, the abductive argumentation scheme – the very engine of qualitative research (Tavory and Timmermans 2014) – and again, the argument from double hierarchy, that of irrelevant difference, that of relevant difference and finally the argument from radical otherness. Each of these arguments is equipped with specific critical questions meant as "pedagogical tools" (Godden and Walton 2007: 280) to improve the soundness of the reasoning. The dialectical dimension of the argumentation schemes is still present in the last tool proposed, the proleptic argumentation, very useful for any steps of qualitative research. The proleptic argumentation (Walton 2009) is a kind of argumentation in which the sequences of dialectical moves constitutive of a persuasive dialogue were advanced by one interlocutor only, who makes a claim, considers the possible objections to it, and reshapes his/her reasoning to defuse the objections considered.

The remaining chapters propose a set of tools to persuade the scientific community of the soundness of the findings acquired through qualitative research. The classic Aristotelian distinction between the means of persuasion is a good guide for my purposes. In Aristotle's *Rhetoric*, we can read:

> Rhetoric may be defined as the faculty of observing in any given case the available means of persuasion. . . . Of the modes of persuasion furnished by the spoken word there are three kinds. The first kind depends on the personal character of the speaker; the second on putting the audience into a certain frame of mind; the third on the proof, or apparent proof, provided by the words of the speech itself.
> (Aristotle Book I 1355b – 1356a, English translation 2015: 7–8)

According to Ricca Edmondson, these three main functions of persuasive argument – "ethos", "pathos", and "logos" – combined, offer the necessary robustness to our arguments (Edmondson 1984: Chapter 1). In her fascinating book, *Rhetoric in Sociology*, Edmondson proposes a convincing redefinition of the three Aristotelian functions that makes them more suitable for researching and writing in sociology. Edmondson redefines the "ethos" function, that which Aristotle attributed to the personal character of the speaker, as "self-presentation" (16). It implies the awareness that any argument must be considered as "someone's argument" (17) and that the personal characteristics of the researcher-author, his/her way of being in the field as well as in the world, contributes to the soundness of the argument proposed. The second Aristotelian mode of persuasion, "pathos", becomes in Edmondson's reflection "sensitisation", namely "putting the audience into a certain frame of mind . . . for the appropriate consideration of a particular argument" (17–18). A few lines later the author confers on this dimension of persuasion the faculty enabling in the reader the resonance (in Wikan's 1992 meaning) of the experience focussed in the argument. The third dimension, that of "logos", refers to the subject matter of discussion and the cognitive aspects

4   Introduction

of the construction of a persuasive argument. Chapters 4 and 5 tackle the logos dimension of argumentation. Chapter 6 elaborates on the two other dimensions of persuasion; "sensitisation", focussing on the multivocality of the writing and "self-presentation", illuminating the reflexive account. The contents of the last three chapters of the book are described more in detail later.

The fourth chapter, the most cumbersome, is devoted to the elaboration of qualitative research design. The chapter is organized as a virtual court trial, in which I try to defend, first, the relevance of the research question, second, the eloquence of the cases selected for the study, and third, the suitability, principally from the epistemic point of view, of the planned methodological path.

With the fifth chapter, we go through qualitative data analysis. The chapter opens with a discussion of the nature, so to speak, of qualitative data, distinguishing among the texts and the artefacts with which we usually analyse different kinds of empirical material (representations, reproductions, and naturalistic data), each with a specific "authenticity range" (Topolski 1977: 434, original edition 1973), with a differentiated capacity to answer our research questions.[2] The following section critically illustrates the logical structure of qualitative data analysis, moving from the notion of "categorisation" elaborated by Douglas Hofstadter and Emmanuel Sander, meant as a "tentative and gradated, gray-shaded linking of an entity or a situation to a prior category in one's mind" (Hofstadter and Sander 2013: 14). This kind of categorization, syntonic with Blumer's idea of "sensitizing concepts" (Blumer 1969), is framed in a lean version of the Template Analysis elaborated by Nigel King (2012), an approach to qualitative data analysis that combines theory-driven and data-driven procedures. Chapter 5 closes with a reflection on the conceptual tools that can suitably represent the relationship detected among our data, the Weberian ideal type that I identified as the best conceptual instrument for this purpose. With some philological liberty, I claimed the metaphorical character of the Weberian ideal type. This qualification is tied to a more general idea of qualitative research for which metaphors play the same role as models play in quantitative research.

The sixth and last chapter discusses the textualization process, first elaborating on the functions and use of one of the distinctive characteristics of qualitative research, the multivocality of writing, and second on the reflexive account. With very few exceptions, the great majority of the texts that present the results of qualitative research are written through the combination of the voice of the researcher with those of the participants. The participants' voices enter the text principally through the quotations that the researchers choose from their textual corpus. This kind of writing serves four diverse aims: i) to convince the scientific community of the robustness of the research results; ii) to evoke in the reader the colours, the emotions of the field, painting them with words; iii) to give voices to the participants; and iv) to expand the sources of the "reflexive account". Section 6.1 deals with all these aspects, framing the multivocality practices into Gregory Bateson's notion of "double description" (Bateson 1936, 1979). The last section of the book tackles the controversial topic of reflexivity (see Lumsden 2019). This issue is discussed with a deliberately low profile, focussing mainly on textualization aspects without any claim of completeness. The reflexive account is defined as an

Introduction 5

ethical responsibility (Altheide and Johnson 1994: 489) of the researcher-author toward the audience of his/her scientific community. The contents of this ethical responsibility emerge convincingly in the definition of reflexivity proposed by Mats Alvesson and Kaj Sköldberg as follows.

> Reflexivity means thinking about the conditions for what one is doing, investigating the way in which the theoretical, cultural and political context of individual and intellectual involvement affects interaction with whatever is being researched, often in ways difficult to become conscious of.
>
> (Alvesson and Sköldberg 2000: 245)

Starting from my first serious writing effort, my master's degree thesis, I have learnt that the introduction of a book must be written last, and this is what I have done. I am writing my last sentences on a special day on which we – with the exception of conspiracy theorists – celebrate the moon-landing of Apollo 11. This enterprise, with all its implications, started some years before with a memorable speech by President John Fitzgerald Kennedy at Rice University. On that occasion, Kennedy said: "We choose to go to the Moon in this decade and do the other things, not because they are easy, but because they are hard". I believe that this mental approach can be applied to practising qualitative research, with all the theoretical and methodological challenges that it implies. We have to do qualitative research not because it is easy because it doesn't need any theoretical nor statistical competences (a reason for doing a qualitative thesis that orients some incautious students), but because it is demanding and because through it we can organize and measure the best of our – both theoretical and methodological – skills.

July 20, 2019

Notes

1 For a reframing of the validity notion in the qualitative field, see Kirk and Miller (1986).
2 The historian Jerzy Topolski defines the range of authenticity of a historical document as "the sum of those questions (problems) to which a given source can provide true answers". The reception of this concept in my theoretical frame required the substitution of the notion of true (referred to answer) with those less demanding of plausibility.

References

Altheide D.L., Johnson J.M. 1994 *Criteria for Assessing Interpretive Validity in Qualitative Research*, in N.K. Denzin and Y.S. Lincoln (eds.), *Handbook of Qualitative Research*, Thousand Oaks and London, Sage Publications, pp. 485–499.
Alvesson M., Sköldberg K. 2000 *Reflexive Methodology: New Vistas for Qualitative Research*, London, Sage Publications.
Aristotle. 2015 *Rhetoric*, English translation by W. Rhys Roberts, Fairhope, AL, Mockingbird Publishing.
Bateson G. 1936 *Naven: A Survey of the Problems Suggested By a Composite Picture of the Culture of a New Guinea Tribe Drawn from Three Points of View*, Cambridge, Cambridge University Press.

6   Introduction

———. 1979 *Mind and Nature: A Necessary Unity*, New York, E.P. Dutton.

Blumer H. 1969 *Symbolic Interactionism*, Englewood Cliffs, NJ, Prentice Hall.

Edmondson R. 1984 *Rhetoric in Sociology*, London, The Macmillan Press Ltd.

Ginzburg C. 2013 *Clues, Myths, and the Historical Method*, Baltimore, The Johns Hopkins University Press (original edition 1978).

Gobo G. 2008 *Re-Conceptualizing Generalization: Old Issues in a New Frame*, in P. Alasuutari, L. Bickman and J. Branner (eds.), *The Sage Handbook of Social Research Methods*, London, Sage Publications, pp. 193–213.

Godden D.M., Walton D. 2007 *Advances in the Theory of Argumentation Schemes and Critical Questions*, in "Informal Logic", Vol. 27, No. 3, pp. 267–292.

Goldthorpe J. 2000 *On Sociology: Numbers, Narratives, and the Integration of Research and Theory*, Oxford, Oxford University Press.

Hofstadter D., Sander E. 2013 *Surfaces and Essences: Analogy as the Fuel and Fire of Thinking*, New York, Basic Books.

King N. 2012 *Doing Template Analysis*, in G. Symon and C. Cassell (eds.), *Qualitative Organizational Research*, London, Sage Publications, pp. 426–450.

Kirk J., Miller M.L. 1986 *Reliability and Validity in Qualitative Research*, Newbury Park, CA, Sage Publications.

Lumsden K. 2019 *Reflexivity: Theory, Method, and Practice*, New York, Routledge.

Madison G.B. 1988 *The Hermeneutics of Postmodernity*, Bloomington, Indiana University Press.

Piasere L. 2002 *L'etnografo imperfetto. Esperienza e cognizione in antropologia*, Roma-Bari, Laterza.

Tavory I., Timmermans S. 2014 *Abductive Analysis: Theorizing Qualitative Research*, Chicago and London, The University of Chicago Press.

Topolski J. 1977 *Methodology of History*, Dordrecht and Boston, D. Reidel Publishing Company (original edition 1973).

Walton D. 1989 *Informal Logic. A Pragmatic Approach*, Cambridge, Cambridge University Press.

———. 2009 *Anticipating Objections in Argumentation*, in H.J. Ribeiro (ed.), *Rhetoric and Argumentation in the Beginning of the XXIst Century*, Coimbra, University of Coimbra Press, pp. 87–109.

Walton D., Reed C., Macagno F. 2008 *Argumentation Schemes*, Cambridge, Cambridge University Press.

Wikan U. 1992 *Beyond the Words: The Power of Resonance*, in "American Ethnologist", Vol. 19, No. 3, pp. 460–482.

Wittgenstein L. 1958 *Philosophical Investigations*, Oxford, Basil Blackwell (first edition 1953).

Zadeh L.A. 1965 *Fuzzy Sets*, in "Information and Control", No. 8, pp. 338–353.

1 A premise about two crucial issues
Invisibility and method

The issue of invisibility, or rather the paradoxical idea of observing the unobservable, seems at least at first glance quite inappropriate for an empirical science like sociology. However, what we know about society is based only to a minor extent on observable phenomena, while the majority of our data refer to unobservable ones. To recognize an authoritarian attitude in a political leader or to identify his/her supporters in a specific social class implies the reference to invisible objects (although with a different kind of invisibility). Authoritarianism, as a trait of the individual personality, cannot be observed directly but only ascribed through "symptoms" gathered from speech behaviours – both online and offline – political decisions (if the leader is part of the government) and other signs. Similarly, nobody can directly observe a social class, social classes being a theoretical construct. The way in which we obtain information about invisible entities seems particularly relevant, and in this respect qualitative research can make a specific contribution to the credibility of the representations of these elusive entities.

The necessity to tackle the issue of invisibility is not specific only to qualitative research. It also invests the other Muse of social sciences, quantitative research. Before tackling the features of qualitative research in detail, a short discussion of the similarities and the differences between these two approaches to social research seems appropriate. This comparison demands for the reshaping of two crucial notions. The first is related to how a distinction between them can be marked out: by using bimodal logic or multimodal logic? The second is related to the notion of method: what notion of method seems more suitable to compare qualitative and quantitative research and – following the new agenda – to combine them?

1.1 The visible and the invisible

From its origins, science has had to confront the intriguing paradox of observing the unobservable, with the necessity of invisible entities invested with the responsibility of describing and/or explain observable phenomena. Starting from the force of gravity, at the heart of *Principia* by Sir Isaac Newton, to the luminiferous aether thought by James Clerk Maxwell to be the mean through which electromagnetic waves propagate, to mention two of the most prominent figures in the history of physics. But, from a cultural point of view, the expression of less

8 *A premise about two crucial issues*

celebrated invisible theoretical entities is also interesting; first of all, the mysterious phlogiston, the principle of inflammability defined by the physician and alchemist Johann Joachim Becher, and then deprived of its ontological status by the father of modern chemistry, Antoine-Laurent de Lavoisier, who substituted the poetical phlogiston with the more prosaic oxygen.

In the broad field of humanities, the paradox of the observation of the unobservable seems a constant, with the interesting exception of psychology, where we can observe a distinctive oscillation between two different orientations. The main expression of invisibility in psychology is the mind or, to be more precise, the cognitive and emotive processes that – silently – take place in the heads of individuals. The first movement of the pendulum goes toward the eradication of the relevance of mental processes. This last was the solution proposed by the Behaviourist School, animated by John Broadus Watson, Edward Lee Thorndike and Burrhus Frederic Skinner. According to these American scholars, the objects of a scientific study of human behaviour must be focussed only on observable properties, mental processes being irrelevant (see the "manifesto" of behaviourist psychology, published by Watson in 1913). In the long run, the stimulus-response approach showed relevant weakness, and psychology scholars oriented their attention to the hyphen that connects stimulus and response, namely the cognitive and emotive mediations between observable properties. Thus, psychologists, particularly social psychologists, invested (and still invest) a lot of time and resources in the measurement of attitudes and cognitive processes, developing a vast amount of validated scales devoted to measuring – through an evidential path (see what follows) – the invisible aspects of the mind.

Starting from the 1980s, a new wave of research has contributed to the reshaping of the issue of invisibility in a challenging although controversial way. Through the use of sophisticated technologies, mental processes – or their shadows (Abend 2017) – become visible, depicted in coloured images of the brain, that show which of its areas are activated when, for instance, an individual faces a moral dilemma (e.g., the trolley problem, Abend 2011: 148–149), experiences spirituality, makes an economic decision or expresses an aesthetic judgment (Guillermo Del Pinal and Nathan 2013; Abend 2017). The area of neural activation of the brain is located by a machine for functional magnetic resonance imaging (fMRI). The working of this machine benefits from the association between what our brain enables us to do – feel, think, perceive, and act – and the oxygen consumption and regional blood flow in a specific area of the brain. This information, associated with a map of the brain that locates mental functions, allows us, for instance, to decide whether the solution of an ethical dilemma is based on cognitive or emotional reasoning (see Guillermo Del Pinal and Nathan 2013: 237). This new tool creates both enthusiastic and extremely sceptical answers. The enthusiastic scholars see in this technology the tool that can guarantee a neural foundation of human behaviour and by doing so to explain everything. The sceptical scholars (see, for instance, Uttal 2001; Abend 2011, 2012; Satel and Lilienfeld 2013), maintain that knowing what brain area is activated during a specific activity is very far from recognizing its meaning.[1]

A premise about two crucial issues 9

Besides the technological sophistication of the "machine" that delivers a coloured image of the brain, suggesting the neural correlates of cognitive activities, the methodological design of these studies is quite basic. Most of the research on this area is based on laboratory experiments in which an individual – in isolation from his/her social world – is interrogated about the appropriateness or inappropriateness, or about the moral acceptability or unacceptability of certain behaviours such as: "Eating people", "Setting a cat on fire", "Cheating on your taxes" (Abend 2011: 149, 152). Thus, the complexity of the machinery that bolsters the myth of the transparency of our minds is coupled with a radical simplification of the research design and the theoretical frame. Studying individuals in perfect isolation parenthesizes what we have learnt from the Symbolic Interactionism School. Adopting a simplified version of cognitive processes, based on the "okay-ness" or "not-okay-ness" (150), does not allow inferences about the neural correlates of more complex cognitive processes which are institutionally or culturally dependent.[2]

In sociology, the field in which I find myself most comfortable, the issue of invisibility has been tackled – at least until now – without any special technology. The temptation of the behaviourist solution opened up, among sociologists, more than one breach, but always avoiding the heroic assumption of the irrelevance of mental processes. What happened in this direction was the choice to focus only on observable "trans-subjective phenomena" (Sorokin 1928: 619) with two different options. The first one is characterized by the explicit renunciation of any interpretation of the association detected among observable variables. This is the way of sociography which delivers surface information, in many cases very useful, at least to orient more in-depth study. In my research experience, I met this kind of approach in several studies on the relationship between social position and health that convincingly document the observable lowering of life expectancy moving from the upper classes to the working class. What is frequently missing here is an explanation of this socially and ethically relevant correlation. The second option moves from the analysis of trans-subjective phenomena, adding to the association detected among the variables a conjectural interpretation or explanation, not always adequately underpinned in empirical evidence. We can recognize this *modus operandi* in the classic study by Émile Durkheim on suicide, at least when the French sociologist skims the individual level of suicidal behaviour and tries to interpret it.

Besides this behaviourist path, mainly present among quantitative researchers, although not only among them,[3] there is a widespread tendency to enter – so to speak – into the minds of individuals to study their internal states such as beliefs, attitudes, values and the meaning they attribute to their actions. This effort unites quantitative and qualitative research, but as I will say in what follows, in the study of invisible, qualitative research has a special advantage. The relevance of entering people's minds is soundly defended in a milestone of sociological theory, *The Polish Peasant in Europe and America*, published about 100 years ago by William Thomas and Florian Znaniecki (1918). This seminal book introduces the notion of "definition of the situation", a cognitive category (defined as attitude by

10   *A premise about two crucial issues*

the authors) which guides the actions of individuals. When deciding the course to be imprinted on one's actions, individuals do not react mechanically to the environment of which they are part (to the stimulus, in behaviourist jargon) but rather to their mental representation of the environment. This idea is expressed with crystal-clear clarity in the famous so-called "Thomas theorem" which states that if an individual defines certain situations as real, they will be real in their consequences. If during a visit to a Scottish castle, out of the blue I become convinced that it is inhabited by a cruel ghost who, for reasons needless to explain, hates Italian tourists and wants to kill them, I will be invaded by a mortal terror. The fright causes me to rush out the castle, running at breakneck speed along some steep stairs, to fall and break my leg. Thus, regardless of the soundness of my conviction, its consequences – the mortal terror, the breakneck running speed and the broken leg – become real. If we assume that at least one of the purposes of sociology (not necessarily the main one) is the "interpretive understanding of social action" (Weber 1922, English translation 1978: 4), the reconstruction of the individual definition of situation and, more broadly, individual internal states that determine his/her way of being in the world seems crucial.[4] The centrality of these internal states is clearly expressed by the French anthropologist Dan Sperber:

> The project of scientific anthropology meets with a major difficulty: it is impossible to describe a cultural phenomenon, an election, a mass, or a football game for instance, without taking into account the ideas of the participants. However, ideas cannot be observed, but only intuitively understood; they cannot be described but only interpreted.
>
> (Sperber 1982, English translation 1985: 9)

The way along which the journey toward the invisible territories, or – less poetically – toward individuals' inner states of mind, shows a close analogy with the *modus operandi* of the nineteenth-century physician. Devoid of the instruments of contemporary medical technology which allow the observation of internal organs, nineteenth-century physicians reached diagnoses through meticulous observation of the signs of the disease accessible to their eyes and of the symptoms reported by patients in their discourses. The physicians observed, for example, the condition of the skin and that of mucous membranes, the patient's posture and gait. Then, with the help of a watch, the physician measured the heart rate, and with a stethoscope auscultated the chest to hear how the respiration worked. These signs were usually integrated with the reconstruction of symptoms through the discourses of patients opportunely solicited for this purpose. In the reading of these discourses, a version of "illness narratives" (Kleinmann 1988; Bury 2001) which emerges in an "institutional context" (Hydén 1997: 62), the physician, besides overcoming his/her scepticism about patients' versions of their suffering experience (48), has to face some obstacles, familiar to any social researcher. Patients can have some difficulties in expressing their experiences in words, particularly if they are not educated or, in broader terms, if they do not

A premise about two crucial issues   11

share the physician's communication code. Memory can be another source of difficulty: patients can forget some relevant details of their bodily experiences or reshape them in a confusing way. Emotions can interfere with the recall of suffering experiences and with their expression in a discourse. Finally, the psychodynamic aspects must be remembered: a patient may deny or modify aspect(s) of his/her illness experience in order to protect the Self.

At any rate, through the combination of this information, the physician arrives at a diagnosis based on a conjectural representation of the conditions of internal organs which allow recognition of a specific syndrome and prescribe a therapy. Helped only by a decidedly rudimentary set of instruments, the physician accesses the invisible following the model of medical semiotics, based on what Carlo Ginzburg (1978, English translation 2013) defines as an "evidential paradigm". Ginzburg recognizes the ancestral roots of this model of knowledge in hunting practice. It was through this model of knowledge that primitive man learned "to reconstruct the shapes and the movements of his invisible prey from the tracks on the ground, broken branches, excrement, tufts of hair, entangled feathers, stagnating odors" (Ginzburg 1978, English translation 2013: 93). It was the same cognitive style which guided the Mesopotamian art of divination and the Hippocratic medical school, access to the invisible through traces, signs, clues. At the end of the nineteenth century, the evidential paradigm emerged with more strength, through the works of three different intellectuals, Giovanni Morelli, Conan Doyle and Sigmund Freud. Giovanni Morelli was the inventor of a singular method for the attribution of pictorial artworks, through which it was possible to distinguish between authentic and false artworks. Morelli concentrated his attention on trifling details that would have been influenced least by the artist's school. Specifically, he focussed on the earlobes, the fingernails, and the shapes of fingers and toes, looking for the personality of the painter "where personal effort is weaker" (Ginzburg 2013: 89). The detective Sherlock Holmes moves in the same way: he is celebrated for his ability to recognize a culprit from marginal and apparently irrelevant clues. Holmes here is also the true hero of abductive inference (see Eco and Sebock 1988), typical of qualitative research (Schwartz-Shea, Yanow 2012: 26–34). Both in Morelli and Sherlock Holmes there emerges an attitude relevant to the qualitative study of social phenomena, investigative sensibility, effectively developed by Jack Douglas through systematic cultivation of "though-minded suspicion" (Douglas 1976: 147).[5] In the same way, reading symptoms, instead of pictorial signs or clues, is the work of the father of the psychoanalysis Sigmund Freud, who recognized – although not so openly – his intellectual debt toward Morelli (Ginzburg 2013: 89–90).

When a quantitative sociologist "measures" the level of the authoritarianism of an individual through the attitude scale of Theodor Adorno, s/he in reality uses clues, signs of this "syndrome" expressed by the structured answer to the items that compose the scale. This way of doing seems not too far from that of the nineteenth-century physician who asks the patient about his/her appetite, or about fatigue in climbing stairs. Similarly, when an ethnographer tries to interpret the subjective meanings of religious rituals, s/he observes the interactions between

12   *A premise about two crucial issues*

the participants in liturgical spaces and then tries to access the participants' meanings of this experience through dialogue with them. Again, this mixture of observation and dialogue seems not so far from the practice of a nineteenth-century physician of observing the posture and movements of patients and, then asking them about their pain experiences. Besides these palpable analogies – invisibility of what happen under the skin for the observer and opacity of their experiences for the observed – a relevant difference emerges. In a medical examination, it is reasonable to assume that the patient provides the doctor with all the cooperation s/he can due to the urgency because of which s/he has decided to see the doctor. The case of social research encounters is, from this point of view, downright different. The degree of cooperation, of compliance, is far from being guaranteed in the context of social research. It is difficult to believe that people interrogated about the way they see the world, their ideals, or – it being impossible to observe them directly – their habitual behaviours respond with the same degree of cooperation as they would during a medical examination. The Canadian sociologist Erving Goffman, who made interaction in everyday life one of his principal objects of study, eloquently documented that what matters most to people in social interactions – and, therefore, in interaction constituted by a specific research – is to "save one's own face", to avoid embarrassment or create a bad impression, even if it is necessary to make a few adjustments in the answers given to an interviewer or to polish, under the indiscreet eye of an observer, the sharpest aspects of one's behaviour (Goffman 1956).

It is quite clear that our data are not only "theory-laden" (Hanson 1958) but also "trust-laden". The quality of the information we collect about participants depends profoundly on the level of trust we have been able to gain. In short, it can be said that, in the study of social phenomena, the cooperation of participants is at the same time indispensable – although not decisive (thinking of the opacity issue) – and uncertain. And it is in this slippery terrain that qualitative research offers an important contribution.

The way in which data are collected in qualitative research, in an intensive, flexible and interactive way, delivers to the researcher not only information about the cultural traits analysed but also the degree of cooperation offered by participants.[6] Due to the kind of relationship that is established in qualitative research between participants and the researcher, the latter can count on a vast number of clues on the participants' degree of cooperation, how it changes (for better or worse) during his/her relationship with them. In a discursive (in-depth) interview, the participants have to express themselves in their own words, combining them with a specific (and thematized by the researcher) emotive colouring, and possibly with some meta-communication on the relationship with the interviewer: "I'm telling you this because you can understand me". A more favourable situation emerges with research methods based on the participation of the researcher in their lives. The longitudinal dimension of these methods (naturalistic and participant observation, field experiment and shadowing) has a double impact on the participants' cooperation. From one point of view, the time spent together allows the researcher to put into practice those investigative virtues, underlined by Jack Douglas, that can help to overcome the barriers the participants raise to protect the borders of their inner world. Whether or not this finding is obtained, the repeated observation of participants' interactions, among themselves and with the researcher – and this is the second point – gives further insight into the degree of participants' cooperation. Quick answers to a questionnaire – or the script-governed behaviours of the individuals involved in a sociological laboratory experiment – do not give the same amount of information.

To conclude, the relevance of the invisible, of the inner world of individuals, seems quite unquestionable and similarly beyond doubt is the necessity of participants' cooperation in grasping something of this world. Because of its special capacity to harmonize data collection procedures to the context of its use, qualitative research has a special edge in the evaluation of the degree of participants' cooperation on which the researcher can count.

1.2 The two Muses of social research: quality and quantity

In this section, the two Muses of social research, quantitative and qualitative approaches, are placed side by side, mainly with the purpose of allowing the specificity of the latter to emerge. With this aim, my description of the features of quantitative research will be incomplete and, probably, a little biased. I started my research career as a quantitative data-cruncher, and my first course – as a contract professor – was about statistics. With my PhD thesis, I moved into the area of qualitative research, in which I continue to work with quantitative scholars doing, with them, my share of qualitative research. Undoubtedly, my heart beats for qualitative research, and this is the reason for possible partiality in my discussion.

In this direction, the first aspect that deserves attention is that of the similarity between qualitative and quantitative research. The previous section was focussed on the first similarity, the common necessity to tackle the issue of invisibility, although with a different kind of involvement. If for qualitative research it is hard to think of a study which does not thematize the meaning that participants assign to their actions, a good portion of quantitative study, following Durkheim's advice, considers only social facts such as death rates, marriages duration and salary differences between relevant sub-populations. Where the issue of invisibility is faced up to, quantitative and qualitative strategies differ greatly. In both cases, the principal logical tool is the argument from sign (Walton, Reed and Macagno 2008: 329) that assumes observable signs as symptoms or as effects of the unobservable property. If the property is authoritarianism, a quantitative symptom can be the answer "strongly agree" to one item of the Authoritarianism California F-scale, like: "Obedience and respect for authority are the most important virtues children should learn". The same topic studied in qualitative research, e.g., ethnography of a populist party in Europe, would consider as signs of authoritarianism the decision processes observed during the first six months of a government, leaders' speeches, their relationship with allied political forces and opposition, and many other aspects of the political climate that can serendipitously emerge during fieldwork. Besides the aspects of the duration of the fieldwork and that of

14 *A premise about two crucial issues*

observable practices thematized, the main logical differences between the two approaches considered is that in quantitative research the definition of the argument from sign precedes data collection procedures; in qualitative research, on the other hand, it is contemporary with or successive to it.[7] In quantitative research the argument from sign is embedded in the operational definition of the variables. In qualitative research the argument from sign is outlined in "sensitizing concepts" (Blumer 1969: 147–148) that guide the gaze of the researcher in the field, and it is rounded off during fieldwork or in the last stage of data analysis.[8]

The second relevant commonality between qualitative and quantitative research refers to their shared vocation toward generality. This idea is soundly expressed by Raimond Boudon and François Bourricaud in their *Critical Dictionary of Sociology*:

> Even when the sociologist analyses a particular phenomenon (whether it is a delinquent gang, a historical episode, or a particular characteristic of a certain society), his or her objective is rarely to account for this object in its particularity but rather to interpret it as the particular realisation of more general structures.
>
> (Boudon and Bourricaud 1982, English translation 2003: 206)

The vocation toward generality embraced by quantitative research is evident. In a survey the sample claims to speak for the population from which it came. In a laboratory experiment results are thought of as general, usually underpinning this claim by on an idea of the ontological homogeneity of the subjects studied (typical of the experiments framed into the rational-choice theory which assumes the universality of the traits proper to *homo oeconomicus*), or invoking a kind of "theoretical inference" (Gomm, Hammersley and Foster 2000: 103).

In the more heterogeneous archipelago of qualitative research (see Chapter 2) there is considerable divergence on this issue. First of all, there is a heated discussion about the viability and suitability of "generalisation" for qualitative results. Some scholars maintain that the extension of the scope from studied to analogous unstudied units is downright inadmissible. There is a sort of deep aversion, sometimes repugnance, toward this logical operation seen as synonymous with a nomological-lawlike generalization, with a pretended trans-contextual applicability (Lincoln and Guba 1985: 110).[9] To avoid this mortal sin, exclusive focus on the studied cases is recommended, a strong commitment to a rich or thick description of the cases analysed (Denzin and Lincoln 2005a: 12), which must be "uniquely adequate" (Denzin and Lincoln 2005b: 379). This position echoes the admonition of Clifford Geertz who, in *The Interpretation of Cultures*, writes: "The essential task of theory building here is not to codify abstract regularities but to make thick description possible, not to generalise across cases but to generalise within them" (Geertz 1973: 26). Demand for nomological-lawlike generalization seems grounded on an exaggerated optimism about what social sciences can actually aspire to. The ontological limit of universal statements is, by now, quite obvious. What we have learnt from anthropological studies is that what we can legitimately aspire to can be only be "local knowledge" bounded by time and space (Geertz 1983); or, moving from anthropology to sociology, some "middle-range theories" focussed on specific issues.[10]

Related to this radical posture is the position of whoever admits the possibility of the extension of the scope of qualitative research findings, but feels uncomfortable with the statistical jargon commonly used to denote it, for example, generalization, sample, and population.[11] In this area we have many different positions proposing alternative terms, and an alternative theoretical frame for the extension of the results acquired from case/cases studied to the unstudied analogous ones. The simpler version of this process is the so-called "naturalistic generalisation" (Lincoln and Guba 1985: 119–120) that – in a nutshell – can be defined as a sort of recognition that what emerges from the study of one case can be applied to other cases. The burden of proof, so to speak, in this case is on the reader who, on receiving the description of the studied case/s, recognizes in its/ their features something that can be applied to other contexts. This idea is developed in the notion of transferability elaborated by Lincoln and Guba (1985). The notion develops the idea of naturalistic generalization to fit it into the process of analogical extension. The authors define the extension of the results of (a) studied case/s to other analogous case/s through the communication metaphor. So we have a sending context, the one studied, and a receiving context, the target of analogical extension. What authorizes the passage from the sending to the receiving context is the "thick description" (Geertz 1973: Chapter 1) of both. The sending-context thick description is the duty of the author of the research, the thick description of the receiving-context is the responsibility of the reader or, in a wider sense, the scientific community, which identifies similarity between the two objects of the argument from analogy.[12] Moving from the approach that we can call "reader-based" to more conventional ones, two main strategies can be briefly illustrated here. The first is rooted in all the different versions of the grounded theory, recourse to the "theoretical saturation" procedure.[13] All the grounded theory schools fully recognize the legitimacy of the logical operation of synecdoche, by which it is possible to say something of the whole, moving from the observation of one of its parts.[14] The main idea of the grounded theory approach is that the size and the profile of the sample cannot be defined in advance. The size of the sample can only be defined in the field through systematic analysis of the progressively acquired empirical material. Through this data analysis, the researcher defines (only inductively for the first generation, also abductively for the others) some empirically grounded categories (codes). As long as the growth of the set of information units produces an enrichment of the category, the sample size must be increased. When, in economics jargon, the marginal utility of the last unit of information added to the sample is zero, the process of sampling can be stopped: theoretical saturation has been reached.

The second strategy substitutes the idea of representativeness of the part as a necessary requisite for the extension of what is observed there to the whole, typical of quantitative research, with the requisite of eloquence. This idea is expressed in a clear and effective way by Janice Morse, who maintains that

16 *A premise about two crucial issues*

in order to obtain "excellent data" it is necessary to locate "'excellent' participants", or in a broader meaning, excellent observation units that can function as "the best examples" of the phenomena studied (Morse 2007: 231, 234).[15] In this perspective, the idea to acquire – through the sample – a miniature of the whole, to be authorized to say something about it (implicitly evoked also by the grounded theory approach), is dismissed. What is sought is to secure some "information-rich cases" (Patton 2015: 264–265) through a purposeful selection of observation units.[16] In this perspective – developed in Chapter 4 – the extension of results obtained through the observation of a handful of cases (sometimes only one or two) is guided by theoretical assumptions which define the limits or the condition of the extension. More correctly, we may speak of *conditional extension*, aware both of the ontological limits that invest social phenomena (see earlier on the local knowledge issue), and on the dependence of our knowledge on a set of assumptions taken for granted for our purposes (Wittgenstein 1969: §205; Hammersley 1999: 582).[17]

To return to the comparison between quantitative and qualitative research, it emerges that in the latter there is vast heterogeneity in the way in which the extension of the scope of the research results is pursued (including the idea of its impossibility). Another important difference is related to the use of synecdoche. In quantitative research the sampling procedure (which can be defined as the operational definition of cases) is planned in all its details before the data-collection procedure. The sample dimension is calculated by considering the variance of the relevant variables and sampling strategies (for instance, simple, stratified, multi-stage and cluster sampling) adopted. When the sampling operations are concluded, no changes in the sampling plan are possible; all that can be done at this stage is to estimate the sample bias due to attrition. In qualitative research case-selection procedures proceed along with data collection and are guided specifically by its in-progress results. Case selection does not finish with the end of the data collection. During data analysis it is still possible to reshape the set of observation units by excluding from the analysis the ones that do not satisfy the eloquence-criteria requirements.[18] The first move in the direction of sample adjustment is what Rosaline Barbour defines as "second stage sampling" (Barbour 2007: 73). Mainly in the methods focussed on individuals, such as in-depth interviews, or on little groups, such as focus groups (see Chapter 2), as well as in all the other qualitative research methods, we select cases, hoping for their eloquence, guided by clues (primarily easily accessible information) such as social role (e.g., single mothers), body or health condition (deaf people or survivors of heart attacks), gender, education, political persuasion, or religious orientation (current or ex-members of a party or of a religious organization). Sometimes it happens that the clues we have chosen are not appropriate and there is insufficient heterogeneity among our cases, discourses or experiences. When this happens, a kind of "refill" seems necessary. Starting from the information acquired in the field, new criteria (clues) for case selection will be adopted, and new cases will be added. The second move is that of "skimming" from the collected cases the ones not eloquent enough for our purposes. The reason for this exclusion ("secondary selection") is that in qualitative analysis a huge amount of data which is irrelevant to the research questions is a real impediment to analysis (see Morse 2007: 233). So in order to tackle better the difficulty of in-depth data analysis, we can decide to reduce the size of the sample (on this point see N. 18 about the cherry-picking bias risk).

The third and last relevant commonality between qualitative and quantitative research worthy of being examined is the common accountability obligation of all research procedures. In quantitative research this obligation is honoured through the display of the empirical definitions that guided the data collection, and through the illustration of the statistical models applied, supplied with the appropriate measures of goodness of fit and statistical significance. The same obligation insists on qualitative research displaying how the representation of the phenomena studied has been arrived at. Qualitative researchers cannot exhibit the operational definitions with which they "measured" the context(s) studied nor measure the "degree of uncertainty" (King, Keohane and Verba 1994: 31–33) with which the statements or the equivalence of quantitative models, the metaphors developed in their research fit the data or can be confidently extended to analogous contexts. What can and must be done in qualitative research is to describe all the relevant research steps in a reflexive account (in Altheide and Johnson's 1994 sense) to allow the scientific community to evaluate the plausibility of the proposed results (see Section 6.2).

Having defined the commonalities between quantitative and qualitative research, and by so doing indicating some of the differences between them, an integrated synthesis of the dissimilarities now seems possible. For this reason, and also for the sake of the rest of my discourse on qualitative research, a reflection on how a distinction can be outlined is necessary. There are two ways to do this: by binary or multimodal logic. Binary logic is the usual way to define a distinction, based on the Aristotelian principle of the excluded middle according to which a subject can be either A or non-A, but not in between; either black or white. The limitations of this way of drawing distinctions have been experienced by all of us, both in everyday experience and in our scientific activity. Discomfort with the law of the excluded middle, "impeccable" binary logic, has been recently expressed by Yvonna Lincoln and Egon Guba, who invoked different "informal rules of logic", a "fuzzy logic" that allows less rigid distinctions (Lincoln and Guba 2013: 28–29). What these authors are seeking, fuzzy logic, was formalized by the engineer Lofty Askar Zadeh in 1965, and for our purposes we can benefit from his contribution although it is distant from the informality of qualitative research. From Zadeh (1965) we learnt that in fuzzy logic the belonging of the generic element x to the fuzzy set A is expressed by a continuous function whose values are included in the continuum between 0 and 1. For the generic element x, a value of belonging to A equal to 0 indicates that x has none of the properties which define A; a membership value of 1 indicates that x fully possesses these properties. Intermediate values of belonging indicate the intensity of the affinity between x and A. The specificity of these two types of logics can be illustrated by an example expressed by means of Set Theory.

18 A premise about two crucial issues

I have already said that in classic binary logic, a generic element *x* may belong or not belong to set *A*. For example, John may or not belong to the set of adults, according to the definition of adult age. If the threshold is 18, and John's eighteenth birthday was yesterday, he definitely belongs to the set of adults. Now let us consider three other people: Clare, Richard, and Eveline. Clare is a 3-year-old baby, Richard is a teenager who celebrated his 17th birthday six months, ago, and Eveline is a 25-year-old mother. In binary logic, since 18 years old is the threshold of adulthood, Clare and Richard are equally not adults regardless of the differences in their ages. John and Eveline are both equally adult. Between the 17-and-a-half-year-old Richard and the 18-year-old John, are there dramatic differences in adulthood, or is it more a question of degree? Clare and Richard are indeed similar in their not being adult? The differences among the four cases considered can be more adequately represented through fuzzy logic. On this basis we could say that Clare, the 3-year-old baby, belongs to the set of adults with a very low membership value, for instance 0.1. The measure of 17-and-a-half-year-old Richard's belonging to the set of adults rises to 0.7, a value that would amount to 0.75 for the 18-year-old John and 0,89 for the 25-year-old Eveline. The two ways to draw a distinction can be illustrated by two figures expressing belonging to the set of adults according, respectively, to binary logic (Figure 1.1), and fuzzy logic (Figure 1.2).[19] The distinctions drawn by adopting bimodal logic have the merit of parsimony, but not that of adequacy (see Kosko 1993: 21).

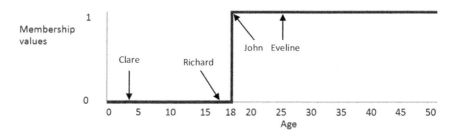

Figure 1.1 Membership of the set of adults in bimodal logic

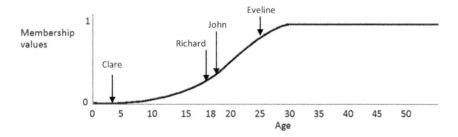

Figure 1.2 Membership of the set of adults in multimodal or fuzzy logic

A premise about two crucial issues   19

To outline the distinction – in a binary or a fuzzy way – between qualitative and quantitative research, the three classical loci of ontology, epistemology, and methodology seem appropriate (see Lincoln and Guba 2013: 28, 37).[20] With regard to ontology, the matter is simple: there are no differences between qualitative and quantitative research. In both areas human beings and social relations are the objects of study. From the second point of view, epistemology, it is difficult to outline a binary, clear-cut distinction between the two kinds of research. Constructivist epistemology seems to be the mainstream of qualitative research, whereas a realist approach seems dominant in quantitative research. But we still have, in the hordes of qualitative research, prominent scholastic figures with well-defended realist epistemology – not the naïve current, but the critical. In my reading, which is not focussed on listing realist scholars, I encountered the work of Martin Hammersley (1992), Matthew Miles and Michael Huberman (1984), Ray Pawson and Nicholas Tilley (1987), Cleve Seale (1999), Joseph Maxwell (2012), and Nick Emmel (2013). Among the majority of constructivist scholars, the team cited earlier is a minority whose mere existence does not authorize drawing a clear-cut distinction between qualitative and quantitative scholars based on the old acritically accepted contrast between positivists and constructivists. Furthermore, the distinction between the two epistemological persuasions is relevant also to the archipelago of qualitative research, with some sound arguments advanced by Peregrine Schwartz-Shea and Dvora Yanow (2012: 5–6). To conclude, from the epistemological point of view, the distinction between qualitative and quantitative research can only be a fuzzy one.

The dimension for which it is possible to outline a clear-cut distinction between qualitative and quantitative research is the methodological one. Here we can see clearly a distinction between an approach based on uniform strategies of data collection, the quantitative one, and another, based on a flexible, context-sensitive approach to data collection, the qualitative one. From the methodological point of view, two other fuzzy differences emerge. First, the preference in qualitative research for small-N studies, shared with laboratory experiments, but without survey research or secondary data analysis. Second, the monovocality of the texts that present quantitative research results, going against the multivocality trend in qualitative texts where – with few exceptions – we can observe an "orchestration" (in the meaning of Bakhtin 1981: 430–431) between the voice of the author(s) and those of participants who join the drama through quotations.[21]

Besides their common features, there are some relevant differences between the two Muses of social research. This fact, the presence of relevant differences, has been frequently contested for various reasons. One of them, not very technical, places the accent on the necessity to overcome the so-called paradigms war, in a sort of methodological ecumenism. Another, more recent, finds its justification in the opportunity to mix qualitative and quantitative methods, in order to obtain all-round representation of social phenomena. Recently the pressure toward mixing the two methods has reached a crescendo, becoming a specific demand for research proposals which compete for national and international funds. In 1959, Carl Wright Mills, in his seminal book, *The Sociological Imagination*, introduces the notion of "methodological inhibition", to contest the mainstream

20   *A premise about two crucial issues*

research which, at that time and in the USA, was surveys. Mills' definition is worth quoting:

> By this [the methodological inhibition] I mean that the kinds of problems that will be taken up and the way in which they are formulated are quite severely limited by The Scientific Method. Methodology, in short, seems to determine the problems.
>
> (Mills 2000: 57, first edition 1959)

Sometimes I have the impression that, if we substitute the phrase "The Scientific Method" with "The Mixed Method", the Mills criticism seems to reconquer its original freshness (and its polemical point of view). A similar position has been expressed by Schwartz-Shea and Yannow who define mixed methods as a "new dogma, that researchers *must*, or *ideally should* incorporate" (Schwartz-Shea and Yanow 2012: 133, italics in the original). A more polemical – if such is possible – interpretation of the mixed-method discourse was Dawn Freshwater's (2007) reading. Starting out from a postmodernist stance (which is not my cup of tea), Freshwater maintains that the mixed-method discourse has become a "mindless mantra" (135) which defends the idea that "there is no space for undecidability in either the text or the method" (141). The underlying idea that seduces most researchers, continues Freshwater, "is that no single method can capture the whole and complex reality" (145). This idea also oriented the earliest advocates of mixed methods, for whom, in John Creswell's words: "All methods had bias and weaknesses, and the collection of both quantitative and qualitative data neutralised the weaknesses of each form of data" (Creswell 2014: 14–15). The idea of mixed methods as a tool that can ensure a sort of epistemological guarantee against uncertainty is what most bothers me, but in addition to this there is another important methodological issue about the conditions under which qualitative and quantitative methods are mixed. This issue demands critical reflection on the notion of the method with which I am going to conclude this chapter.

1.3 Method: principles vs orders

The idea of method that best suits qualitative research and any possible form of combination between this way of doing social research with those adopted by the neighbouring field of quantitative research emerges from Gary Brent Madison's reflection, introduced in a Thomas Schwandt essay, part of the first edition of the *Sage Handbook of Qualitative Research* (Schwandt 1994: 121–122). In a chapter devoted to the issue of more appropriate methods for phenomenological hermeneutics, that contrasts the Hirsch and Gadamer points of view, Madison proposes a definition of method as a *set of principles* that receive a different interpretation according to the context in which they are applied, instead of a *collection of rules* that act as orders (1988: 28–29). These principles, guiding the method, are more similar to ethical or juridical norms of jurisprudence than to laws of physics; principles for which there is no single correct application, but more than one which depends on context; principles whose application, not

A premise about two crucial issues 21

unlike a sentence handed down in court, must be defended with appropriate arguments. Thinking of method in this way implies that, for instance, the principle of accountability informing any scientific research will be honoured differently in qualitative and quantitative research, but – and this is the most relevant point – the two very different procedures have to be considered as being equivalent. Based on this idea of method, I believe that it is possible to benefit by mixing qualitative and quantitative methods, accepting that each "game" (cf. Wittgenstein) follows its own rules, both considered as legitimate expressions of more general principles (to be pompous, the principles that govern the game of scientific research). The same idea of method, meant as an art with which to define the best way to harmonize our practices with changeable contexts, will inspire the rest of the book.

Notes

1 As far as I have understood neuroimaging procedures, my view is definitely closer to the sceptical than the enthusiastic scholars.
2 On this last point, the contribution of Gabriel Abend is particularly relevant. Abend focusses on a specific area of neural correlates study, that of morality, at the centre of the sociological theory starting from Émile Durkheim's studies. Abend maintains that the study of morality through the search of neural correlates can offer only a partial contribution to the explanation of moral judgements, due to its theoretical framework based on "thin" instead of "thick" concepts of morality (Abend 2011: 151). The distinction between these two categories of concepts is developed based on Bernard Williams's reflections (Williams 1985) which lead us in a different direction as regards the Geertzian one. In Abend's words: "Thin concepts – for example, right, good, and permissible – evaluate an object. But they don't describe it. If you say, 'That action was wrong', you aren't conveying any further information about it, other than its being wrong in your view. Conceptually and semantically, you are free to say that any action is wrong. By contrast, thick concepts – for example, dignity, fanaticism, or moderation – do a dual job. They simultaneously evaluate and describe an object. Take the sentences 'That was a brutal action' and 'That was a materialistic action.' There are semantic constraints on what you can call 'brutal' and 'materialistic,' because these words are describing that action besides negatively evaluating it" (Abend 2012: 179–180). Due to this theoretical simplification, this science of the invisible "whatever other merits and flaws it might have . . . is a science of one part of morality only" (Abend 2011: 162). I would like to thank Iddo Tavory for pointing out to me the studies of Gabriel Abend.
3 An exclusive focus on behaviours, specifically speech behaviours, characterizes Conversation Analysis (Sacks 1992). The variegated attention paid to the interpretive dimension of qualitative research practices is thematized in the fine book by Peregrine Schwartz-Shea and Dvora Yanow, who distinguish between "qualitative positivist methods" and "qualitative interpretive methods" (2012: 5–6).
4 Max Weber defines the purpose of sociology as follows: "Sociology (in the sense in which this-highly ambiguous word is used here) is a science concerning itself with the interpretive understanding of social action and thereby with a causal explanation of its course and consequences. We shall speak of 'action' insofar as the acting individual attaches a subjective meaning to his behaviour – be it overt or covert, omission or acquiescence. Action is 'social' insofar as its subjective meaning takes account of the behaviour of others and is thereby oriented in its course" (Weber 1922, English translation 1978: 4).
5 The adjective "investigative" does not refer to police or disciplinary connotations of social research, but to investigative journalism, which Douglas sees emblematically

22 A premise about two crucial issues

represented by Lincoln Steffens, author of important reports on the political and economic corruption of America at the beginning of the last century. What Douglas encourages is, first of all, the adoption of a critical disposition, of systematic scepticism about what we observe and hear in the field.

6 These aspects of qualitative data collection will be further elaborated in Chapter 2.

7 In the text I am referring to the majority of empirical procedures in quantitative research. There are, as can be imagined, some exceptions to this rule. For instance, in *explorative* factor analysis, the argument from sign emerges during the reading of the output, interpreting the factor loading, the correlations between observed and latent variables, to give a name (a very interpretative procedure) to the factors extracted.

8 "Whereas definitive concepts provide prescriptions of what to see, sensitizing concepts merely suggest directions along which to look" (Blumer 1969: 148).

9 Strangely enough, the mantra of non-generalizability, usually recited by quantitative researchers to belittle the qualitative ones, becomes a reason of pride among postmodernist scholars.

10 Robert Merton defines middle-range theories as "theories that lie between the minor but necessary working hypotheses that evolve in abundance during day-to-day research and the all-inclusive systematic efforts to develop a unified theory that will explain all the observed uniformities of social behavior, social organization and social change" (Merton 1968: 39). Merton illustrates this notion through a set of theories which he defines as middle-range, among which the clearest (and probably best-known) is the theory of reference groups (40–41). The referene groups theory explains the sense of relative deprivation of an individual as a consequence of the comparative reference group adopted (if in evaluating my salary, I compare myself with the other members of my department, I might be quite satisfied; if, on the other hand, I elect as my comparative reference group Harvard full professors, is it possible to feel deep relative deprivation). In an essay devoted to the analysis of law in a comparative perspective, Clifford Geertz defines the notion of local knowledge in these terms: "Like sailing, gardening, politics, and poetry, law and ethnography are crafts of place: they work by the light of local knowledge" (Geertz 1983: 167). What Geertz relates to ethnography can legitimately be extended to all qualitative research: anthropologists label as ethnography all the research practices that sociologists distinguish in participant observation, in-depth interviews, documentary analysis, naturalistic observation, shadowing, and so on. The analysis elaborated by Geertz is focussed on a specific issue, the law, developed in a comparative perspective. Combining – with some philological liberty – the ideas expressed by Merton and Geertz, is it possible to maintain that the areas in which is it possible to recognize some regularities and apply the logical procedure of extension of scope – these areas are bound by space and time.

11 In a book on sampling in qualitative research, the author Nick Emmel, distant from the postmodernist perspective that underpins the radical rejection of generalisation, opens his Introduction with what follows: "I am really not sure that the verb 'sampling' does justice to the act of choosing cases in qualitative research. Sampling in the sense most often used in research refers to two activities: first, defining a population from which a sample will be drawn and of which the sample will be representative; and secondly, ensuring that every person or thing from this predefined population has the chance of inclusion that is greater than zero and can be measured. Neither of this rules . . . applies to the choosing of cases in qualitative research" (Emmel 2013: 1).

12 The argument from analogy will be spelled out in Chapter 3.

13 It is usual to distinguish three generations of grounded theory scholars, indicated by three important books. The first is that of the founders, Barney Glaser and Anselm Strauss, with *The Discovery of Grounded Theory* (1967). The second generation is that which originated from a minor schism; the book that inspired this generation is that by Anselm Strauss and Juliet Corbin, *Basics of Qualitative Research* (1990). The third generation is that of Kathy Charmaz, who defended a constructivist version of

A premise about two crucial issues 23

the grounded theory in the book *Constructing Grounded Theory* (2006). The bread-and-butter interpretation of the evolution of grounded theory can be identified in the role played by pre-comprehension: excluded by the founders, tolerated by the second generation, fully accepted by the third.

14 The use of the classical trope of the synecdoche to define the procedure of sampling is due to Howard Becker (Becker 1998: 67). In Section 4.2, a specific, diminished version of synecdoche, more suitable to qualitative research, will be discussed.

15 Janis Morse embeds this notion – which I have framed into that of eloquence – in an essay devoted to elaborating the grounded theory procedure of sampling, guided by the goals of theoretical saturation. The essay presents two sets of principles meant to guide sampling procedures: general principles for qualitative inquiry and specific principles thought out for grounded theory. The principle – in my words – of eloquence (locating excellent participants) belongs to the first set of principles (Morse 2007: 229).

16 In qualitative methodology literature, the adjective "purposive" is normally preferred to the "purposeful" adopted here. Michael Quinn Patton offers two good reasons, with which I agree, for this (Patton 2015: 265). First, the meaning of purposeful is clearer than purposive among lay participants. Second, the term purposive, related to a kind of sample, is used by statisticians to define a type of quota sample meant to represent – although not probabilistically – the population.

17 In Section 3.2, these ideas will be framed within the notion of conditional plausibility.

18 All these operations have to be accounted for and defended as to their suitability, to avoid the cherry-picking bias, or, more formally, the *ad hoc* selection of cases that can corroborate the statements we defend.

19 The two figures are an adaptation to those presented by Bart Kosko in his intriguing introduction to "fuzzy thinking" (Kosko 1993: 35).

20 Lincoln and Guba introduce another important dimension, the axiological, which I believe is not relevant here.

21 The multivocality of the writing is one of the distinctive features of qualitative research (see Section 2.1). One important exception to the rule of multivocality is represented by Erving Goffman's book *Asylums*. A ponderous volume – of almost 400 pages – it contains a lot of quotations taken from diaries, autobiographies, novels, film screenplays, and, obviously, from scientific literature; but only a few pages contain the voice of the inmates and staff. In a deliberate rereading of the original version, published in 1961, I only met eight pages in which the participants' voices are reported (Goffman 1961: 152, 153, 154, 161, 292, 293, 302, 311).

References

Abend G. 2011 *Thick Concepts and the Moral Brain*, in "European Journal of Sociology", Vol. 52, No. 1, pp. 143–172.

——. 2012 *What the Science of Morality Doesn't Say about Morality*, in "Philosophy of the Social Sciences", Vol. 43, No. 2, pp. 157–200.

——. 2017 *What Are Neural Correlates Neural Correlates of?*, in "BioSocieties", Vol. 12, No. 3, pp. 415–438.

Altheide D.L., Johnson J.M. 1994 *Criteria for Assessing Interpretive Validity in Qualitative Research*, in N.K. Denzin and Y.S. Lincoln (eds.), *Handbook of Qualitative Research*, Thousand Oaks and London, Sage Publications, pp. 485–499.

Bakhtin M.M. 1981 *The Dialogical Imagination: Four Essays*, Austin, University of Texas Press.

Barbour R. 2007 *Introducing Qualitative Research: A Student's Guide to the Craft of Doing Qualitative Research*, London, Sage Publications.

24 *A premise about two crucial issues*

Becker H.S. 1998 *Tricks of the Trade. How to Think About Your Research While You're Doing It*, Chicago and London, The University of Chicago Press.

Blumer H. 1969 *Symbolic Interactionism*, Englewood Cliffs, NJ, Prentice Hall.

Boudon R., Bourricaud F. 2003 *Critical Dictionary of Sociology*, New York and London, Routledge (original edition 1982).

Bury M. 2001 *Illness Narratives: Fact or Fiction*, in "Sociology of Health and Illness", Vol. 23, No. 3, pp. 263–285.

Charmaz K. 2006 *Constructing Grounded Theory*, London, Sage Publications.

Creswell J.W. 2014 *Research Design: Qualitative, Quantitative, and Mixed Methods Approaches*, Thousand Oaks, Sage Publications.

Denzin N.K., Lincoln Y.S. 2005a *The Discipline and Practice of Qualitative Research*, in N.K. Denzin and Y.S. Lincoln (eds.), *The Sage Handbook of Qualitative Research*, Thousand Oaks, Sage Publications, pp. 1–32.

———. 2005b *Strategies of Inquiry*, in N.K. Denzin and Y.S. Lincoln (eds.), *The Sage Handbook of Qualitative Research*, Thousand Oaks, Sage Publications, pp. 375–386.

Douglas J.D. 1976 *Investigative Social Research: Individual and Team Field Research*, London, Sage Publications.

Eco U., Sebock T.S. (eds.). 1988 *Dupin, Holmes, Peirce: The Sign of Three*, Bloomington and Indianapolis, Indiana University Press.

Emmel N. 2013 *Sampling and Choosing Cases in Qualitative Research: A Realist Approach*, London, Sage Publications.

Freshwater D. 2007 *Reading Mixed Methods Research: Contexts for Criticism*, in "Journal of Mixed Methods Research", Vol. 1, No. 2, pp. 134–146.

Geertz C. 1973 *The Interpretation of Cultures: Selected Essays*, New York, Basic Books.

———. 1983 *Local Knowledge: Further Essays in Interpretive Anthropology*, New York, Basic Books.

Ginzburg C. 2013 *Clues, Myths, and the Historical Method*, Baltimore, The Johns Hopkins University Press (original edition 1978).

Glaser B.G., Strauss A. 1967 *The Discovery of Grounded Theory: Strategies for Qualitative Research*, London, Aldine Transaction.

Goffman E. 1956 *The Presentation of Self in Everyday Life*, Edinburgh, University of Edinburgh.

———. 1961 *Asylums: Essays on the Social Situation of Mental Patients and Other Inmates*, New York, Anchor Books Doubleday & Company, Inc.

Gomm R., Hammersley M., Foster P. (eds.). 2000 *Case Study Method*, London, Sage Publications.

Guillermo Del Pinal G., Nathan M.J. 2013 *There and Up Again: On the Uses and Misuses of Neuroimaging in Psychology*, in "Cognitive Neuropsychology", Vol. 30, No. 4, pp. 233–252.

Hammersley M. 1992 *What's Wrong with Ethnography? Methodological Exploration*, London, Routledge.

———. 1999 *Not Bricolage But Boatbuilding: Exploring Two Metaphors for Thinking about Ethnography*, in "Journal of Contemporary Ethnography", Vol. 28, No. 5, pp. 574–585.

Hanson N.R. 1958 *Patterns of Discovery: An Inquiry Into the Conceptual Foundations of Science*, Cambridge, Cambridge University Press.

Hydén L.C. 1997 *Illness and Narrative*, in "Sociology of Health and Illness", Vol. 19, No. 1, pp. 48–69.

King G., Keohane R.O., Verba S. 1994 *Designing Social Inquiry: Scientific Inference in Qualitative Research*, Princeton, NJ, Princeton University Press.

Kleinmann A. 1988 *The Illness Narratives: Suffering, Healing and the Human Condition*, New York, Basic Books.

Kosko B. 1993 *Fuzzy Thinking: The New Science of Fuzzy Logic*, New York, Hyperion.

Lincoln Y.S., Guba E.G. 1985 *Naturalistic Inquiry*, Beverly Hills, CA, Sage Publications.

———. 2013 *The Constructivist Credo*, Walnut Creek, CA, Left Coast Press Inc.

Madison G.B. 1988 *The Hermeneutics of Postmodernity*, Bloomington, Indiana University Press.

Maxwell J.A. 2012 *A Realist Approach for Qualitative Research*, London, Sage Publications.

Merton R.K. 1968 *Social Theory and Social Structure*, Enlarged Edition, New York, The Free Press.

Miles M.B., Huberman A.M. 1984 *Qualitative Data Analysis: A Sourcebook of New Methods*, Thousand Oaks, CA, Sage Publications.

Mills C.W. 2000 *The Sociological Imagination*, Fortieth Anniversary Edition, Oxford and New York, Oxford University Press (original edition 1959).

Morse J.M. 2007 *Sampling in Grounded Theory*, in A. Bryant and K. Charmaz (eds.), *The Sage Handbook of Grounded Theory*, London, Sage Publications, pp. 229–244.

Patton M.Q. 2015 *Qualitative Research & Evaluation Methods*, Fourth Edition, Thousand Oaks, CA, Sage Publications.

Pawson R., Tilley N. 1987 *Realistic Evaluation*, London, Sage Publications.

Sacks H. 1992 *Lectures on Conversation*, Vol. 1, Oxford, Blackwell.

Satel S., Lilienfeld S. 2013 *Brainwashed: The Seductive Appeal of Mindless Neuroscience*, New York, Basic Books.

Schwandt T.A. 1994 *Constructivist, Interpretivist Approaches to Human Inquiry*, in N.K. Denzin and Y.S. Lincoln (eds.), *Handbook of Qualitative Research*, Thousand Oaks and London, Sage Publications, pp. 118–137.

Schwartz-Shea P., Yanow D. 2012 *Interpretive Research Design: Concepts and Processes*, New York and London, Routledge.

Seale C. 1999 *The Quality of Qualitative Research*, London, Sage Publications.

Sorokin P. 1928 *Contemporary Sociological Theories*, New York and London, Harper & Brothers.

Sperber D. 1985 *On Anthropological Knowledge: Three Essays*, Cambridge, Cambridge University Press (original edition 1982).

Strauss A., Corbin J. 1990 *Basics of Qualitative Research*, London, Sage Publications.

Thomas W., Znaniecki F. 1918 *The Polish Peasant in Europe and America: Monograph of an Immigrant Group*, Boston, Richard G. Badger, The Gorham Press.

Uttal W.R. 2001 *The New Phrenology: The Limits of Localizing Cognitive Processes*, Cambridge, MA, MIT Press.

Walton D., Reed C., Macagno F. 2008 *Argumentation Schemes*, Cambridge, Cambridge University Press.

Watson J.B. 1913 *Psychology as the Behaviorist Views It*, in "Psychological Review", Vol. 20, No. 2, pp. 158–177.

Weber M. 1978 *Economy and Society: An Outline of Interpretive Sociology*, Berkeley, Los Angeles and London, University of California Press (original edition 1922).

Williams B.A.O. 1985 *Ethics and the Limits of Philosophy*, Cambridge, MA, Harvard University Press.

Wittgenstein L. 1969 *On Certainty*, Oxford, Basil Blackwell.

Zadeh L.A. 1965 *Fuzzy Sets*, in "Information and Control", No. 8, pp. 338–353.

2 Qualitative research

A portrait

Qualitative research is anything but a monolith, a solid set of research practices carved out of the same theoretical and epistemological matter. This heterogeneity was proudly defended in what can be defined as the "manifesto" of the last generation of qualitative researchers, the first edition of the *Handbook of Qualitative Research*, where the editors use the Bourdieusian metaphor of the field to underline the "essential tensions" that characterize this community of practices.

> It did not take us long to discover that the "field" of qualitative research is far from a unified set of principles promulgated by networked groups of scholars. In fact, we have discovered that the field of qualitative research is defined primarily by a series of essential tensions, contradictions and hesitations. These tensions work back and forth among competing definitions and conceptions of the field.
>
> (Denzin and Lincoln 1994: ix)

Norman Denzin and Yvonna Lincoln also add that qualitative research "has no theory or paradigm that is distinctly its own" (3). A rapid reading of recent qualitative literature and a closer analysis of the most cited methodological handbooks confirm this conclusion. The theoretical roots of qualitative research include, with some historical traditions, such as symbolic interactionism, phenomenology, and the Frankfurt School of critical theory (see Kincheloe and McLaren 1994), and some more recent perspectives such as ethnomethodology, feminist theory, racial and ethnic theories, queer theories, and postcolonial theories. To all this, it is necessary to add the most recent versions of the critical theory, inspired by French philosophers such as Michel Foucault, Jacques Derrida, Félix Guattari, and Gilles Deleuze.[1] Furthermore, for some of the earlier -mentioned theoretical approaches, besides the cognitive version, oriented to describe the social phenomena studied, there is an intervention version, which means transforming society or specific social contexts, usually with the participants' cooperation – technically participatory action research involving additional theoretical references (Lewin 1946; Reason 1994).

An analogous heterogeneity can be recognized among epistemological postures (Pernecky 2016: 183). If the epistemological mainstream can be identified in the constructivist stance, this space is inhabited by diverse persuasions, e.g.,

Qualitative research 27

pragmatism, hermeneutics, and the whole spectrum of constructivism from the moderate to the radical versions. The first version recognizes the right of social phenomena the to "talk back" against our representations (Blumer 1969: 22); of the text, the capacity to rise up against the interpretive project of the reader, compelled to "accept some things that are against [him/her], even though no one else forces [her/him] to do so" (Gadamer 1960, English translation 2004: 355).[2] The radical versions of constructivism are eloquently expressed by the postmodernist position for which there is no reality at all.[3] With the constructivist posture cohabits the critical realist perspective characterized with a constructivist epistemology, but also with a realist ontology (Maxwell 2012).

Among these diverse theoretical and epistemological postures, there are some "tensions", but nothing that can be paralleled with the paradigms war between quantitative and qualitative research that has characterized recent decades. This climate can be credited only partially to shared ethics of theoretical and epistemological freedom, but more to the fact that the epistemological, and in a minor measure, the theoretical postures are usually part of the "tacit knowledge" (Polanyi 1958), not reflexively thematized, which marks out every scientific community.[4]

Considering the level of practices, heterogeneity in qualitative research is vaster (see Pernecky 2016: 196): moving from unobtrusive documentary analysis, like the study of the letters and the archive materials of Polish peasants in America (Thomas and Znaniecki 1918), to the over-intrusive shadowing of some women engineers in a firm (Fletcher 1999); or from the collecting of illness narratives with a set of single individuals involved in in-depth interviews (Estroff, Lachicotte, Illingworth and Johnston 1991), to the study of the interaction between gangs in America (Jankowski 1991). For all these reasons qualitative research, more than a continent that – coherent and united – views suspiciously the border that separates it from the land of quantitative research, is an archipelago made up of distinct islands, linked together by – now tenuous, now more intense – "family resemblances" (Wittgenstein 1953, English translation 1958: § 66–67). Ludwig Wittgenstein used the notion of "family resemblances" to define what games, like board-games, card-games, ball-games, Olympic Games, and so on have in common. The Viennese philosopher recognized among them some resemblance of the same kind as the ones that characterized the members of a family, where the last born has the nose of his grandfather, the build of his mother, the eyes with the same intense blue of the father, and, perhaps, the gait of his older brother. These members of the family do not share a set of traits *uniformly;* they, so to speak, are not cut from the same cloth, but among them, we recognize family resemblances.[5] In some of them, the "air" of the family is more easily recognizable; in some others, we must look more carefully to detect it. Remaining with the Wittgenstein metaphor, we can imagine some "forms of life", some social activities that share only a few elements with the game. Let's think of the simulation of a fight or aggression between male teenagers – a game – that can become an act of bullying – not a game, at least not for all the people involved. To tackle this problem of distinction, that echoes the sorites, or heap paradox, we can use the tools of multimodal logic (see Section 1.2).[6] For each research method, membership of

28   *Qualitative research*

the "game" of qualitative research can be expressed through a continuous function from 0 to 1. In doing so, the quintessential qualitative method, participant observation, belongs to the qualitative game with a value very close to 1, and, for instance, the content analysis applied to social network data, belongs to the same game with a value, let's say, 0.2 or less. *Within* this logical frame, it is possible to identify the features that define the family air shared by qualitative research.

2.1 Three main features of qualitative research

There are, in my view, three characteristics that identify the family resemblance of qualitative research: i) context-sensitivity of data collection procedures; ii) details-focalization; iii) multivocality of the writing. These three traits, while contributing to sketch the portrait of qualitative research, also mark the distinction that separates qualitative and quantitative research. Let's see what these dimensions refer to.

Context-sensitivity of data collection procedures

The context-sensitivity of data collection procedures, the harmonization of the method with the context in which it is applied, constitutes the only trait shared by all the family members of qualitative research. This point is clearly expressed by Barbara Czarniawska, who writes: "If there is one rule of field research, it is that all techniques must be context-sensitive" (2004: 44). This trait expresses with clarity the naturalistic vocation of qualitative research i.e., its orientation toward the *mensuratio ad rem* (Gadamer 1960, English translation 2004: 251), the will to adapt the reading strategies of the text which constitutes the social action (in the meaning of Ricoeur 1971), recognizing the priority of text over the interpreter. In qualitative research, it is not the participants who – in order to allow us to represent their way of being in the world – have to adapt their expressions (words or actions) to the method proposed to them, but it is the method that has to be harmonized with the participants. The necessity to respect the nature of the empirical world under study is clearly expressed in one of the milestones of theory and methods for qualitative research, *Symbolic Interactionism* by Herbert Blumer (1969: vii, 27–28). This peculiarity neatly emerges if we compare the two main versions of data collection based on the interlocution between researcher and participants, the questionnaire, in quantitative research, and the in-depth interview, in qualitative research. In a survey, all the people interviewed receive the same verbal solicitations, with the same wording, in the same fixed order, and, to respond, they have to adapt their views to the predefined possible answers (part of the operational definitions of the variables measured) thought out by the researcher. The situation is totally different in an in-depth interview, eloquently described by Tim Rapley's advice to the interview beginner.

> You don't have to ask the same question in the same way in each interaction. You often cover the same broad themes in different interviews – either through

Qualitative research 29

the interviewee or you raising it as a subject for talk. This is a central rationale of qualitative interviewing – *that it enables you to gather contrasting and complementary talk on the same theme or issue.*

(Rapley 2004: 18, italics in the original)

This disposition toward respect for the nature of the studied phenomena has an evident cognitive value. According to Yvonna Lincoln and Egon Guba, social phenomena "take their meaning as much from the contexts as they do from themselves" (Lincoln and Guba 1985: 189). Thus, it is awareness of the context-dependency of social phenomena that underpins the effort to mould data collection methods to the context where the action is. This orientation guarantees the wealth of the information collected, both with regard to the social phenomena studied, and to the participants' degree of cooperation with our cognitive efforts. From these two sources flows the accuracy of the representation of the phenomena studied.

From a practical point of view, the context-sensitivity of data collection procedures implies a peculiar openness and flexibility of the research path. The conceptual tools employed to guide the research must be flexible to allow their adapting to the changing contexts of qualitative research. Instead of operational definitions, what are requested are "sensitizing concepts" (Blumer 1969: 147–148) suited to implement the suggestions that derive from interaction with the participants and the study of their life contexts.

In quantitative research, the golden rule is that of invariance of the operational definitions: measure all the social properties you are interested in, always in the same way. In qualitative research the golden rule is "find, moment by moment, the right measure for your measurement" and learn from each of your immersions in the context studied the best way to represent it. In doing so, the procedures of data collection evolve day by day, case by case; improving their "validity", to postpone the issue of "reliability" (Kirk and Miller 1986) at the end of the research when, in the reflexive account (Altheide and Johnson 1994), the story of the changing procedures of data collection will be eventually told.[7]

The flexibility and the openness of data collection procedures in qualitative research can be paralleled with the hermeneutical experience of the reading of a text in which, according to Gadamer, it is possible to experience "being pulled up short by the text" (Gadamer 1960, English translation 2004: 270); the experience of meeting something surprising, requiring interpretation or explanation. This kind of experience, made possible by openness, is what triggers off the abductive reasoning typical of qualitative research (see Schwartz-Shea and Yanow 2012: 27 ff.; Tavory and Timmermans 2014). The first clear definition of abductive inference was elaborated by Charles Sanders Peirce as follows (see Chapter 3).

The surprising fact, C, is observed;
> But if A were true, C would be a matter of course,
> Hence, there is reason to suspect that A is true.

(Peirce 1935–1966: § 5.189)

30 *Qualitative research*

The openness of the data collection procedures prepares researchers to meet the unexpected and often brings them face-to-face with surprising facts, which nurture the creativity and the invention of qualitative research through a dialogue between theory and data.[8]

Details-focalization

The second trait of qualitative research identifies its main cognitive purpose, clearly expressed by Jennifer Mason: to grasp "*how things work in particular contexts*" (Mason 2002: 1, italics in the original). For this purpose, to grasp any little detail, all the nuances that define the "how" of the phenomenon studied, attention is focussed on a handful of cases, sometimes only one, recognized as particularly eloquent.[9] In qualitative research, intensive studies are preferred to extensive studies, in wide populations or samples, typical of quantitative research. The reference to the other Muse of social research, the quantitative one, allows specifying the logical nature of this distinction. Although all qualitative studies are carried out focussing on a small number of cases, not all quantitative pieces of research are performed on vast samples or populations. Laboratory experiments, typically, are carried out on a small number of cases, of which a narrow set of variables is considered and measured through a uniform procedure. In laboratory experiments – in sociology, psychology and economics – attention to details, to the nuances that distinguish participants' behaviour, is usually sacrificed on behalf of the homogeneity of the measurement procedures and the control of third variables. Therefore, the second trait of qualitative research here considered allows only a fuzzy distinction between qualitative and quantitative research. This feature of qualitative research frequently becomes the target of a criticism that underlines the anecdotal character of this kind of research. Michael Quinn Patton reports this criticism, quoting the words of an American author, Ophelia Benson, not properly a methodologist, but able to express this point in a lapidary style: "The plural of anecdote is not evidence" (Benson 2013, quoted in Patton 2015: 31). I think that in a book entitled *Defending Qualitative Research*, this argument deserves attention. Before tackling it, I will consider the specular criticism advanced by William Bruce Cameron against quantitative research in an equally lapidary style: "Not everything that can be counted counts, and not everything that counts can be counted" (Cameron 1966: 13). The point here is that the number of observations cannot – alone – determine the quality of an argument, this number being one or 1000. Moving from this premise, instead of contesting the allegation of anecdotalism, I will celebrate it following one of the "ruminations" of Michael Quinn Patton, in his handbook on qualitative evaluation (Patton 2015: 31–33). Patton's thesis, which I adopt, is that an individual event, a small thing upon which one decides to focus attention, may be particularly eloquent, may shed light upon a set of extremely relevant social and cultural aspects. Patton convinces me by telling a tale that takes us to colonial India. The story is about what happened to Mrs Montgomery who, one night, when returning home by a long road, preceded, as usual, by her servant, came across one of the most poisonous snakes in India.

The servant, who had seen it, ordered the lady to stop; she did not listen to him, and the servant was obliged to break the rule that prevented servants from touching the body of their masters: he pushed Lady Montgomery back by placing his hand on her shoulders. Even though she knew that she owed her life to the servant, Mrs Montgomery was determined to dismiss him, for he had disregarded the sacred rule which prevented physical contact between a servant and the master. Although the Lady Montgomery tale has small beginnings, it is emblematic of the English settlers of that time and their representation of the Indian population. So the point is not the anecdotal approach, as Alan Bryman complained (1988: 77), but the eloquence of details selected to support the argument proposed.[10] Mirroring the Cameron quotation, "not all anecdote counts, but some are very eloquent". The eloquence of a description of the single case is underpinned by the position of this case in its field (in Bourdieu's meaning), and the richness of the details presented. Therefore, combining a thought selection of cases with their thick description, it is possible to guarantee the eloquence of our claims. The preference for intensive study is justified by the awareness of the ontological limits of our knowledge of social phenomena. What can be soundly underpinned by our data is only "local knowledge" bounded by time and space (Geertz 1983), within the scope of research focussed on details and nuances (see Section 1.2).

Multivocality of the writing

The third trait that characterizes qualitative research emerges from the last stage of our activity, the textualization of the research results, the organization of the – hopefully rich – dialogue between empirical materials and theory. The great majority of the texts that present the results of qualitative research are written through a combination of the voice of the researcher-author with the voices of participants. The participants' voices enter the text principally through the quotations that the researchers choose from their empirical material: interview or focus group transcripts, field notes, texts collected or solicited in the field. This writing style serves four diverse aims, variously pursued by each author or by the same author in different situations. The most important aim of the orchestration between the voice of the author and that of the participants is to convince the reader of the soundness of the interpretation proposed. The second function of multivocality is to evoke in the reader the colours of the field, painting them with words. It is through the combination of our academic, courteous, sometimes posh voice, with the undisciplined, informal, sometimes rude participants' voices that we can write texts evoking strong emotions in the reader. The third function performed by the multivocality of qualitative texts relates to the possibility, given to participants, to express – although with different degrees of autonomy – their voices. The fourth and last aim of the multivocality of the writing is that of a special type of reflexivity which, in agreement with Enzo Colombo (personal communication to the author), can be labelled as an enlarged version. In the previous chapter, I insisted on characterizing qualitative research as a way to produce a sound representation of social phenomena through procedures of data

32 *Qualitative research*

collection and analysis that evolve, grow through their applications. This great flexibility does not excuse us from our accountability obligation (see Mason 2002: 7). Researchers are free to define their way of collecting and analysing data, but in defending the soundness of the research results they have to describe – after the event – how they have acquired the evidence that underpins their conclusions. The usual way in which the accountability obligation is honoured is based only on the gaze and the voice of the researcher committed to the production of a reflexive account of his/her experience which obviously implies a relation with the participants. The participants' voices can expand the area of reflexivity when the author decides to benefit from their description of the relationship maintained with the researcher. This kind of participants' voice can be promoted through the well-known member-check procedures, properly meant as a tool to deliver new information and not as a test of the validity of our interpretation. In addition to this kind of solicited feedback, it is possible to get information about our relationship with participants through their spontaneous communications. Even short meta-communications between interviewer and respondent can be useful, something like: "I am saying this to you because I feel that I can trust you". To conclude, a combination of the plain, direct reflexive account by the researcher with some comments on the observational relation by the participants can give the reader a deeper representation of the field experience. All these aspects of the multivocality of writing will be developed in greater detail in the last chapter of the book (Section 6.2).

The three features just presented – context-sensitivity, details-focalization, and multivocality – define the family resemblance that qualitative methods share and, at the same time, mark their distance from quantitative research. These traits are sometimes more and sometimes less pronounced in the islands of the archipelago of qualitative research whose geography can be traced considering, through closer observation, how data are collected. To do so and outline a map of the archipelago I will consider three important aspects of data collection: i) the degree of perturbation induced; ii) the main focus; individuals versus social interactions; iii) the context, natural versus artificial, where the observational relation takes place. These three dimensions will be combined in a taxonomy that allows distinguishing five different islands in the archipelago of qualitative research.

With the first criterion, the degree of perturbation induced by the data collection procedures, three conditions are distinguished: the absence of perturbation, interactive perturbation, and observational perturbation. The perturbation is absent if the data collection procedure does not have any impact on what we mean to observe. There is observational perturbation when, during the data collection procedures, the participants are aware of the attention paid to them by the researcher, and for this reason, they may change their behaviour or modulate the measure of their cooperation. We have interactive perturbation when it is the simple presence of the researcher in the context observed – not perceived as such, but a bona fide member – that induces alterations in the behaviour of other bystanders, simply by the fact of being among them (we experience this kind of perturbation every time we share a short stay in an elevator with an unknown person). The second criterion is intuitive; it distinguishes data collection procedures focussed on a single individual from procedures that pinpoint interaction among individuals. The last criterion considers the context in which the relationship between the researcher and participants takes place. The context is natural if it is the common theatre where the action takes place; otherwise it is artificial. The application of these three criteria generates the taxonomy illustrated in Figure 2.1.

The first island, that of nonintrusive methods, includes documentary analysis and distance observation. If documentary analysis is widely used in qualitative research, either on its own or combined with other methods, distance observation, based on the use of powerful telephoto lenses (close to ethological observation) is not so common.[11] The second island, in which data are collected through interactive perturbation, includes naturalistic observation, covered participant observation and field experiment.[12] The third island includes open (uncovered) participant observation, autoethnography, and shadowing. I think that participant observation is so well-known that it does not need an example to illustrate it. Autoethnography is quite a recent qualitative method, in which researchers observe their own experience. Two main versions of autoethnography cohabit in the qualitative research field, an analytical and an evocative or introspective one (for the distinction between them see Adams, Holmes Jones and Ellis 2015). Shadowing is a kind of observation focussed on an individual; the researcher follows like a shadow for some days or weeks. It can be considered the most intrusive method in social research, allowing one to rebuild, through the eyes of the participant followed, his/her social contexts of life.[13] In the fourth – separate – island, we find the focus group, a research method designed to study the interaction of small groups committed to discussion, guided by two researchers, of a specific topic (see Krueger 1994).[14] The fifth and last island combines the in-depth interview with solicited diaries. Like participant observation, the in-depth interview is well known in social research, and does not need an introduction. The use of solicited diaries, on the other hand, is not a common data collection procedure in qualitative research. The purpose of this method is to collect longitudinal data about a specific

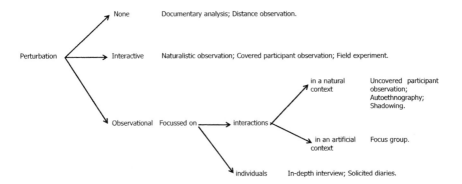

Figure 2.1 Islands in the archipelago: a map of qualitative methods

34   Qualitative research

experience, notwithstanding the defect that the information received is moulded by the participant individual's self-censorship.[15]

When I present to my students this map of qualitative research, almost invariably some of them ask: "Where are visual methods in this map?" and, after a while, an apparently "digital native" adds: "What about the internet research?". Both questions are pertinent, but – at least in my view – do not impose a radical reshaping of the proposed taxonomy. Starting from the first question, visual methods resides in each of the five islands, in a double role as an instrument to produce data and as material on which data analysis is performed.[16] The documentary analysis is applied not only to written materials but also to images, both fixed (photos) and mobile (videos). Erving Goffman's classic study of the representation of women in advertising is a clear example of documentary analysis of images (Goffman 1976). Another classic example of documentary analysis, applied this time to moving pictures, namely videos, is Gregory Bateson's study of the Hans Steinhoff movie *Hitlerjunge Quex*, realized in 1933. Bateson's study belonged to a broad project meant to study culture at a distance, and his contribution was devoted to an analysis of Nazi culture (Bateson 1953). In the sociological context, the research of Randall Collins, *Violence* (2008), based on the analysis of video-surveillance cameras, constitutes another eloquent example. Most distance observations produce images to be analysed, and this is the case of the research cited earlier on the body strategies of collision avoidance on a crowed pedestrian crossing (Collett and Marsh 1974). In the second island, that of naturalistic observation, covert participant observation and field experiment, the use of images is not easy because it can produce the disclosure of researcher identity and – no less important – can generate an ethical violation of the privacy right of participants. Having said that, some usage of visual methods in this island is possible, and actually are adopted in so-called commercial ethnography (Gobo 2009), particularly in the study of consumption behaviour in supermarkets. In this sanctuary of shopping, closed circuit video-recording systems (CCTV) are used, more than to prevent thefts, to video record the behaviour of the clients, to learn how to sell their products more and better (see Underhill 1999, cited in Gobo 2009). In the third island, that of uncovered participant observation, autoethnography and shadowing, the use of images, and visual methods is quite common. Starting from Bronisław Malinowski (2002: 418–473, first edition 1922) use of the photograph to illustrate his theory and to document his "being there" (2002: 418–473, first edition 1922), through more aware and critical use of photographs in Gregory Bateson and Margaret Mead's work on Balinese character (1942), ending with the classic work of Douglas Harper on Tramp culture (1996), participant observation boasts a long tradition in the use of images. In autoethnography the use of combinations of tools to represent the researcher's personal experience is quite common, particularly in the evocative stream. Thus, with the more traditional ethnographic notes we can find the visual diary through which the researcher's experience is recorded and transmitted; that is "visual autoethnography" (Chaplin 2011). Shadowing is, in itself, the most intrusive method of research, and adding visual methods to this scenario seems too demanding for both the researcher and the participant. Consulting the ProQuest archive with the keywords "shadowing" and "visual methods", I failed to find any pertinent entries. In the fourth scarcely inhabited island, that of the focus group, the use of visual methods is common. When the issue discussed is not too delicate, it is customary to videotape the discussion between the participants involved in a focus group, although not all scholars agree on this solution (Krueger 1994: 49).[17] Finally, on the fifth island, that of the in-depth interview and solicited materials, visual methods are at home. For the in-depth interview, visual methods can be used both to trigger participant discourses and to record the speech acts of the two main characters of the conversation (interviewer and respondent). For the former, the interview includes the photo-elicitation tool, with which the participant reacts using free discourse to images proposed by the interviewer (Lapenta 2011). The videotaping of an in-depth interview adds to the linguistic dimension of the speech as well as information on the paralinguistic and extralinguistic dimensions that can improve accuracy in the interpretation of the text.[18] Among the solicited materials, along with texts we can consider participants' production of photos or videos, facilitated by the diffusion of smartphones. These approaches belong to what is commonly defined "participatory visual methods" (Chalfen 2011), through which it is possible to get a vivid view of participants' lives, with the self-censorship limitations associated with all kinds of delegated data collection procedures.

For the second question, about the internet research, it is possible to find an answer moving from a distinction – perhaps approximate – among the main kinds of data available on the web: virtual data and digital data. Data that we can get from the web using – adapted for that context – qualitative methods used offline are virtual. An interview or a focus group carried out on the web can be placed in some island designed for the more traditional version of these methods. Digital data, on the other hand, are natively digital objects, originating on the internet and analysed with digital methods (Rogers 2013). The world of digital data is all but homogenous, and data analysis procedures are equally heterogeneous. Considering the quota of information that can be analysed using qualitative methods, the internet offers mainly texts, made up of words and images, that can be analysed in perspective and with the tools of documentary analysis. The internet also offers the possibility to observe how a text is created through the interaction of web surfers. We have this opportunity when following a discussion in a forum. If we decide not to intervene in the discussion, as a "lurker", our activity is just like naturalistic observation in the offline world. If we decide to intervene in the discussion evolving before our eyes, we move in an area very close to that of field experiment or participant observation. The kind of field experiment that can be carried out is close to the Garfinkel breaching experiments. To give an idea of what I mean, think of entering an anti-vaxxer forum and publishing a post which says something like: "My son is immunosupressed and cannot take any vaccines, but he risks his life every day by living with your healthy son, a proud anti-vaxxer!". In the area of participant observation or, with an expression more in tune with the context, digital ethnography, the two main options of the offline version are still present: covert or overt observation. We are in the area of digital

36 *Qualitative research*

ethnography if, and only if, we virtually interact with the participants. If not, we move back to documentary analysis or naturalistic observation. If what I have just said is sound, we do not need to reshape the proposed map of qualitative research to include visual or internet research methods.

The main features of qualitative research having been defined, with a draft map of the archipelago of qualitative research, what is missing is an evaluation of the strengths and the alleged weakness of this way of doing social research.

2.2 The strengths of qualitative research

The main strength of qualitative research lies in information accuracy. The context-sensitivity of data collection procedures allows participants to express themselves in their own words, to act in their natural environments. Again, the openness of the conceptual tools permits meeting the unexpected, triggering abductive processes that guarantee a more accurate representation of the phenomena studied. The availability of a profusion of clues to participants' degree of cooperation (see Section 1.1) still further increases the accuracy of the information collected. The accuracy of the representation of the phenomena studied, of the answers we attribute to the way in which things work in a particular context, assumes a distinctive shape when a longitudinal perspective is adopted. When time enters equation, qualitative research offers a specific contribution to the reconstruction of the social phenomena, giving a narrative account of processes and causality (cf. Becker 1998: 57–63).

Some of the research methods earlier presented in the map have an intrinsic longitudinal character. It is the case of naturalistic and participant observation (both overt and covert), of autoethnography and shadowing. For all these data collection procedures, attention toward the evolution of the phenomena in time is intrinsic. We observe the action – our action included – moment by moment, for a long enough time to allow us to find an acceptable answer to our questions. The other qualitative methods, namely documentary analysis, distance observation, focus groups, in-depth interviews, and solicited diaries, can be carried out in a longitudinal version through repeated application. This happens when – in the same context or with the same individuals – we repeat our observation or dialogue two or more times. That is the case of the repeated interviews or repeated focus groups or the case of repeated reading of pages on the internet (which change their contents).[19] We can do a repeated reading of the posts of an influencer on a specific topic but also the self-presentation page of a company or a political party over the years. For the solicited diary, the repetition is almost implicit but is still repetition. In filling in their diaries, participants define one or more moments in the day in which they look at recent past events to describe and comment on them in the diary. In a diary, there is not a moment-by-moment description of lived experiences: it is impossible to act and – simultaneously – observe and describe our actions.

A visual metaphor can illustrate the differences between the two groups of qualitative methods. The intrinsically longitudinal methods, naturalistic and participant observation, autoethnography and shadowing, deliver a film clip for the actions analysed; the methods that can have a longitudinal version, documentary analysis, distance observation, focus group, in-depth interview, and solicited diaries, deliver a set of snapshots taken in a sequence of time points.[20] The field experiment is in between these two main categories. In the ethnographic version, the experiment is properly a longitudinal tool. This was the case of the Rosenhan experiment on the epistemological status of psychiatric diagnosis, carried out by eight researchers who pretended to hear voices in their head and therefore to be schizophrenic. They were hospitalized for a period ranging from seven to 52 days, during which they performed an ethnographic study of the ward in which they were confined (Rosenhan 1973). The version of qualitative experiment inspired by Garfinkel's breaching experiments can assume a longitudinal shape only through a repetition of the same experiment in a similar context two or more times. Sensitivity to time produces two specific assets for qualitative research: the prolonged observation guaranteed by naturalistic and participant observation and, although to a lesser extent, by shadowing, allows analysis of the burning issue of the relationship between what we say and what we do (see Deutscher 1973). Time, moreover, can be a good remedy for the participants' distrust, a tool with which we can gain their cooperation.

2.3 The weaknesses of qualitative research

The criticisms levelled against qualitative research compose an old and well known adagio that points out three inexcusable lacunae, those of impersonality, uniformity, and generalizability. The charge of lack of impersonality relates to so-called subjectivity of the qualitative research results. The argument that underpins this allegation maintains that due to the relevance of the researcher's personal attributes, it is quite improbable that two different scholars could reach the same results studying the same phenomenon.[21] The second accusation in a way offers an explanation for the subjectivity of qualitative research results. The lack of uniformity in data collection procedures is mainly responsible for the dependence of the person of the researcher on the results acquired. The third charge, that of lack of generalisability, maintains that due to the limited number of cases studied, they do not have enough statistical power to defend the extension from the cases studied to other unstudied ones. All these lacunae or weaknesses are usually synthesized with the unappealable accusation of lack of rigour. Before analysing and trying to deconstruct these charges, it is important to underline that the idea of rigour that guides this accusation is the one that characterizes quantitative research, based on standardization, and through it, on impersonality, and on the use of the "logic of inference" based on the theory of probability (see King, Keohane and Verba 1994: 15; Goldthorpe 2000: 67, 88). But now is time to consider, point by point, all these alleged weaknesses.

Lack of impersonality

The charge of lack of impersonality is totally founded, but it doesn't identify a weakness. The impact of the researcher's persona, that of observational relationship of the study results, is one of the issues of the "reflexive account" (Altheide

38   *Qualitative research*

and Johnson 1994) that all qualitative researchers maintain as their epistemological and ethical duty (see Section 6.1). Focussing on this aspect changes a source of bias into an information resource. Moreover, among the methodological tools developed in the archipelago of qualitative research, there are some explicitly directed toward improving the intersubjectivity of research results. Team ethnography (Erikson and Stull 1998) is one of the more efficient in this regard. Doing team ethnography means working in a team of ethnographers that share (to various degrees) experience of the same site and build a representation of it through a dialectical confrontation, from which some germs of inter-subjectivity can flourish.

Lack of uniformity

The charge of lack of uniformity is totally founded, but – again – it doesn't identify a weakness, rather one of the most relevant distinctive traits of qualitative research. The lack of uniformity, opportunely reworded as context-sensitivity, is what guarantees the special accuracy of qualitative research. The harmonization of data collection procedures with the singular features of the cases studied can create some difficulties during the data analysis phase when we must compare different cases regarding the same properties registered through different procedures. This is what Tim Rapley recommended by saying: "You don't have to ask the same question in the same way in each interaction". In any case, for this problem – not always adequately thematized in methodological reflection – there are some convincing solutions. These solutions will be plainly presented in Chapters 3 and 5. For now, it is possible to hint that these solutions rest on the use of a multimodal logic (see Section 1.2) realized by the Weberian tool of the ideal type, and on some tools drawn from the theory of argumentation. Concerning the accusation of lack of uniformity, it is necessary to add that adhering to the alternative rule of harmonization does not imply the renounce to fulfil the duty of accountability. If it is true that the simplest way to guarantee the accountability of the data collection procedures is through recourse to the operational definition, the solution typically adopted by quantitative research, this is not the only way possible (and may not even be the best). Through the reflexive account is it possible to satisfy the accountability principle with equivalent results.[22]

Lack of generalizability

If by lack of generalizability we mean the impossibility to extend the scope of qualitative research results *through statistical inference* or, more generally, through the theory of probability again this is totally true, but not relevant. The theory of probability is not the only tool to guarantee the soundness of the extension of the scope of our research results. This important job can be done, in the archipelago of qualitative research, by the theory of argumentation, whose essential features will be illustrated in the next chapter. The theory of argumentation

Qualitative research   39

allows us to satisfy the scientific requisite of rigour in a different way, combining rigour with creativity.

Notes

1 To compile the list of theoretical roots tabled in the text, I consulted Lincoln and Guba (1985), Denzin and Lincoln (1994), Mason (2002), Flick, von Kardoff and Steinke (2004), Creswell (2013), Lincoln and Guba (2013), Patton (2015), Pernecky (2016). About the more recent versions of critical theory, the influence on qualitative research of scholars as Foucault and Derrida is well known. The other two French thinkers, Guattari and Deleuze, have had an important impact in Latin America, where they inspired the cartography approach (see Ferigato and Carvalho 2011).
2 These two instances of constructivism oriented to a *mensuratio ad rem*, to the recognition of the reasons of the phenomena studied, are – at least in my reading – expressed in these two passages, respectively drawn out by *Symbolic Interactionism* by Blumer and *Truth and Method* by Gadamer. "One errs if he thinks that since the empirical world can exist for human beings only in terms of images or conceptions of it, therefore reality must be sought in images or conceptions independent of an empirical world. Such a solipsistic position is untenable and would make empirical science impossible. The position is untenable because of the fact that the empirical world can 'talk back' to our pictures of it or assertions about it – talk back in the sense of challenging and resisting, or not bending to, our images or conceptions of it" (Blumer 1969: 22). "In human relations the important thing is, as we have seen, to experience the Thou truly as a Thou – i.e., not to overlook his claim but to let him really say something to us. Here is where openness belongs. But ultimately this openness does not exist only for the person who speaks; rather, anyone who listens is fundamentally open . . . openness to the other, then, involves recognizing that I myself must accept some things that are against me, even though no one else forces me to do so" (Gadamer 1960, English translation 2004: 355).
3 For a concise illustration of the possible versions of the constructivist stance see Lincoln and Guba (1985: 83–87).
4 The observations of Peregrine Schwartz-Shea and Dvora Yanow (2012: 5) point in the same direction.
5 Ludwig Wittgenstein defined as follows the notion of family resemblances: "Consider for example the proceedings that we call 'games'. I mean board-games, card-games, ball-games, Olympic games, and so on. What is common to them all? – Don't say: 'There *must* be something common, or they would not be called 'games' – but *look and see* whether there is anything common to all. – For if you look at them you will not see something that is common to *all,* but similarities, relationships, and a whole series of them at that. To repeat: don't think, but look! – Look for example at board-games, with their multifarious relationships. Now pass to card-games; here you find many correspondences with the first group, but many common features drop out, and others appear. When we pass next to ballgames, much that is common is retained, but much is lost. – Are they all 'amusing'? Compare chess with noughts and crosses. Or is there always winning and losing, or competition between players? Think of patience. In ball games there is winning and losing; but when a child throws his ball at the wall and catches it again, this feature has disappeared. Look at the parts played by skill and luck; and at the difference between skill in chess and skill in tennis. Think now of games like ring-a-ring-a-roses; here is the element of amusement, but how many other characteristic features have disappeared! And we can go through the many, many other groups of games in the same way; can see how similarities crop up and disappear. And the result of this examination is: we see a complicated network of similarities overlapping and crisscrossing: sometimes overall similarities, sometimes similarities of detail . . . I can think

40   *Qualitative research*

of no better expression to characterize these similarities than 'family resemblances'; for the various resemblances between members of a family: build, features, colour of eyes, gait, temperament, etc. etc. overlap and criss-cross in the same way. – And I shall say: 'games' form a family" (Wittgenstein 1953, English translation 1958 § 66–67). For the application of this concept to define what qualitative methods have in common, see Cardano (2011: 16); Schwartz-Shea and Yanow (2012: 13).

6   The term "sorites" derives from the Greek word *sōritēs*, meaning "heap". This paradox is usually credited to the Megarian philosopher Eubulides (fourth century BC), and relates to the vague predicates, like being a heap, a bald or tall person and so on. The gist of this paradox can be expressed this way: if a heap of sand is reduced by a single grain at a time, at what exact point does it cease to be considered a heap? (see https://plato.stanford.edu/entries/sorites-paradox/).

7   In the classic book, which may be outdated, by Jerome Kirk and Marc Miller, *Reliability and Validity in Qualitative Research*, they define these two concepts as follows: "Loosely speaking 'reliability' is the extent to which a measurement procedure yields the same answer however and whenever it is carried out; 'validity' is the extent to which it gives the correct answer. These concepts apply equally well to qualitative observation" (Kirk and Miller 1986: 19). In the statement that closes the book, they write: "The fundamental gist of this book is that the problem of validity is handled by field research and the problem of reliability is handled by documented ethnographic decision making" (73).

8   In the text, I have hinted at the Heraclitian maxim: "If you do not expect the unexpected you will not find it". It is the openness of qualitative research that that makes possible the encounter, sometimes the clash, with the unexpected.

9   The focus on a single eloquent case characterizes the critical case design that will be elaborated in detail in Section 4.2.1.

10   In Bryan's book, devoted to mapping the debate on qualitative and quantitative methods, we can read: "There is a tendency towards an anecdotal approach to the use of 'data' in relation to conclusions or explanations in qualitative research. Brief conversations, snippets from unstructured interviews, or example of a particular activity are used to provide evidence for a particular contention. There are grounds for disquiet in that the representativeness or generality of these fragments is rarely addressed" (Bryman 1988: 77).

11   A good example of documentary analysis is represented by the classic study by William Thomas and Florian Znaniecki of Polish immigrants in America. Thomas and Znaniecki analysed a collection of 754 letters of Polish immigrants received in response to an advertisement in a Polish newspaper, and some more empirical materials from archival data, institutional documents, and the long autobiography of a young Pole, Wladek Wisznienski. For distance observation, a good example is that of Collet and Marsh on the body strategies of collision avoidance on a crowded pedestrian crossing (Collett and Marsh 1974).

12   Among the studies with which I am most familiar, a good illustration of naturalistic observation is the study by Jeff Nash of the "community on wheels", commuters on suburban buses (Nash 1975). One of the best known and, at the same time, most controversial pieces of research based on covered participant observation is the study by Laud Humphreys of impersonal sex in public toilets (Humphreys 1975). For an updated presentation of this way of doing research, see Calvey (2017). Experiments are not so common in qualitative research, but two good examples come to mind. The first is the breaching experiments devised by Harold Garfinkel to allow tacit rules to be evident by means of their violation (Garfinkel 1967). The second example is the ethnographic experiment carried out by David Rosenhan in American psychiatric hospitals. Eight scholars, pretending to be mad, succeeded in being hospitalized, observing how psychiatric diagnosis and cure work (Rosenhan 1973).

13 The best known study based on autoethnography is that carried out by Carolyn Ellis on her experience of the chronic illness and death of her husband (Ellis 1995). For a plain presentation of shadowing, see the fine book by Barbara Czarniawska (2007). Among the research based on shadowing my favourite is that by Joyce Fletcher, *Disappearing Act. Gender, Power, and Relational Practice at Work* (1999). Following six women engineers in their daily activities, Fletcher aims to document the "invisible" organizational practices, carried out mainly by women, that keeps the members of an organization together.

14 My favourite research based on focus groups is the study of the precocious initiation to tobacco smoking among pre-adolescents in Canada, carried out by Katherine Frohlich, Louise Potvin, Patrick Chabot, and Ellen Corin. These scholars used focus groups with natural groups and elaborated a very intriguing theoretical notion, that of "collective lifestyle", which offers an interesting contribution on the study of health behaviours (Frolich, Potvin, Chabot et al. 2002).

15 A good example of the use of solicited diaries is the study by Felicity Thomas (2006), carried out in Namibia. Thomas focussed on HIV-infected people and on their caregivers. She asked seven patients and their caregivers to compile a diary of their daily experiences for a period ranging from one to six months.

16 In writing the pages dedicated to visual method, I was greatly assisted by colleague Luigi Gariglio, whom I warmly thank.

17 On the use of videotaping, Richard Krueger in his highly cited handbook, *Focus Groups. A Practical Guide for Applied Research,* writes: "Videotaping is obtrusive and usually not worth the effort. I have found that it may change the environment and affect participant spontaneity. Videotaping usually requires several cameras plus camera operators who attempt to swing the camera quickly to follow the flowing conversation. The fuss and fury of videotaping make the focus group appear more like a circus than a discussion" (Krueger 1994: 49).

18 The linguistic dimension pertains to what is said during the interview through the exclusive use of spoken language. The paralinguistic dimension pertains to the modalities in which speech is modulated by tone, timbre, intensity, and the volume of the voice. The extralinguistic dimension concerns intentional and unintentional forms of communication that are expressed by what, in a broad sense, can be defined as body language – for instance, posture, movement, crying, laughing, and coughing.

19 The repeated interview is one of the tools of the life course approach, particularly in prospective studies oriented to follow a sample of individuals through their life. For an illustration of the qualitative version of this approach, see Laub and Sampson (1998).

20 The view of longitudinal qualitative research adopted here is less strict that those proposed by Johnny Saldaña (2003), who considers the presence of a change and a specific duration as a condition to consider research longitudinal.

21 The disagreement between the studies is interestingly represented by Karl Heider with the Kurosawa metaphor of the "Rashomon effect" (Heider 1988).

22 In the text, I implicitly refer to the idea of the method proposed by Gary Brent Madison and exposed in Section 1.2.

References

Adams T.E., Holmes Jones S., Ellis C. 2015 *Autoethnography*, Oxford, Oxford University Press.

Altheide D.L., Johnson J.M. 1994 *Criteria for Assessing Interpretive Validity in Qualitative Research*, in N.K. Denzin and Y.S. Lincoln (eds.), *Handbook of Qualitative Research*, Thousand Oaks and London, Sage Publications, pp. 485–499.

42 *Qualitative research*

Bateson G. 1953 *An Analysis of the Nazi Film Hitlerjunge Quex*, in M. Mead and R. Metraux (eds.), *The Study of Culture at a Distance*, New York and Oxford, Berghahn Books, pp. 331–350.

Becker H.S. 1998 *Tricks of the Trade. How to Think About Your Research While You're Doing It*, Chicago and London, The University of Chicago Press.

Benson O. 2013 *Whose Pattern?*, in "Free Inquiry", Vol. 33, No. 6, p. 11.

Blumer H. 1969 *Symbolic Interactionism*, Englewood Cliffs, NJ, Prentice Hall.

Bryman A. 1988 *Quantity and Quality in Social Research*, London, Unwin Hyman.

Calvey D. 2017 *Covert Research: The Art, Politics and Ethics of Undercover Fieldwork*, Los Angeles, Sage Publications.

Cameron W.B. 1966 *Informal Sociology: A Casual Introduction to Sociological Thinking*, New York, Random House.

Cardano M. 2011 *La ricerca qualitativa*, Bologna, Il Mulino.

Chalfen R. 2011 *Differentiating Practices of Participatory Visual Media Production*, in E. Margolis and L. Pauwels (eds.), *The Sage Handbook of Visual Research Methods*, London, Sage Publications, pp. 186–200.

Chaplin E. 2011 *The Photo Diary as an Autoethnographic Method*, in E. Margolis and L. Pauwels (eds.), *The Sage Handbook of Visual Research Methods*, London, Sage Publications, pp. 241–262.

Collett P., Marsh P. 1974 *Pattern of Public Behaviour: Collision Avoidance on a Pedestrian Crossing*, in "Semiotica", Vol. 12, No. 4, pp. 281–299.

Creswell J.W. 2013 *Qualitative Inquiry and Research Design: Choosing among Five Approaches*, Third Edition, Thousand Oaks, Sage Publications.

Czarniawska B. 2004 *Narrative in Social Science Research*, London, Sage.

Czarniawska B. 2007 *Shadowing and Other Techniques for Doing Fieldwork in Modern Societies*, Malmö and Sweden, Liber AB.

Denzin N.K., Lincoln Y.S. (eds.). 1994 *Handbook of Qualitative Research*, Thousand Oaks, London and New Delhi, Sage Publications.

Deutscher I. 1973 *What We Say/What We Do*, Glenview, IL, Scott Foresman & Company.

Ellis C. 1995 *Final Negotiation: A Story of Love and Loss, and Chronic Illness*, Philadelphia, Temple University Press.

Erikson K., Stull D. 1998 *Doing Team Ethnography: Warnings and Advice*, London, Sage Publications.

Estroff S.E., Lachicotte W.S., Illingworth L.C., Johnston A. 1991 *Everybody's Got a Little Mental Illness: Accounts of Illness and Self among People with Severe, Persistent Mental Illnesses*, in "Medical Anthropology Quarterly", Vol. 4, pp. 331–369.

Ferigato S.H., Carvalho S.R. 2011 *Pesquisa qualitativa, cartografia e saúde: conexões*, in "Interface–Comunicação Saúde Educação", Vol. 15, No. 38, pp. 663–675.

Fletcher J.K. 1999 *Disappearing Acts: Gender, Power, and Relational Practice at Work*, Boston, MA, MIT Press.

Flick U., von Kardoff E., Steinke I. (eds.) 2004 *A Companion to Qualitative Research*, London, Thousand Oaks and New Delhi, Sage Publications.

Frolich K.L., Potvin L., Chabot P., Corin E. 2002 *A Theoretical and Empirical Analysis of Context: Neighbourhoods, Smoking and Youth*, in "Social Science & Medicine", Vol. 54, pp. 1401–1417.

Gadamer H.G. 2004 *Truth and Method*, London and New York, Continuum (original edition 1960).

Garfinkel H. 1967 *Studies in Ethnomethodology*, Englewood Cliffs, NJ, Prentice-Hall Inc.

Geertz C. 1983 *Local Knowledge: Further Essays in Interpretive Anthropology*, New York, Basic Books.

Gobo G. 2009 *La società dell'osservazione. Nuove opportunità per la ricerca etnografica*, in "Rassegna Italiana di Sociologia", Vol. 50, No. 1, pp. 101–132.

Goffman E. 1976 *Gender Advertisement*, New York, Harper & Row Publisher.

Goldthorpe J. 2000 *On Sociology: Numbers, Narratives, and the Integration of Research and Theory*, Oxford, Oxford University Press.

Heider K.G. 1988 *The Rashomon Effects: When Anthropologists Disagree*, in "American Anthropologist", Vol. 90, No. 1, pp. 73–81.

Humphreys L. 1975 *Tearoom Trade: Impersonal Sex in Public Places*, Enlarged Edition, New York, de Gruyter.

Jankowski M.S. 1991 *Islands in the Street*, Berkeley and Los Angeles, University of California Press.

Kincheloe J.L., McLaren P.L. 1994 *Rethinking Critical Theory and Qualitative Research*, in N.K. Denzin and Y.S. Lincoln (eds.), *Handbook of Qualitative Research*, Thousand Oaks, London and New Delhi, Sage Publications, pp. 138–157.

King G., Keohane R.O., Verba S. 1994 *Designing Social Inquiry: Scientific Inference in Qualitative Research*, Princeton, Princeton University Press.

Kirk J., Miller M.L. 1986 *Reliability and Validity in Qualitative Research*, London, Sage Publications.

Krueger R.A. 1994 *Focus Groups: A Practical Guide for Applied Research*, London, Sage Publications.

Lapenta F. 2011 *Some Theoretical and Methodological Views on Photo-Elicitation*, in E. Margolis and L. Pauwels (eds.), *The Sage Handbook of Visual Research Methods*, London, Sage Publications, pp. 201–213.

Lewin K. 1946 *Action Research and Minority Problems*, in "Journal of Social Issues", No. 2, pp. 34–46.

Laub J., Sampson R. 1998 *Integrating Quantitative and Qualitative Data*, in J.Z. Giele and G.H. Elder Jr.(eds.), *Methods of Life Course Research: Qualitative and Quantitative Approaches*, Thousand Oaks, London and New Delhi, Sage Publications, pp. 213–230.

Lincoln Y.S., Guba E.G. 1985 *Naturalistic Inquiry*, Beverly Hills, CA, Sage Publications.

———. 2013 *The Constructivist Credo*, Walnut Creek, CA, Left Coast Press Inc.

Malinowski B. 2002 *Argonauts of the Western Pacific: An Account of Native Enterprise and Adventure in the Archipelagoes of Melanesian New Guinea*, London, Routledge (first edition 1922).

Mason J. 2002 *Qualitative Researching*, Second Edition, London, Sage Publications.

Maxwell J.A. 2012 *A Realist Approach for Qualitative Research*, London, Sage Publications.

Nash J. 1975 *Bus Riding: Community on Wheels*, in "Urban Life", Vol. 4, No. 1, pp. 99–124.

Patton M.Q. 2015 *Qualitative Research & Evaluation Methods*, Fourth Edition, Thousand Oaks, CA, Sage Publications.

Peirce C.S. 1935–1966 *Collected Papers of Charles Sanders Peirce*, in C. Hartshorne, P. Weiss, and A.W. Burks (eds.), 8 vols. Cambridge, MA, Harvard University Press.

Pernecky T. 2016 *Epistemology and Metaphysics for Qualitative Research*, Thousand Oaks, London and New Delhi, Sage Publications.

Polanyi M. 1958 *Personal Knowledge: Towards a Post-Critical Philosophy*, London, Routledge & Kegan Paul Ltd.

Randall C. 2008 *Violence: A Micro-Sociological Theory*, Princeton and Oxford, Princeton University Press.

44 *Qualitative research*

Rapley T. 2004 *Interviews*, in C. Seale, G. Gobo, J.F. Gubrium and D. Silverman (eds.), *Qualitative Research Practice*, London, Sage Publications, pp. 15–33.

Reason P. 1994 *Three Approaches to Participative Inquiry*, in N.K. Denzin and Y.S. Lincoln (eds.), *Handbook of Qualitative Research*, Thousand Oaks and London, Sage Publications, pp. 324–339.

Ricoeur P. 1971 *The Model of the Text: The Meaningful Action Considered as a Text*, in P. Rabinow and W.M. Sullivan (eds.), *Interpretive Social Science: A Reader*, Berkeley, Los Angeles and London, University of California Press, pp. 73–101.

Rogers R. 2013 *Digital Methods*, Boston, MIT Press.

Rosenhan D.L. 1973 *On Being Sane in Insane Places*, in "Science", Vol. 179, No. 4070, pp. 250–258.

Saldaña J. 2003 *Longitudinal Qualitative Research: Analyzing Change Through Time*, Walnut Creek, Lanham, New York and Oxford, Altamira Press.

Schwartz-Shea P., Yanow D. 2012 *Interpretive Research Design: Concepts and Processes*, New York and London, Routledge.

Tavory I., Timmermans S. 2014 *Abductive Analysis: Theorizing Qualitative Research*, Chicago and London, The University of Chicago Press.

Thomas F. 2006 *Stigma, Fatigue and Social Breakdown: Exploring the Impacts of HIV/AIDS on Patient and Carer Well-Being in the Caprivi Region, Namibia*, in "Social Science & Medicine", Vol. 63, pp. 3174–3187.

Thomas W., Znaniecki F. 1918 *The Polish Peasant in Europe and America: Monograph of an Immigrant Group*, Boston, Richard G. Badger, The Gorham Press.

Underhill P. 1999 *Why We Buy: The Science of Shopping*, New York, Simon & Schuster.

Wittgenstein L. 1958 *Philosophical Investigations*, Oxford, Basil Blackwell (first edition 1953).

3 The theory-of-argumentation survival kit

The theory of argumentation is a multidisciplinary area that ranges from philosophy to social and cognitive sciences, law, artificial intelligence research, and many others. The objects of the theory of argumentation are the nature, functions, and limits of persuasive discourse. This kind of discourse is widespread both in everyday life and in social research, although not necessarily framed as argumentative. The following three fragments illustrate this kind of discourse:

> During my last stay in Brazil, as visiting scholar, Luciane, Aline, Jaqueline and many other colleagues were very hospitable. This is probably a trait of Brazilian academic culture.
> Paul cannot tolerate open-ended questions in a questionnaire; how can he accept a research project based on in-depth interviews?

> Yesterday I went to Luigi's office door but – strangely enough – he wasn't in. I assumed that he was in the library.

The first fragment illustrates the so-called "argument by example" (Perelman and Olbrechts-Tyteca 1958, English translation 1969: §78; Walton, Reed and Macagno 2008: 314). This kind of reasoning is the basis of all sampling procedures through which we attribute properties to a set, starting from the observation of a sub-set of cases belonging to it.[1] The second quotation illustrates the "double hierarchy argument" (Perelman and Olbrechts-Tyteca 1958, English translation 1969: §76). This argument moves from an assumption about the structure of reality, in which two classes of phenomena, two hierarchies, are distinguished. The double-hierarchy argument usually expresses an idea of direct or inverse proportionality between the elements that belong to the ordered group considered. This kind of reasoning was codified in Aristotle's *Rhetoric*, in which we can read this statement: "if the harder of two things is possible, so is the easier" (Aristotle II (b) 19, English translation 2015: 107). This kind of reasoning, also called the *a fortiori* (with greater reason) argument, resides at the root of critical-case design, particularly relevant in qualitative research (see Section 4.2.1). The third and last quotation is an example of one of the most relevant kind of reasoning in qualitative research (Tavory and Timmermans 2014; Vaughan 2014; Schwartz-Shea and Yanow 2012), abduction.

46 *The theory-of-argumentation survival kit*

There are plenty of illustrations of this kind of reasoning in social sciences, but being the author of this chapter, I will take the liberty of choosing an example from one of my own research experiences. I wrote my PhD thesis on a somewhat unusual topic, the sacralization of nature, through a comparative ethnography carried out on two small communities based in Italy (Cardano 1995, 1997). The comparison involved an esoteric spiritual community, Damanhur (Cardano and Pannofino 2018), and a lay, rural community, The Elves of the Great Ravine (*Elfi del Gran Burrone*). The purpose of the comparison was to discover core differences and similarities between a spiritual and a lay community in the process of sacralizing nature. What is pertinent here happened during my fieldwork with the community of Elves. The Elves of the Great Ravine was (and still is) an anarchic community whose members expressed their devotion toward nature through a choice of simplicity and with a gentle touch in the agricultural activities in which they were involved. They did not use fertilizers or tractors for farming and tended to reduce contacts with the market society to a bare minimum. Studying their attitudes toward nature, I directed my attention toward the rites that punctuated the community's life. Among them, the most important were the rite of the "sweat lodge" and that of the "magical beverage", borrowed, respectively, from Native American and Druidic traditions. Participating in and observing the diverse instances of both rites, what surprised me was the huge heterogeneity of what we can call liturgy. Bearing in mind the liturgy of the Catholic Church in which I was nurtured (to leave it as soon as I reach adulthood) and all that I had learned about rituality through my academic reading, I wondered whether was observing were really spiritual rites. I emerged from this situation of doubt by intuiting an interpretive hypothesis, based on my knowledge at that time – in Umberto Eco's words, my "semiotic encyclopaedia" (Eco 1988: 206). Some months before I had to tackle this problem, I fortuitously discovered the music of Bruno Maderna, who had recently passed away; he composed a kind of aleatory music which grated on my uneducated ear. The gist of this musical style was to open up musical performances to chance so that each performance acquired its own peculiarities, and none could be considered the same as the first. Aleatory music is based on a very essential, meagre score which leaves performers great liberty of interpretation, allowing chance to dictate the form that the performance will assume. I assumed that the Elves' rituality was – like aleatory music – based on an essential liturgical score which was, again in the words of Umberto Eco (1962, English translation 1989) an "open work". This interpretive hypothesis fitted in with the anarchic profile of the community and allowed surprising heterogeneity of ritual practices to become a matter of course. As I wrote in the book:

> The staging of a rite recalls, in many respects, a performance of Maderna's music; music constantly open to the aleatory, to chance, built on a thin, allusive, deliberately fragmented score: rite as an open work. The erosion of liturgical rules is combined with the weakening of the symbolic content of community rituals. The Elves' ritual practices actually depend on a relatively narrow set of symbols, linked to one another by an extremely simple plot.

The theory-of-argumentation survival kit   47

Furthermore, the use of symbols is mainly oriented towards expression and production of feelings rather than assertion, to the staging of a discourse on the world. This image can be traced back to two specific rituals in which I was able to participate during my stay in the community: the rite of the sweat lodge and that of the magical beverage.

(Cardano 1997: 234)

Abduction is the kind of reasoning that best represents the features of qualitative research, creativity in the production of concepts and theories, and the presumptive nature of the result acquired.[2] Starting from the second half of the twentieth century, we have all had to renounce the myth of truth (particularly the Correspondence Theory of Truth), accepting cohabitation with uncertainty, which is variously expressed through the notion of probability or that of plausibility (see what follows). The presumptive character of social-phenomena representation – in both qualitative and quantitative research – hinges upon the invisibility of the internal states that so frequently appear as subjects of our statements, and on the difficulty connected with gaining participants' cooperation (see Section 1.1).

Returning to abductive reasoning, it may be useful to recall the classic definition of this kind of reasoning proposed by Charles Sanders Peirce:

The surprising fact, C, is observed;
But if A were true, C would be a matter of course,
Hence, there is reason to suspect that A is true.

(Peirce 1935–1966: § 5.189)

In the case of the Elves' rituality, what surprised me was the degree of the liturgy's heterogeneity (C in the Peirce formula). The notion of the rite as open work, as the metaphorical equivalent of aleatory music, was the conjectural Inference to the Best Explanation (A). This interpretive hypothesis fitted in with the anarchist cultural profile of the community, and no alternative explanation seemed more appropriate for it to be judged plausible.

A more serviceable version of the Peircean abductive argument scheme in the context of our discourse was proposed by Douglas Walton.

D is a set of data or supposed facts in a case.
Each one of a set of accounts $A_1, A_2, \ldots, A_n$ is successful in explaining D.
A_1 is the account that explains D most successfully.
Therefore A_1 is the most *plausible* hypothesis in the case.

(Walton 2004: 217–218, italic mine)

Walton's version of abductive reasoning underlines the plausible nature of the conclusion of this kind of inference. Furthermore, Walton's definition focusses on one of the most relevant aspects of abductive reasoning, the consideration of a set of possible explanations for the "surprising fact" in the case; evoking the necessity to nurture our abductive reasoning with a special theoretical sensitivity

48   *The theory-of-argumentation survival kit*

that allows comparison among different explicative hypotheses (Tavory and Timmermans 2014: 41, 113–114; Vaughan 2014: 66–67). The presumptive nature of this kind of reasoning does not impede our ability to evaluate its soundness. Some suggestions on the criteria through which to evaluate its plausibility emerge from two scholars of Artificial Intelligence, John and Susan Josephson. In their book dedicated to abductive inference, these criteria are presented:

1   how decisively A_1 surpasses the alternatives
2   how good A_1 is by itself, independently of considering the alternatives (we should be cautious about accepting a hypothesis, even if it is clearly the best one we have if it is not sufficiently plausible in itself)
3   judgments of the reliability of the data
4   how much confidence there is that all plausible explanations have been considered (how thorough was the search for alternative explanations).

(Adapted from Josephson and Josephson 1994: 16)[3]

The evaluation criteria proposed by Josephson and Josephson work as "critical questions", which in our context – as we can see in what follows (Section 3.3) – carry out two different functions. The first, clearly expressed by the authors, is that which allows evaluation of the argument's acceptability degree. The second function, relevant in a methodological frame, is to offer a "pedagogical tool" (Godden and Walton 2007: 280) to improve the soundness of the reasoning.

In order to recognize better the specificity of abductive reasoning, which can be defined as "inference to the best explanation" (Walton 2004: 4; Tavory and Timmermans 2014: 36), a rapid comparison with the other two types of reasoning – induction and deduction – may be useful. In what follows I reproduce – partly adapted – the comparison scheme proposed by Peirce (1935–1966: §§ 2.623, 5.171) based on the famous white beans. Instead of beans, I will consider children; instead of bags, I consider schools. The whiteness of beans becomes here an ethnic attribute: being white instead of black.

Deduction

All the children in this school are white.
These children are enrolled in this school.
These children – *necessarily* – are white.

Induction

These children are enrolled in this school.
These children are white.
All the children from this school are – *probably* – are white.

Abduction

All the children in this school are white.
These children are white.
These children – *plausibly* – are from this school.[4]

The creativity of abductive reasoning – according to Tavory and Timmermans (2014: 37) – emerges through from comparison of the three inference procedures because the conclusion, "These children – plausibly – are from this school" is neither assumed before the fact (as in deduction) nor observed (as in induction). The hypothesis that transforms a surprising fact into a matter of course is invented, sometimes in a creative way (see Eco 1988).

I have just introduced the issue of uncertainty as the necessary price to be paid in the representation of social phenomena, both in qualitative and quantitative research. The idea of uncertainty is clearly expressed by Charles Sanders Peirce when, in a reflection on the translation of cuneiform inscriptions, observes that any representation "not standing upon the bedrock of fact. It is walking upon a bog, and can only say, this ground seems to hold for the present. Here I will stay till it begins to give way" (Peirce 1935–1966: § 5.589). There are two main ways to express uncertainty in social sciences, one in terms of probability, the other in terms of plausibility. These two concepts are very similar, but a distinction between them – a fuzzy one – can be made, and this is particularly useful to define the specificity of qualitative research reasoning as compared to that of quantitative research.

The relationship between probability and plausibility is discussed in one of the appendices of the Josephson and Josephson book. The issue is controversial (on the same point, see Walton 2004: 28). Three main points allow distinguishing plausibility from probability. First, probability expresses uncertainty in a formalized fashion; on the contrary, plausibility does it in an informal way similar to ordinary language (Josephson and Josephson 1994: 266). Second, the measure of uncertainty through probability requires a clear definition (enumeration) of the alternatives considered. To operate with probability, it is also necessary to make specific assumptions on the relationship between alternatives, and the assumption adopted is usually that of independence. When we are involved in argumentative reasoning – abductive reasoning or by analogy, for instance – the sets of possible alternatives cannot be strictly measured, and the assumption of independence between them seems deeply to impoverish our discourses.[5] To avoid the fallacy of misplaced precision, which we fall into "when exact numbers are used for inexact notions" (Pirie 2015: 76), in the frame of plausibility uncertainty or confidence is expressed in a "coarse-scale" measurement (Josephson and Josephson 1994: 268). Third, although not so decisive, some of argumentative reasoning, abduction for example, calls for a causal explanation for which probability and statistics seem ill-equipped (270–271). All these reasons converge toward a distinction between probability and plausibility, and in defining plausibility the proper idiom for both the theory of argumentation and qualitative research.

Having said this, it is time to go deeper into the definition of argument and the theory of argumentation. It is not my objective to provide a synopsis of the huge field of the theory of argumentation, but only to share with the reader some tools, taken from this area of study, useful for developing the idea of rigour in qualitative research without being subjected to the dictates of the so-called "logic of inference" (Goldthorpe 2000).

50   *The theory-of-argumentation survival kit*

3.1 A quick overview of argumentation theory

The distinction between argument and argumentation could be an appropriate start. In a nontechnical way, we can define an argument as the product of a specific activity of reasoning, and argumentation the process through which a set of arguments is advanced, contested, and defended. With Douglas Walton we can move toward a more analytical definition of both notions. In Walton's words: "*Argument* is a social and verbal means of trying to resolve, or at least to contend with, a conflict or difference that has arisen or exists between two (or more) parties" (Walton 1990: 411). The use of arguments in reasoning activity – meant as a process through which the acceptability of premises is tentatively transferred to the conclusion in a dialogical context – constitutes argumentation.

Argumentation is a social process, even when it takes the form of a solo discourse, the oration (cf. van Eemeren, Grootendorst and Henkemans 2009: 5). Both in everyday and academic discourses, an argument is addressed to a real or imaginary audience. In the context of qualitative research, the arguments are advanced before what Charles Sanders Peirce defined as the "community of inquiry" (Tavory and Timmermans 2014: Chapter 7).[6] The acceptability of argumentative reasoning is not assessed against the bedrock of facts (as it is for the correspondence theory of truth) but before a rational judge in a context closer to the court trial than to the experimental laboratory.

In recent decades, argumentation theory has become increasingly relevant after being marginal for a very long time. The roots of argumentation theory are to be found in ancient Greece, particularly in the thought of Aristotle who, in the first book of *Topics*, defined the nature of dialectics, namely argumentative reasoning. The dialectical argumentation was born from the necessity to tackle, by means of rational discussion, cognitive fields in which the truth of the reasoning premises could not be taken for granted. In addition to dialectics, Aristotle developed another form of reasoning, rhetoric, as the faculty to discover in each argument what can persuade the audience. For a long time, both dialectics and rhetoric, along with grammar, were the foundation of higher education. In the seventeenth century, starting from publications of the Port-Royal School of Logic and the progressive affirmation of modern sciences, both dialectics and rhetoric were ostracized for their alleged obscurity and reduced to nothing more than tools for the study of stylistic devices of speech, so-called rhetorical figures of speech. The study of reasoning became the monopoly of logic, and all the reasoning forms that do not fit in with the abstract trans-contextual rules of formal logic were considered fallacies.[7]

The marginalization of argumentation theory continued until the second half of the twentieth century when, in 1958, two seminal books marked the so-called argumentative turn: *Traité de l'argumentation. La nouvelle rhétorique*, by Chaïm Perelman and Lucie Olbrechts-Tyteca – already cited – was one of them; the other was *The Uses of Argument*, by Stephen Edelston Toulmin (van Eemeren and Grootendorst 2004: 45). Albeit with different scopes and reasoning strategies, both books contest the monopoly of formal logic in the study of reasoning. Perelman and Olbrechts-Tyteca, starting from the title chosen for their book, propose

The theory-of-argumentation survival kit 51

a renaissance of ancient Greek dialectics and rhetoric, openly contesting Cartesian rationalism, based on *more geometrico* (geometrical) reasoning rooted in mathematics and logic. Stephen Toulmin moves in the same direction by refuting what he called the "geometrical" concept of validity (van Eemeren, Grootendorst and Henkemans 2009: 131). Specifically, Toulmin contested the view that there are universal norms for the evaluation of an argument and that these norms are provided by formal logic (130). As a model for the evaluation of the soundness of an argument, Toulmin proposed substituting formal logic with jurisprudence, a context-sensitive practice to express judgement. This last idea, that of context sensitivity, with which qualitative research feels very comfortable, was clearly expressed through the notion of audience, in Perelman and Olbrechts-Tyteca, and with that of field, in Toulmin. The acceptability of an argument is tied to the context in which it is advanced, although it is possible to define some general trans-contextual rules for the structure of an argument. In this direction the clearest contribution is that of Stephen Toulmin, who proposed a general structure of reasoning (field-independent), that necessarily curves according to the specific field in which it is implemented (see Toulmin 1958: Chapter 3).

These two books revived the attention toward argumentative reasoning, but they didn't mark a real break with the classical tradition (van Eemeren and Grootendorst 2004: Chapter 3). What is missing in both theses is a specific appreciation of the dialogical and dialectical dimensions of the process of making an argument (Cantù and Testa 2006: 12–13; van Eemeren and Grootendorst 2004: Chapter 3), which is particularly relevant in the context of scientific practice. Moreover, in Toulmin's model, which is the closest to scientific sensitivity, the argumentation process takes the form of an oration rather than that of dialectical confrontation.

Attention toward the dialogical and dialectical dimensions of the argumentative process is shown in a more recent approach, that of informal logic. The informal logic approach is a variegated one where it is possible to notes the two waves that – at least in my view – can contribute to the scientific reasoning developed in qualitative research. According to Paola Cantù and Italo Testa (2006: 52), In this area I situated both the pragma-dialectical school, oriented by Frans van Eemeren (van Eemeren, Grootendorst 2004) and the Canadian school that refers to the works of Douglas Walton (Walton 1989; Walton and Krabbe 1995). Interestingly enough, these approaches have their roots in pragmatist culture, particularly in the Peircean version. The dialogical and dialectical confrontation that gives and evaluates the acceptability of reasoning takes place in the "community of inquiry" (Tavory and Timmermans 2014: Chapter 7). The two approaches here considered shed light on the kind of dialectical dialogue that characterizes the production of plausible accounts in qualitative research. In the van Eemeren model, it is critical discussion; in the Walton approach, persuasive dialogue. Van Eemeren and Grootendorst define the feature of critical discussion:

> A critical discussion can be described as an exchange of views in which the parties involved in a difference of opinion systematically try to determine

52 *The theory-of-argumentation survival kit*

> whether the standpoint or standpoints at issue are defensible in the light of critical doubt or objections.
>
> (van Eemeren and Grootendorst 2004: 52)

In Walton's approach, persuasive dialogue is only one of a wider set of dialogues that can be thought of as many "linguistic games" in the Wittgenstein meaning (Cantù and Testa 2006: 102). Each dialogue is characterized by three main features: the initial situation, the main goal, and the participants' aims; and comes with a set of rules that allow the participants to reach the defined goal. These rules are related to the kind of commitments that the participants in dialogue have to take or reject. For persuasive dialogue, the initial situation is characterized by conflicting points of view; the main goal is the resolution of such conflict by verbal means; and the participants' aims consist in persuading the other(s) (Walton and Krabbe 1995: 66).[8]

The dialectical context in which qualitative research is planned and developed and its main results are defended through their textualization can be adequately framed either in critical discussion or in persuasive dialogue. To choose between these two equally solid alternatives, I have considered – in a pragmatic posture – the set of instruments that is most-immediately serviceable that accompanies each of them. The Canadian school offers a set of useful tools for qualitative research, namely presumptive argumentation schemes. Such schemes can appropriately guide the formulation of specific reasoning central to carrying out qualitative research, such as case selection (with the argument from example), information interpretation, both in the field and during data analysis (with the argument from sign, or the abductive argument). Each scheme is equipped with specific critical questions (Hastings 1963, cited in Walton, Reed and Macagno 2008: 3), a tool which covers a double dialectical function. Critical questions allow evaluation of the acceptability of premises and the plausibility of conclusions.[9] Moreover, critical questions can work as a decision medium, guiding researchers in the construction of their argument. This last function is carried out by another instrument from the Walton repertoire: proleptic argumentation (Walton 2009).

To illustrate the presumptive nature of argumentative reasoning, the canonical example from Douglas Walton, the Tweety argument, is a good start.

The Tweety argument

Birds fly.
> Tweety is a bird.
> Therefore Tweety flies.

> (Walton 2004: 26)

As Douglas Walton observes, the Tweety argument can be considered rationally acceptable assuming that we do not have any information about Tweety except that it is a bird. But if we obtain some additional information and we discover that Tweety is a penguin or an ostrich, we must admit that the conclusion of the argument is unacceptable. The conclusion is invalid, although both premises seem reasonable. To deal with this problem, we can introduce an exception clause listing all the known birds that do not fly (penguins, ostriches, cocks, turkeys, emus, kiwis, rheas, and perhaps some others). But what if Tweety is not an exception and has a broken wing? In this way the Tweety argument persists as being defeasible because not all the possible exceptions can be defined in advance. Starting from this example, it is possible to define the features of a presumptive argument: an argument whose premises are questionable and/or the inferences drawn from them in order to reach the conclusion are not always valid.

All social research – not only qualitative – focussing on invisible properties such as beliefs, values, and the meaning of actions (see Section 1.1) necessarily reach their conclusion through reasoning that starts from at least one defeasible premise, the one that describes the internal state of individuals through a conjectural combination of clues acquired without the full guarantee of the participants' cooperation. This seems – in my view – a good reason to consider argumentative reasoning as the common form of our way of thinking in social sciences.

Presumptive argumentation is framed in a dialectical register in Douglas Walton's thought; he indirectly calls into question the community of inquiry in a dispute (sometimes only virtual) about the plausibility of a claim. The two main tools that give the argumentation its dialectical curvature are proleptic argumentation (Walton 2009) and argumentation schemes (Walton, Reed and Macagno 2008). Before indicating the qualitative research contexts in which these two instruments can be effectively applied, a short definition of their general structure is desirable.

3.2 Proleptic argumentation

Proleptic argumentation is a kind of argumentation in which the sequences of dialectical moves constitutive of a persuasive dialogue are advanced by one interlocutor only, who makes a claim, considers the possible objections to it, and reshapes his/her reasoning to defuse the objections considered (see Walton 2009). The ordinary sequence of moves in persuasive dialogue entails that the proponent put forward an argument, and then the respondent advance one or more objections to that argument. Then, in a third move, the proponent replies to the respondent's objections. This sequence is repeated until both – and this is a virtual "both" – proponent and respondent find a resolution that can be an agreement about a claim or a motivated disagreement. To give an example:

PROPONENT: In qualitative research, the writing is characterized by a clear multivocality.
RESPONDENT: Have a look at *Asylum*, by Erving Goffman. It is 390 pages long but the participants' voices can be seen in only 8 of them.
PROPONENT: OK, I see your point. *Asylum* is a significant exception, but it was published at the beginning of the 1960s. Considering the most recent works in qualitative research, let's say from what Norman Denzin and Yvonne Lincoln

54 *The theory-of-argumentation survival kit*

define the third moment in the history of qualitative research, starting from the 1970s, the writing in qualitative research becomes *basically* multivocal.[10]

In the proleptic argumentation, the speaker covers both roles, that of proponent and that of respondent. S/he makes a claim, advances some reasonable objections to it, and reacts to these objections, either through a counterargument that leaves the original argument unchanged or through a reshaping of the original argument that defuses the objections. As in a "peopled" dialogue, in which the proponent faces flesh-and-blood respondents, in proleptic argumentation the role of the respondent can be performed with different assertiveness. Objections can be oriented to deconstruct the original claim (dissent type of discussion) or they can be oriented to advance an alternative claim (dispute type of dialogue). Apart from the metaphor of dialogue, proleptic argumentation is reasoning in which the proponent dialectically anticipates the possible objections to her/his claim by answering some imagined critical questions inviting a reshaping of the argument.[11]

Every answer to the respondents' (dialectically anticipated) objections implies a proposition commitment by the proponent. In the earlier example, the respondent commits herself/himself on the plausibility of the distinction of the history of qualitative research in the main moments defined by Denzin and Lincoln. More precisely, s/he assumes a discontinuity in the writing habits of the qualitative researcher's community before and after the 1970s.

Every propositional commitment acts as an assumption that marks the boundary of the reasoning conclusion. In the example that opens this discussion, the answer to the respondent reshapes the scope and the qualification of the original claim: the multivocality of qualitative writing is recognized only by the most recent works (starting from the 1970s), and an informal modal qualifier, *basically*, is introduced. In a more general way, every propositional commitment becomes a factor that introduces a form of conditional plausibility. Conditional plausibility can be thought of as the analogical equivalent, in the area of argumentative reasoning, of the conditional probability proper to statistical inference. In statistics, the conditional probability of an event B is the probability that the event will occur, given the knowledge that an event A has already taken place. It is normally expressed by the notation $P(B|A)$. In the argumentative version of this kind of thought, conditional plausibility, instead of events we have statements. The plausibility of the statement "The writing in qualitative research is characterized by multivocality" is subordinated to the plausibility of distinction of the history of qualitative research proposed.[12] Therefore the plausibility of argumentative reasoning is subordinated to the plausibility of the assumptions on which it hinges. We shall see the practical implications of this feature particularly clearly in cases-selection procedures (see Section 4.3).

3.3 Argumentation schemes

Argumentation schemes (Walton, Reed and Macagno 2008) offer an organized version of the dialectical form of reasoning expressed by proleptic argumentation. In the words of Walton Reed and Macagno: "Argumentation schemes are forms of argument that represent the structure of common types of argument used in everyday

The theory-of-argumentation survival kit   55

discourses, as well in special contexts like those of legal argumentation and scientific argumentation" (1). These structures of inference are defeasible in nature; they produce conclusions that, although plausible, can be defeated as new evidence is considered. In the classic books of logic, arguments like those from analogy or from sign were considered fallacies, but they regain full citizenship rights in the context of informal logic. Walton, Reed and Macagno propose a repertoire of 60 argumentation schemes. Each scheme combines a set of premises which authorize a conclusion and a series of critical questions (Hastings 1963) that – dialectically – allow the improvement and the evaluation of the argument's cogency.[13]

Following in Walton and Colleagues' footprints, the structure of argumentation schemes can be illustrated through the most relevant way of reasoning in qualitative research, the argument from analogy (Tavory and Timmermans 2014; Vaughan 2014). The argument from analogy is the foundation of all case-based reasoning (Walton, Reed, Macagno 43) which is the core business of qualitative research.

ARGUMENT-FROM-ANALOGY SCHEME[14]

MAJOR PREMISE	GENERALLY, CASE C1 IS SIMILAR TO CASE C2.
MINOR PREMISE	PROPOSITION A (PROPERTY) IS TRUE IN CASE C1.
CONCLUSION	PROPOSITION A (PROPERTY) IS TRUE IN CASE C2.

A tricky application example eloquently demonstrates the reason for which critical questions are essential. Consider the argument: this apple is red and tastes good; this billiard ball is red; therefore, it will taste good. Tasting good is the property which we mean to transfer from the Analogue – the apple – to the Principal Subject – the billiard ball (Walton, Reed and Macagno 2008: 56; Macagno 2017). What is wrong with this reasoning? The answer is quite obvious: the colour resemblance is not sufficient to convince us to bite into a billiard ball.

The matching critical questions that accompany the argument-from-analogy scheme focus on this and on other issues to be considered in order to reach a plausible conclusion. Walton and Colleagues offer a set of five critical questions (CQ):[15]

CRITICAL QUESTIONS FOR THE ARGUMENT-FROM-ANALOGY SCHEME

CQ_1	Is A true in C_1?
CQ_2	Are C_1 and C_2 similar in the respect cited?
CQ_3	Is the similarity between C_1 and C_2 observed so far relevant for the further similarity that is in question?
CQ_4	Are there important differences (dissimilarities) between C_1 and C_2?
CQ_5	Is there some other case C_3 that is also similar to C_1 except that A is false in C_3?

The first critical question addresses the *minor premise* of the reasoning, namely, the issue of the conditions that gave the apple a good taste. This allows us to consider the conservation state of the fruit, and also – accidentally – to remember the sad story of Snow White and the poisoned apple. The second critical question focuses on the *major premise* and invites to consider the similarity between the apple and the billiard ball in a broader sense. Both are red; both are spherical; both can be held in one's hand, and so on. The answers to this last question lead to the

56 *The theory-of-argumentation survival kit*

third decisive critical question about the relevance of the similarity. Is the common red colour of these objects enough to assume that both taste good? To answer this question, we can move in two opposite directions. We can ask ourselves if there are others red, spherical objects that we can hold in our hand that do not taste good. There are many such objects, but among them it could be useful to contemplate briefly Indian liquorice (*Abrus precatorius*). Indian liquorice is a small red fruit (being a fruit seems an important feature in the economy of our reasoning) which is highly toxic. Complementarily, we can consider green and yellow apples. They are not red but taste good similarly to the red apple. Both anecdotal evidence seem to call into doubt the relevance of the colour red as a clue to the tastiness of objects that share this property. The fourth critical question, about dissimilarities, invites us to consider whether there are some relevant differences between our apple and our billiard ball that can challenge the conclusion of our reasoning. Our sense of smell – which can also help us to detect dissimilarities – can tell us if something tastes good. A red apple has a pleasant smell; a red billiard ball does not have any smell, if not in some cases, an unpleasant enamel paint smell. In their being spherical, we can recognize a perfect correspondence with the sphere form of a billiard ball rather than the imperfectly spherical shape of an apple. This statement of fact could suggest that the billiard ball is a manufactured article, where as an apple is a natural product. If we still wish to bite into the billiard ball, we can taste the two red objects and find out that one is tender and the other tough.[16] The fifth critical question challenges argument-from-analogy plausibility with a Popperian approach, focussing on a counter-analogy (Walton, Reed and Macagno 2008: 63) which shows that resemblance with regard to one property (being red) does not necessarily imply resemblance with regard to another (tasting good). Answering this critical question implies seeking red objects that do not taste good. As a matter of fact, there are many of them, from the aforementioned Indian liquorice and a Ferrari car to a UK phone box. The more the object listed resembles an apple, the better the counter-analogy works. So the Indian liquorice, in the same dimensional scale of the apple, and with a property far distant from a good taste, is a more suitable example than the Ferrari or the phone box.

Discussion of the five critical questions earlier illustrates how the argument from analogy integrates a logical and a semantic dimension (Macagno 2017). The argument from analogy is a "twofold reasoning process" in which the transfer of a property from the Analogous to the Principal Subject (logical dimension) is based on the recognition of a "functional genus" (semantic dimension) which guarantees the "reasonableness of such a transfer of predication" (466, 471, 467). This functional genus does not coincide with the definitional one of the two objects compared but is rather creatively invented. This functional genus is absent in the apple-billiard-ball example, therefore, to describe its profile we need a successful example of analogical reasoning. To develop this point, Fabrizio Macagno reintroduces the classical Aristotelian argument about ruling-class selection:

> Public officials ought not to be selected by lot. That is like using the lot to select athletes, instead of choosing those who are fit for the contest; or using

The theory-of-argumentation survival kit   57

the lot to select a steersman from among a ship's crew, as if we ought to take the man on whom the lot falls, and not the man who knows most about it.

(Aristotle, *Rhetoric* 1393b4–1393b8)

The transfer from athletes (Analogous) to public officials (Subject) of the property of the disaster of their selection by lot hinges upon the identification of a "functional genus", different from what identifies the two "species" at hand. Athletes practice sports; public officials govern public affairs. The functional genus emerges through an abstraction process which recognizes in both athletes and public officials a commitment to an activity which requires expertise and skill (Macagno 2017: 472). Thinking about this abstraction step in the context of qualitative research allows recognizing the relevance of theoretical sensitivity to sustain the creative leap that ends with the detection of the functional genus which guarantees the soundness of the analogical reasoning (cf. Tavory and Timmermans 2014; Vaughan 2014).

Returning to the apple-billiard-ball example, we can define the functions of the critical question by quoting the Walton and Colleagues. According to Bart Verheij (2003, quoted in Walton, Reed and Macagno 2008: 62), critical questions have four functions.

1   They can be used to question whether a premise of a scheme holds.
2   They can point to exceptional situations in which a scheme should not be used.
3   They can set conditions for the proper use of a scheme.
4   They can point to other arguments that might be used to attack the scheme.

(Walton, Reed and Macagno 2008: 62)

Answers to all the relevant critical questions can become additional premises in argumentation schemes. For instance, the original Argument-from-analogy scheme can be modified by incorporating answers to the critical questions:

ARGUMENT-FROM-ANALOGY SCHEME: EXTENDED VERSION[17]

Major premise	Generally, case C1 is similar to case C2.
Similarity basis premise (from CQ2)	The similarity between C1 and C2 is evident for the features $f1, f2, f3, \ldots fn$.
Relevant similarity premise (from CQ3)	The similarity between C1 and C2 observed so far is relevant to the further similarity that is in question.
Irrelevance of differences premise (from CQ4)	The differences between C1 and C2 observed so far do not constitute a strong enough reason to dismiss the idea of their similarity.
No known counter-analogy premise (from CQ5)	No C3 case is known so far that shares with C1 the features $f1, f2, f3, \ldots fn$ but for which A is false.
Minor premise:	Proposition A is true in case C1.
Stability of feature premise (from CQ1)	The observation of a theoretically relevant set of C1 instances for a wide enough time span so far allows us to say that proposition A is true in C1.
Conclusion	Proposition A is true in case C2.

58   *The theory-of-argumentation survival kit*

All the premises, both original and additional, constitute a set of propositional commitments that give substance to the notion of conditional plausibility (see earlier). Namely, the conclusion of the argument for which A is true in case C_2 is acceptable on condition that all the premises are true. Moreover, about the conditions not considered in the stated premises nothing can be said.

The argument from analogy is very relevant in qualitative research. According to Peirce (1935–1966: § 5.277), the argument from analogy combines the features of induction and abduction, the two most important inferential strategies in qualitative research. The plainest definition of analogy proposed by Peirce suggests the presence of an abductive dimension quite clearly.

> Analogy is the inference that a not very large collection of objects which agree in various respects may very likely agree in another respect. For instance, the Earth and Mars agree in so many respects that it seems not unlikely they may agree in being inhabited.
>
> (Peirce 1935–1966: § 1.69)

The truly presumptive character of the hypothesis about the peopled red planet guides us in the better-known territory (at least compared with Mars) of abduction.

> Hypothesis is where we find some very curious circumstance, which would be explained by the supposition that it was a case of a certain general rule, and thereupon adopt that supposition. Or, where we find that in certain respects two objects have a strong resemblance, and infer that they resemble one another strongly in other respects.
>
> (Peirce 1935–1966: § 2.624)

> Among probable inferences of mixed character, there are many forms of great importance. The most interesting, perhaps, is the argument from Analogy, in which, from a few instances of objects agreeing in a few well-defined respects, inference is made that another object, known to agree with the others in all but one of those respects, agrees in that respect also.
>
> (Peirce 1935–1966: § 2.787)[18]

Analogical reasoning plays an important role in the field during the data-collection process. It is through the combination of analogy and abduction that we build our "passing theory" (Wikan 1992: 468), with which we try to make sense of our experiences. Through inductive sensibility, we find similarities, resemblances in what we observe and/or hear; then through abduction we creatively postulate something that strongly connects all the instances observed.

Analogical reasoning comes once again to the forefront during the analysis of our data. In Chapter 2, the context sensitivity of data collection procedures has been defined as the DNA of qualitative research. The application of this constitutive principle of our research practices implies that we collect a heteroclite set of

The theory-of-argumentation survival kit 59

empirical materials to compare and contrast. This aspect is particularly clear when we contrast an in-depth interview with its quantitative equivalent, the structured interview guided by a questionnaire. In survey research, comparison among individuals in our sample is quite easy and direct. Operational definitions had guided the data collection, and all the individuals had tried to express themselves through the words defined in advance according to the previously defined multiple-choice options. John's "totally agree" to the question about the necessity of closing all European psychiatric hospitals can be statistically added to with the "totally agree" of Michael, Rosaline, Mary, and many others (at least if we do not consider the different nuances implicit in individuals' positions). John, Michael, Rosaline, and Mary, involved in the same topic through an in-depth interview would express their views through four different discourses (see Rapley 2004: 18), requiring subtle work of interpretation before being counted as instances of a specific stand which may be compared with others.

To impose order on these discourses, to find the main threads among them, requires analogical reasoning. We must identify resemblances among discourses expressed with different words, different emotional tones, and different argumentative forms. The best way to tackle this conundrum passes through the construction of an ideal type (Weber 1904, English translation 1949: 90) through which we manage the problem in order to group together different discursive instances bonded by more-or-less strong family resemblance.[19] Inventing a Weberian ideal type realizes Peirce's definition of analogy through which we find that in certain respects some objects "have a strong resemblance, and infer that they resemble one another strongly in other respects" (Peirce 1935–1966: § 2.624). This theme will be analysed in more detail in Chapter 5.

All the argumentation schemes proposed by Walton and Colleagues have the same structure as the argument from analogy: a set of premises, from which a conclusion derives, matched with a series of critical questions through which the reasoning can be evaluated and improved (through the dialectical anticipation of criticisms) in its cogency. The list of argumentation schemes is open. The first version of this reasoning tool proposed by Walton in 1996 gathered 26 schemes (Walton 1996, cited in Walton, Reed and Macagno 2008: 3). The most recent version, composed with Chris Reed and Fabrizio Macagno, includes – as said earlier– more than 60 schemes.[20]

In my attempted application of these instruments to the epistemic problems of qualitative research, I have added to the list two new schemes (see Sections 4.2.2, 4.2.3), the argument from irrelevant difference and the argument from relevant difference, both inspired by comparative methods, i.e., most-different-systems design and most-similar-system design formulated by Adam Przeworski and Henry Teune (1982: 31–39; original edition 1970). Not all the schemes proposed by Walton and Colleagues are immediately exploitable for qualitative research's epistemic or ethical needs. Some of them even seem most useful, and in the concluding section of this chapter, they will be listed, whereas their analytic illustration will be postponed to the following chapters.

60   *The theory-of-argumentation survival kit*

3.4 Argumentation schemes for qualitative research: where they are useful

To locate argumentative tools in the flow of qualitative research practices, its subdivision into four canonical steps may be useful: i) design; ii) data collection; iii) data analysis; and iv) textualization.[21] Proleptic argumentation, due to its generality, is applied to all steps of qualitative research. This dialectical device serves to defend the research question's relevance and the epistemic and ethical suitability of the research method(s) chosen. Proleptic argumentation still helps in making many of the analytical choices which punctuate data-collection, data-analysis, and writing procedures.

In the design step, the argumentative tools play an important role in defence of the eloquence of the cases selected for study. For this purpose the most general tool is the argument from example, used both to build and to illustrate knowledge (Willer, Ruchatz and Pethes 2007; cited in Šorm 2010).[22] For the definition of the research design through case selection, four argumentation schemes are fundamental: the double-hierarchy argument, the argument from irrelevant difference, the argument from relevant difference and the argument from radical otherness. Proleptic argumentation also offers an important contribution to case selection. In the data-collection phase, three arguments are particularly useful: the argument from sign, the abductive argumentation scheme, and the argument from analogy through which we create our "passing theory" (Wikan 1992: 468). Finally, the eloquence of the information acquired from a key informant can be defended through the argument from position-to-know.

For the two last steps of qualitative research, analysis and textualization, all the argumentative schemes mentioned earlier are decisive. As mentioned in Section 3.3, the features of qualitative data, their deliberate heterogeneity, require the argument from sign and that of analogy for a very decisive – although not always thematized – role. In the next three chapters, the utility of the theory of argumentation tools will be tested in detail.

Notes

1   Howard Becker defines this procedure as "a version of the classical trope of synecdoche" (Becker 1998: 67).
2   With regard to the creation of new concepts, Mary Morgan's remarks on case studies seems to apply to all qualitative research. Morgan maintains that one of the most promising features of case study rests on its capacity to produce, frequently in a serendipitous way, new evidence-based concepts (Morgan 2014: 299, 302).
3   To make this quotation coherent with Douglas Walton's previous one, the symbol used by Josephson and Josephson to denote the generic explanatory hypotheses, H, has been substituted with A_1.
4   In line with Walton (2004: 3), in the scheme proposed in the text I have added – in italics – the three qualifiers: necessarily, probably and plausibly. This seems coherent with Pierce's position on this point: "Deduction proves that something ***must*** be; Induction shows that something ***actually is*** operative; Abduction merely suggests that something ***may be***" (Peirce 1935–1966 Collected Papers 5.171, bold type in the original).
5   On this point, we can recognize similarities with the Baconian notion of probability (see Weinstock, Goodenough and Klein 2013: 3 and passim). I would like to thank Fabrizio Macagno for calling this aspect to my attention.

The theory-of-argumentation survival kit 61

6 Peirce (1935–1966: § 5.265) used the locution "community of philosophers" instead of "community of inquiry". Nevertheless, here I will follow the actualization proposal advanced by Tavory and Stephen Timmermans, who adopted the notion of "community of inquiry".

7 For the short synthesis exposed in the text, I took inspiration from Boniolo and Vidali (2011: Chapter 2).

8 The other kinds of dialogue considered by Walton and Krabbe are negotiation, inquiry, deliberation, information-seeking dialogue, and the eristic (Walton and Krabbe 1995: 66).

9 A working definition for premise acceptability can be borrowed from Leo Groarke and Christopher Tindale, reproduced in what follows. "A premise is judged acceptable if (1) it would be accepted *without further support* by the audience for which it is intended, given the background knowledge of its members and the beliefs and values they hold, *and* (2) it conforms to (does not violate), alone or in combination with other premises, the principles of good reasoning" (Groarke and Tindale 2004: 256, italic in the original).

10 In the imaginary dialogue in the text, the proponent refers to the periodization of qualitative research proposed by Denzin and Lincoln (Denzin and Lincoln 1994: 7–11).

11 In a recent well-written book on research writing, inspired by the theory of argumentation, Arnold Wentzel introduces a procedure very close to proleptic argumentation, teaching students how to develop their arguments (Wentzel 2018: 59).

12 In the development of this idea I took inspiration from the reflection on case studies by Martyn Hammersley, Roger Gomm, and Peter Foster (2000: 251).

13 "Difficult Questions for Qualitative Research", developed by Jennifer Mason (Mason 2002: 205–212), presents something very close to the idea of critical questions applied in the context of qualitative research.

14 Adapted from Macagno (2017: 470).

15 Adapted from Walton, Reed, and Macagno (2008: 58–62).

16 The fourth critical question recalls the procedure defined by Mary Hesse to evaluate the suitability of an analogical model in science – strangely enough – again involving billiard balls in the reasoning (Hesse 1970). On this aspect, see Chapter 5, n. 27.

17 Adapted from Walton, Reed, and Macagno (2008: 55–64). Walton and colleagues propose a modified version of the argument from analogy scheme (58) which includes in analogical reasoning the answer to only one critical question (CQ_3), the most relevant. For the sake of completeness, the modified version of the scheme presented here considers all critical questions thematized.

18 In the quoted extract (Peirce 1935–1966: § 2.787), the author uses the adjective "probable" to refer indistinctly to what has been distinguished above through the probability/plausibility pair. In the theoretical frame I am proposing, I understand the adjective "probable" as a generic expression of non-deductive inference.

19 On the Weberian notion of ideal type, see Section 5.2.

20 A more compact presentation of the argumentation schemes "aimed at meeting both the need of specificity and effectiveness" is presented in Walton and Macagno (2015).

21 I agree with Arnold Wentzel (2018) about the centrality of the argumentation process for all steps of social research, and the distinction introduced goes in the same direction as he indicates.

22 The distinction proposed in the text mirrors that between strategic and illustrative sampling advanced by Jennifer Mason (Mason 2002: 123–127).

References

Aristotle. 2015 *Rhetoric*, English translation by W. Rhys Roberts, Fairhope, AL, Mockingbird Publishing.

Becker H.S. 1998 *Tricks of the Trade: How to Think about Your Research While You're Doing It*, Chicago and London, The University of Chicago Press.

62 The theory-of-argumentation survival kit

Boniolo G., Vidali P. 2011 *Strumenti per ragionare. Logica e teoria dell'argomentazione*, Milano-Torino, Bruno Mondadori.

Cantù P., Testa I. 2006 *Teorie dell'argomentazione. Un'introduzione alle logiche del dialogo*, Milano-Torino, Bruno Mondadori.

Cardano M. 1995 *Natura sacra. Uno studio etnografico*, in "Rassegna Italiana di Sociologia", Vol. 36, No. 4, pp. 587–624.

———. 1997 *Lo specchio, la rosa e il loto. Uno studio sulla sacralizzazione della natura*, Roma, Edizioni Seam.

Cardano M., Pannofino N. 2018 *Taking Leave of Damanhur: Deconversion from a Magico-Esoteric Community*, in "Social Compass", Vol. 65, No. 3, pp. 433–450.

Denzin N.K., Lincoln Y.S. 1994 *Introduction: Entering the Field of Qualitative Research*, in N.K. Denzin and Y.S. Lincoln (eds.), *Handbook of Qualitative Research*, Thousand Oaks, London and New Delhi, Sage Publications, pp. 1–17.

Eco U. 1988 *Horns, Hooves, Insteps: Some Hypotheses on Three Types of Abduction*, in U. Eco and T.A. Sebeok (eds.), *The Sign of Three: Dupin, Holmes, Peirce*, Bloomington and Indianapolis, Indiana University Press, pp. 198–220.

———. 1989 *The Open Work*, Cambridge, MA, Harvard University Press (original edition 1962).

Godden D.M., Walton D. 2007 *Advances in the Theory of Argumentation Schemes and Critical Questions*, in "Informal Logic", Vol. 27, No. 3, pp. 267–292.

Goldthorpe J. 2000 *On Sociology: Numbers, Narratives, and the Integration of Research and Theory*, Oxford, Oxford University Press.

Groarke L.A., Tindale C.W. 2004 *Good Reasoning Matters! A Constructive Approach to Critical Thinking*, Oxford and New York, Oxford University Press.

Hammersley M., Gomm R., Foster P. 2000 *Case Study and Theory*, in M. Hammersley, R. Gomm and P. Foster (eds.), *Case Study Method*, London, Sage Publications, pp. 234–258.

Hastings A.C. 1963 *A Reformulation of the Modes of Reasoning in Argumentation*, Ph.D. dissertation, Northwestern University, Evanston, III.

Hesse M. 1970 *Models and Analogies in Science*, Chapel Hill, University of Notre Dame Press (first edition 1966).

Josephson J.R., Josephson S.G. (eds.). 1994 *Abductive Inference: Computation, Philosophy, Technology*, Cambridge, Cambridge University Press.

Macagno F. 2017 *The Logical and Pragmatical Structure of Argument from Analogy*, in "Logique & Analyse", No. 240, pp. 465–490.

Mason J. 2002 *Qualitative Researching*, Second Edition, London, Sage Publications.

Morgan M.S. 2014 *Case Studies*, in N. Cartwright and E. Montuschi (eds.), *Philosophy of Social Sciences: A New Introduction*, Oxford, Oxford University Press.

Peirce C.S. 1935–1966 *Collected Papers of Charles Sanders Peirce*, in C. Hartshorne, P. Weiss, and A.W. Burks (eds.), 8 vols., Cambridge, MA, Harvard University Press.

Perelman C., Olbrechts-Tyteca L. 1969 *The New Rhetoric: A Treatise on Argumentation*, London, University of Notre dame Press (original edition 1958).

Pirie M. 2015 *How to Win Every Argument: The Use and Abuse of Logic*, London and New York, Continuum.

Przeworski A., Teune H. 1982 *The Logic of Comparative Social Inquiry*, Malabar and Florida, Krieger Publishing Company (original edition 1970).

Rapley T. 2004 *Interviews*, in C. Seale, G. Gobo, J.F. Gubrium and D. Silverman (eds.), *Qualitative Research Practice*, London, Sage Publications, pp. 15–33.

Schwartz-Shea P., Yanow D. 2012 *Interpretive Research Design: Concepts and Processes*, New York and London, Routledge.

The theory-of-argumentation survival kit 63

Šorm E. 2010 *The Good, the Bad and the Persuasive: Normative Quality and Actual Persuasiveness of Arguments from Authority, Arguments from Cause to Effect and Arguments from Example*, Utrecht, Lot.

Tavory I., Timmermans S. 2014 *Abductive Analysis: Theorizing Qualitative Research*, Chicago and London, The University of Chicago Press.

Toulmin S.E. 1958 *The Uses of Argument*, Cambridge, Cambridge University Press.

Van Eemeren F.H., Grootendorst R. 2004 *A Systematic Theory of Argumentation: The Pragma-Dialectical Approach*, Cambridge, Cambridge University Press.

Van Eemeren F.H., Grootendorst R., Henkemans F.S. (eds.). 2009 *Fundamentals of Argumentation Theory: A Handbook of Historical Backgrounds and Contemporary Developments*, New York and London, Routledge.

Vaughan D. 2014 *Analogy, Cases, and Comparative Social Organization*, in R. Swedberg (ed.), *Theorizing in Social Science: The Context of Discovery*, Stanford, Stanford University Press, pp. 61–84.

Verheij B. 2003 *Dialectical Argumentation with Argumentation Schemes: Toward a Methodology for the Investigation of Argumentation Schemes*, in F. van Eemeren, A. Blair, C. Willard and F. Snoeck Henkemans (eds.), *Proceedings of the Fifth Conference of the International Society for the Study of Argumentation (ISSA 2002)*, Amsterdam, Sic Sat, pp. 1033–1037.

Walton D. 1989 *Informal Logic: A Pragmatic Approach*, Cambridge, Cambridge University Press.

———— 1990 *What Is Reasoning? What Is an Argument?*, in "Journal of Philosophy", Vol. 87, No. 8, pp. 399–419.

————. 1996 *Argumentation Schemes for Presumptive Reasoning*, Mahwah N.J., Erlbaum.

————. 2004 *Abductive Reasoning*, Tuscaloosa, The University of Alabama Press.

————. 2009 *Anticipating Objections in Argumentation*, in H.J. Ribeiro (ed.), *Rhetoric and Argumentation in the Beginning of the XXIst Century*, Coimbra, University of Coimbra Press, pp. 87–109.

Walton D., Krabbe E.C.W. 1995 *Commitment in Dialogue: Basic Concepts of Interpersonal Reasoning*, Albany, State University of New York Press.

Walton D., Macagno F. 2015 *Classifying the Patterns of Natural Arguments*, in "Philosophy and Rhetoric", Vol. 48, No. 1, pp. 26–53.

Walton D., Reed C., Macagno F. 2008 *Argumentation Schemes*, Cambridge, Cambridge University Press.

Weber M. 1949 *The Methodology of Social Sciences*, Glencoe and Illinois, The Free Press (original edition 1904).

Weinstock C.B., Goodenough J.B., Klein A.Z. 2013 *Measuring Assurance Case Confidence Using Baconian Probabilities*, 1st International Workshop on Assurance Cases for Software-Intensive Systems (ASSURE), pp. 7–11.

Wentzel A. 2018 *A Guide to Argumentative Research Writing and Thinking: Overcoming Challenges*, London and New York, Routledge.

Wikan U. 1992 *Beyond the Words: The Power of Resonance*, in "American Ethnologist", Vol. 19, No. 3, pp. 460–482.

Willer S., Ruchatz J., Pethes N. 2007 *Zur Systematik des Beispiels*, in J. Ruchatz, S. Willer and N. Pethes (eds.), *Das Beispiel: Epistemologie des Exemplarischen*, Berlin, Kulturverlag Kadmos, pp. 7–59.

4 The qualitative research design

The whole process of carrying out qualitative research can be thought of a formulation of an argument, meant to persuade the scientific community about the plausibility of the conclusions reached.[1] The making of this argument varies in its form and its contents in the different constitutive phases of qualitative research. It is common to distinguish four phases in the realization of qualitative research: i) planning or design; ii) data collection; iii) data analysis; iv) textualization. The phase for which the major effort to define "how" the argument must be advanced have been made is that of data collection. In the current methodological literature, there are a lot of handbooks – generally very useful – that advice on how to do ethnography, researching through in-depth interviews or focus groups, and surfing the net to realize good qualitative digital analysis. Less attention has been devoted to the steps that precede and follow the fieldwork: research design and textualization. The data analysis phase occupies an intermediate position. For this phase of qualitative research a lot of handbooks and a very rich supply of Computer Aided Qualitative Data Analysis Software (CAQDAS) are available, many of them inspired by the grounded theory approach (Glaser and Strauss 1967). All these tools guide the so-called process of coding but not always with due attention to the heterogeneity of the information coded and to the logical process necessary for the comparison of not-uniformly collected data. Without prejudice to the indisputable contribution which grounded theory has made to the development of qualitative research, some of the assumptions that guide its employment raise perplexities. Among them, the one with which I am least comfortable is the banning of theory, the blank sheet admonition that characterizes the "naturalisation" (in the meaning of Moscovici 1961) of grounded theory, the reception of Glaser and Strauss's original ideas in the wider community of scholars.[2] The unjustifiable exclusion of any theory not inductively produced imposes taking leave from what can be defined as the current mainstream in qualitative research (Morse 2009: 13; Tavory and Timmermans 2014: 3, 10) to suggest an approach that grounds sufficient space to the theory (see Chapter 5). Therefore this book, as has been said (see *Introduction*), is focalized on what happens before and after the fieldwork, focussing more on the logical aspects and less in how to give advice, of the design (in this chapter), and analysis and textualization (in the following chapters).

The research design step, that of research process planning, occupies a central role in quantitative research. No quantitative researcher doubts the necessity to

The qualitative research design 65

decide in advance *the way in which* the study will be carried out, starting from the operational definition of variables and cases and arriving at the formulation of the research hypothesis or, at least, of a research question to be tested against data.[3]

The situation is totally different in the field of qualitative research, informed by habits of mind that maintain sometimes the pointlessness and sometimes the dangerousness of research planning. The topic of the pointlessness of research design rests on a conception of fieldwork in qualitative research that is both romantic and heroic. Qualitative research, in this perspective, is an experience that necessarily sabotages every plan, something that asks the researcher-hero to invent, moment by moment, their cognitive and practical trajectories. This view seems to me clearly expressed in one of the first handbooks that introduced a reflection on qualitative research into Italy (my country), that of Howard Schwartz and Jerry Jacobs (1979, translated into Italian in 1987). In *Qualitative Sociology. A Method to Madness*, we can read:

> One of the reasons this book was difficult to write has to do with the nature of qualitative sociology itself. While quantitative sociologists have achieved a certain stardardization of their techniques, many qualitative sociologists find it necessary to avoid standardization because of the kinds of topics to study. For them, research is an art form that requires the use of a large variety of very different research tools. More important, it requires that the researcher *be able to improvise* his own concepts and research methods in order to deal effectively with the *novel situations that invariably arise* in this kind of undertaking.
> (Schwartz and Jacobs 1979: xiv, italics mine)

This attitude – that by the way, authorizes escaping from any serious methodological training – has recently found deeper motivation in postmodernist thought, namely in the rejection of method meant as a disciplining instance, the "method-o-centrism" that restricts creativity by punishing those "who would want to experiment with something new and different under the sun" (Ellis, Bochner, Denzin et al. 2008: 326).

The second source of opposition toward research design is based on a sort of *horror doctrinae* (fear of theory), that reminds us of the Aristotelian theory of *horror vacui*, fear of the void.[4] Therefore, to avoid the theory contamination unavoidably implied by the prefiguration of the research path, through the sketch of a theoretical frame that can allow the definition of the research question, the research design assumes a very sober form, sometimes with the simple designation of the social context to be studied. Incidentally, we can observe, according to Rosaline Barbour, that the radical refusal of theory, typical of the grounded theory vulgate, becomes a good excuse to escape from reading relevant theoretical literature (Barbour 2007: 196).

A very convincing objection to the pointlessness of the argument of research design comes from two other scholars who have made a decisive contribution to the development of qualitative research, Yvonna Lincoln and Egon Guba. In their seminal book, *Naturalistic Inquiry*, they maintain that the fact that not all elements of qualitative research design can be pre-specified does not imply that none of them

66 *The qualitative research design*

can (Lincoln and Guba 1985: 226). What can be defined in advance – continue Lincoln and Guba – are, at least, the focus of inquiry; where and from whom data will be collected; the methodological instruments used, the chronological and logistic plan of the research activities (226–249). The spirit of this observation reminds me of the words of the American economist, Robert Solow, for whom, saying that since a perfectly aseptic environment is impossible does not imply that we can conduct surgery in a sewer (quoted in Geertz 1973: 30). Analogically, from the fact that it is impossible to plan every aspect of qualitative research, we cannot conclude that we have to improvise every move. On the menace to creativity represented by method, I totally agree with Iddo Tavory and Stefan Timmermas, who maintain that "method is not the enemy of creative theorization, but its closest ally" (Tavory and Timmermans 2014: 51).

Against the argument of the dangerousness of qualitative research design, moulded on the fear of theory, it seems to me that to perform qualitative research we need a research question, and that to have a good research question we must have a good command of the pertinent theoretical and empirical literature. Good qualitative research needs a theoretical frame that can be challenged by the evidence, but that is a necessary starting point (see Tavory and Timmermans 2014: 10–17). It is within a theoretical frame that is possible to define the "intellectual puzzle" (Mason 2002: 17) that guides our experiences of the social world. Again, it is theory that is the source of our abductive inventions.

This constitutes a good reason to define the structure of qualitative research design. To do so, this chapter is organized as a virtual court trial, in which I try to defend, first, the relevance of the research question, second, the eloquence of the cases selected for the study, and third, the suitability, principally from the epistemic point of view, of the planned methodological path.[5]

4.1 Defending the relevance of the research question

The title of this chapter moves from a premise – not unanimously accepted – that precisely for this reason requires to be discussed. What follows is based on the persuasion that what can set up qualitative research (and perhaps other kinds of research too) should be a definition of a question, and the prefiguration of a methodological itinerary that can hopefully allow the elaboration of an answer to it.[6] For the qualification of the nature of, both the question and the answer, it could be useful to borrow the words of the American epistemologist Larry Laudan, whom with certain philological liberty, I allow myself to extrapolate from the broader context of his theoretical reflection. In *Progress and Its Problems* (1977), Laudan, in qualifying the requirements of the most mature expression of scientific research, a theory, observes:

> The first and essential acid test for any theory is whether it provides *acceptable answers* to *interesting questions*: whether, in other words, it provides satisfactory solutions to important problems.
>
> (Laudan 1977: 13, *italics mine*)

The qualitative research design 67

The characterization of what makes a question interesting and worthwhile hunting for one or more answers to, contributes to the reflection of Andrew Abbott on the method of discovery (2004). In the first pages of his intriguing book about the frequent bewilderment that grabs many good students when they sit down to write their bachelor's or PhD dissertation, and they are racked by despair because they have nothing to say, Abbott maintains:

> What then does it take to have something to say? It takes two things. The first is a puzzle, something about the social world that is odd, unusual, unexpected, or novel. The second is a clever idea that responds to or interprets or solves the puzzle. Everything else – the methods, the literature, the description of data – is really just window dressing. The heart of good work is a puzzle and the idea.
>
> (Abbott 2004: xi)[7]

Assuming that an interesting question is the necessary trigger of good qualitative research, it seems appropriate to elaborate on what makes a question interesting and research guided by it worthwhile (see Schwartz-Shea and Yanow 2012: Chapter 1).[8]

So what makes a research question interesting? In the methodological literature, there are many pieces of advice on this issue that focus either on the relevance or the significance of the question and on the originality of the expected answer. The issue of relevance seems to me a good starting point to establish how interesting a research question can be. To progress in the definition of the "interest formula" can be useful to consider the audience, or in a broader view, the perspective from which a research question can be interesting. For this purpose, we can distinguish two different sources of relevance: sociology and society.[9] A research question is relevant for sociology if it can contribute to the progress of our discipline, in a theoretical or in a methodological way. A research question is relevant for society if it can contribute to what James Coleman defines as "institutional design" (1993); if through the expected results of the research guided by this question we can contribute to a more efficient, equitable and ethic architecture of social institutions.[10]

The writing of this book has been interwoven with the carrying out of a study on the use of coercion in Italian acute psychiatric wards, focussing on the recourse of physical restraint, with which patients in a severe crisis are tied to their beds. The study is a team ethnography (see Erickson and Stull 1998) that involves a group of scholars, some of them in the field, others involved in the in progress discussion of the research results.[11] The research questions that oriented this study can be reduced – in a nutshell – to: "What cultural and organizational aspects of the ward determine the recourse to physical restraint to tackle the severe crisis of hospitalised patients?" This question can be considered relevant to society. We plan to accompany the scientific publications of our results with some guidelines through which a redesigning of intensive psychiatric wards, oriented to reducing or eliminating physical restraint, will be possible. Besides the main question posed earlier, another question has oriented our study, a methodological one: "How

68 *The qualitative research design*

can team ethnography contribute to the plausibility of the representation of the phenomena studied?" This last question can be considered relevant for sociology, mainly for the methodological community. At the end of the study, we hope to be able to add some evidence and arguments to defend the suitability of a team approach compared with the more common model of the so-called "Lone Ranger", in which a solitary ethnographer, through his/her experience, represents the social context studied.

The example also allows elucidating that the two kinds of relevance are not mutually exclusive. The first research question, that on the cultural and organizational factors related to the use of mechanical restraint, can be considered relevant also for sociology, although not principally. Symmetrically, we can imagine that the results on team ethnography can – with considerable effort – be extended through the argument from analogy to some activities for which a solo or a group performance (for instance, teaching, curing, inventing a new format for a TV programme) is possible.

Following the grammar of sociological imagination rules (Mills 2000: 213, original edition 1959) or, alternatively, the animal instinct that forces any sociologist who meets a couple of properties to cross them and create a typology, we can consider the relationship between the two sources of relevance (see Figure 4.1).

To be worthwhile as a research guide, a question must be relevant at least from one point of view, either sociological or societal. These are the cases represented by Types 1, 2, and 3, where the situation in Type 1 is the most promising. A Type 4 research question is the one for which research investment seems inappropriate. To detect the position of our research question in the property space defined by the crossing of the two kinds of relevance, a dialectical self-reflection, guided by the model of proleptic argumentation (see Section 3.2), can be useful. Systematic discussion with a member of the community of inquiry (Tavory and Timmermans 2014: Chapter 7) to which we belong, would seem to be more decisive.

For all the first three types of research questions, additional scrutiny is necessary. To decide if the research investment is worthwhile, we have to consider the expected originality of the answer to our research question (Wentzel 2018: Chapter 3). A research question can be considered original if it challenges the tacitly accepted knowledge of the reference community of practices, which may be that of our research field (for instance, that of the sociology of mental health) or that of the social context studied (for instance, that of intensive psychiatric ward staffs).[12]

		Relevance for sociology	
		Yes	*No*
Relevance	Yes	Type 1	Type 2
for society	No	Type 3	Type 4

Figure 4.1 Relevance of a research question for sociology and society

The qualitative research design 69

Having passed the relevance and originality test, the research question has to be evaluated from the ethical and practical points of view, namely on their ethical admissibility and on their practical feasibility. Starting with the ethical issue, according to Peregrine Schwartz-Shea and Dvora Yanow, we must consider the ethical aspects of our research as inherent dimensions of the research design (Schwartz-Shea and Yanow 2012: 22). As for methodological aspects of qualitative research (see Section 1.2), its ethical issues must be tackled in a context-sensitive way and not lining up a collection of rules that act as orders (Madison 1988: 28–29). To guide the necessary context-sensitive ethical decisions, starting from the ethicality of our research question, three general principles can be useful, that of minimization of harm, respect for autonomy, and that of confidentiality, namely of protection of privacy (Hammersley and Traianou 2012: 52–55). The principle of minimization of harm requires that the implementation of our research question in the field does not produce either severe harm to the participant or significant disruption of the setting (Marshall and Rossman 1999: 62). This ethical attention must be deeper when one's research question concerns vulnerable people, like children, the elderly, individuals at the end of their lives, and people characterized by some kind of stigmatizing otherness, mental, physical, or sensory disability (Barbour 2007: 78). The principle of autonomy requires that the carrying out of our research question gives participants the possibility to decide the degree of their collaboration with our study. In this case, we have to consider whether, with a low level of cooperation, the information collected allows us to elaborate an acceptable answer to the research question. The principle of confidentiality requires that the information collected to answer the research question be analysable and reported without prejudice to participants' right to privacy. This last aspect shows its relevance through the connection between the research question and the identification of the empirical context to be studied. In this case, we have to ask ourselves if the empirical context appropriate for generating an acceptable answer to our question can rendered sufficiently anonymous to protect the participants' privacy.[13]

The last step toward the definitive approval of the research question passes through the evaluation of the feasibility of the research activities required for the production of the information that we need to articulate an answer. For instance, besides any ethical considerations, a study such as covert observation of mafia initiation rituals, although original enough cannot be carried out, if we want the research results to be presented by the researcher involved and not, in the best case, by her widower/his widow.

The research question eventually defined prompts both the empirical context in which we can reasonably find an answer to it and the methodological path that seems more appropriate for our purposes. The way through which we harmonize research question, empirical context, and method is anything but deterministic. The typical flexibility of qualitative research also emerges in this case. What usually happens can be represented as a reciprocal adaptation among the three main ingredients of qualitative research design, as illustrated in Figure 4.2.

70   The qualitative research design

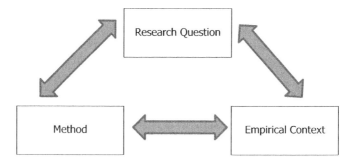

Figure 4.2 Reciprocal adaptations among research question, empirical context, and method

Applied to a specific empirical context, the research question sometimes must be reformulated, by the consideration of the will and capacity of the participants to cooperate with the acquisition of the requested information. Again, through the definition of the data collection methods, for instance, in-depth interview or participant observation, the profile of the original research question can further change through the consideration of the limits and potentialities of the selected method. It is part and parcel of the circular research question – empirical context – method, the possibility to meet the unexpected, to find something that imposes on us to totally *reshape* our research design. In the following sections, the aspects of the research design definition that consider the selection of the empirical context (Section 4.2) and that of the choice of method (Section 4.3) will be analysed.

4.2 Defending the eloquence of the context studied

The analytical passage that follows the definition of the research question is the singling out of the empirical context where it is possible to find an acceptable answer for it. For empirical context, I mean any observational instances, or cases, that allow picking up relevant information for our purposes: organizations, formal or informal groups, people, texts, events, and any other expressions of living in a society. So the cases, broadly speaking, are selected by their relevance to our research question, for their capacity to contribute to the construction of our argument (cf. Mason 2002: 124).

This aim is all but specific to qualitative research. In quantitative research, as well, the cases are selected for their capacity to answer the research question or to test the formulated hypothesis. But the two Muses of social research adopt a different strategy. In quantitative research – usually – the cases are randomly selected in a number big enough to get an accurate microcosm of the context (technically population) studied. So the aim of obtaining a miniature of the phenomenon studied and random selection of the tesserae that compose the picture are the key features of cases selection in quantitative research. Through this procedure, the

The qualitative research design 71

most dangerous selection biases are bridled, and the representativeness of the sample is assured, and with this last condition reached, the argument with which the research results are generalized to the population as a whole acquires a special cogency. These features of the quantitative sampling procedures are so attractive that some authors invite qualitative researchers to follow this "logic of inference" (King, Keohane and Verba 1994; Goldthorpe 2000). Unfortunately, this is not possible.

One of the distinguishing traits of qualitative research, namely details-focalization, imposes a close reading of a small number of observational instances which does not allow consideration of a large number of cases. When the number of cases is small – as it must be in this version of the game of scientific research – there are no advantages in their random selection: neither are possible selection biases controlled, nor the goal of getting a miniature of the phenomenon studied reached.[14] In qualitative research, the aim of representativeness is replaced by that of eloquence. Eloquent means a sample composed of information-rich cases, "those from which one can learn a great deal about issues of central importance to the purpose of the inquiry" (Patton 2015: 264).

In the current methodological literature, case selection oriented toward gaining an eloquent sample is defined either as "purposive sampling" or as "theoretical sampling". These two expressions are frequently considered synonymous since the purpose orienting case selection is usually theoretically guided (see Silverman and Marvasti 2008: 167). Both the adjectives adopted to connote this sampling procedure address relevant aspects that deserve to be elucidated. "Purposive" points out the technical practices that hand over the sample and underline one important difference between quantitative and qualitative sampling, so it contrasts "random" as a way to choose among a set of eligible observational instances.[15] "Theoretical", on the other hand, points out the criteria which guide a reasoned choice among eligible observational instances. These criteria are oriented by a substantive theory, a theory about how some aspects of society work, instead of a theory of probability. Every choice of observational instances implies a specific claim on the relevance of the criterion that has guided the selection. In the lexicon of the theory of argumentation, these claims are propositional commitments defining the outline of the conditional plausibility (see Section 3.2) of the extension of the scope of the research findings. The scope extension is plausible if the claim for the relevance of the criteria adopted for the cases' selection is adequately defended.

An example can help to elucidate this last point. I ask the reader to follow me, once again, to the acute psychiatric wards of my region, where – while I am writing this book – I am carrying out a team ethnography on coercive practices in psychiatric cure, focussing on physical restraint (see earlier Section 4.1). The team I am leading compares six acute psychiatric wards, selected for their different attitudes and practices regarding the use of physical restraint. The practice of physical restraint – in Italy and also elsewhere – is prescribed by psychiatrists but put into effect by nurses, sometimes with the help of the paramedical staff. Moreover, on many occasions, it is the nurses who ask the psychiatrists to apply

72 The qualitative research design

physical restraint to an inpatient perceived as dangerous to himself/herself, to other patients and/or the staff. This organization aspect makes crucial the role of nurses and the centrality of their cultural orientation, including their training and their perception of madness. For all these reasons, we decided to interview the nurses working in the acute psychiatric wards studied, but how many? All of them, or a subset? Having to compare the nurses' interviews with those planned for psychiatrists and patients hospitalized during the observational period, the choice of one subset of nurses becomes compulsory, at least if we really want to focalize our analysis on any little details of the texts collected. The nurses and the paramedical staff in the six sites studied number more than 150 people, so the selection of some information-rich participants seems essential. It goes without saying that the random selection of a subset of individuals is definitely inappropriate. What the field requires is a purposive selection of nurses, guided by some theoretical criteria.

The literature on physical restraint in acute psychiatric wards underlines three main relevant aspects of nurses' practices: gender, length of service, and experience of some contested application of these measures. The impact of socio-demographic characteristics of the staff on the use of physical restraint is well known (Bregar, Skela-Savic and Kores Plesničar 2018), but the issue of gender assumes in this context a specific curvature. Among nurses, being a woman or a man entails not only diverse physical endowment but also a diverse embodied "emotional habitus" (Virkki 2008: 76), strictly related to the capacity to defuse, copy, and avoid the escalation of violence in a psychiatric ward.[16] The second dimension, length of service, in the context studied, is related to the burnout experience. The work of nurses in an acute psychiatric ward is very demanding, both because of the nature of the job – more relational than technical – and because of the characteristics of the inpatients, sometimes undergoing a deep crisis.[17] Burnout is quite common among psychiatric nurses, particularly among those who have been long in service in acute psychiatric wards.[18] The burnout condition, if not tackled, remains quite stable over time, and it is commonly associated with impairment in physical and mental health (Morse, Salyers, Rollins et al. 2012: 343). More important here is that the condition of burnout reduces the capacity to be empathetic, collaborative and attentive, both with colleagues and inpatients, and creates a negative feeling toward psychiatric inpatients (344). Related to the use of physical restraint, the condition of burnout seems to increase the adoption of this practice, even when it is not strictly necessary. The third dimension, the experience of contested practices of physical restraint, is relevant for two different reasons. First, "being there" when this extreme measure has been applied models the nurses' individual ontologies on madness and cure, their perception of what madness is and what must be the way to tackle the crisis that mental distress sometimes implies (Dahan, Levi, Behrbalk et al. 2018). Second, the availability of this information to researchers – possible in ethnographic research – allows ethnographers to pick up information-rich cases directly and to orient the interviews on the level of actual practices and not only on the virtual condition in which mechanical restraint can or must be used.

The qualitative research design 73

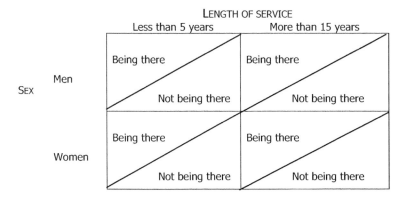

Figure 4.3 Partition of the property space of nurses working in an acute psychiatric ward

Moving from these theoretical criteria,[19] we decided to focus only on staff with either quite short or quite long periods of service, nurses whose seniority is less than five years or longer than 15. Given this choice, the number of nurses eligible for interview was dramatically reduced, so allowing close reading of the texts obtained through the interviews. Among this subset we decided to include a balanced number of men and women, giving precedence to those involved in contested or contestable physical restraints. We decided to consider as contested or contestable the application of a physical restraint when the so-called state of necessity was not so clearly recognizable or when its duration surpassed what we – as a team – defined as reasonable. The scheme that guided case selection is illustrated in Figure 4.3.

Framing this empirical procedure within the more general discussion on the selection of observational instances, we can schematically observe what follows.

1   Through this procedure, we aimed to get a set of information-rich cases that eloquently illustrated the cultural traits of nurses' work in an acute psychiatric ward (with regard to whom, among psychiatric nurses, see Point 5). The sample selected is all but a miniature of the population considered. Its eloquence is underpinned on a deliberately biased selection.
2   The choice of the cases was guided by theoretical considerations related to "emotional habitus" (Virkki 2008), burnout theory (Morse, Salyers, Rollins et al. 2012) and the critical issue of "being there" when a contestable physical restraint had taken place (Dahan, Levi, Behrbalk et al. 2018).
3   In introducing these criteria, we formulated a set of arguments meant to defend their relevance for our research question.[20]
4   The arguments advanced to defend the relevance of the criteria adopted are propositional commitments that define the conditions under which the research results can be extended to unobserved instances. In a nutshell, these arguments model the conditional plausibility of the breadth of the extension of the research results.

74   *The qualitative research design*

5   The soundness of the criteria adopted and that of arguments with which their relevance is defended define the breadth with which the research results can be extended. For the example here proposed, the breadth of the extension relates to three main levels:

i)   All the nurses of the six acute psychiatric wards studied;
ii) The nurses working in the acute psychiatric wards of Piedmont, the North-Western Italian region where all six wards are situated;
iii) The nurses working in any Italian acute psychiatric wards.

What allows us to speak about unobserved cases, starting from what we have learnt from our sample, is – at least, in my view – an argumentative scheme. For the example of psychiatric nurses, it is the argument from analogy (see Section 3.3), where our propositional commitments define the limits of the analogical extension, i.e., what can be said about unobserved case changes, moving from the closer observational instances (nurses not interviewed in the six wards) to the more distant (Italian nurses working in any acute psychiatric wards). The closer to the observed cases is the target of our extension; the wider is the contents of what we can establish on it. Anyway, as I have said previously (see Section 1.2 and Chapter 2), there are good reasons to limit our aspirations to the general, considering the ontological limits that insist on knowledge of social issues which, according to Geertz, must be local, namely bounded by time and space (Geertz 1983).

The issue of the extension of the scope of the research findings can be expressed in a more general way through the notion of "range of authenticity" proposed by Jerzy Topolski for the analysis of historical documents. Topolski defines the range of authenticity of an historical document as the "the sum of those questions (problems) to which a given source can provide *true* answers" (1977: 434, original edition 1973, italics mine). In the epistemological frame adopted in this book, the notion of truth must be abandoned for the more suitable notion of plausibility. Applied to a sample defined through the use of the relevance criteria adopted, the range-of-authenticity notion sets limits to the questions to which the empirical material can offer a plausible answer. In other words, the consideration of the authenticity range of the empirical material collected excludes a set of questions to which it cannot give a proper answer because of the criteria that informed its selection. In the example of the psychiatric nurse's sample, the exclusion from the criteria to which we entrusted the objective to generate a relevant heterogeneity among cases of, for instance, political or religious attitudes, does not allow questioning the empirical material on these aspects.[21]

The theory of argumentation offers a set of instruments: i) for making as transparent as possible the formulation of relevance claims and the propositional commitments that guide a theoretical selection of observational instances and determine the "authenticity range" of the empirical material collected;[22] ii) for the singling out the best information-rich cases that allow a wider extension of the research results from studied to unstudied cases; iii) for clearly defining the conditional plausibility of the reasoning through which we advance our claims

The qualitative research design   75

about the extension of the scope of our research results. The main argumentative levers for these purposes are the argument from example and the argument from analogy in their diverse declinations that will be presented in what follows. Before doing so, a reflection on what makes a case information-rich seems appropriate.

The eloquence of a case, or a set of cases, rests upon its/their position in a property space whose coordinates are defined mainly by theoretical considerations.[23] The simplest configuration of this property space is the one characterized by the presence of an extreme or deviant case. What makes a case a deviant one is its position confronted with that of the totality (usually numerous) of other cases: the black sheep among a flock of white sheep; or the nurse contrary to physical restraint among a psychiatric staff inclined to an ethically indifferent use of this measure. The eloquence of an extreme or deviant case does not rest upon its representativeness of the whole set of cases on which the focus is concentrated. It allows defining the rule that governs the majority through the analysis of its patent violation. It informs us about the resistance practices adopted to survive as a black sheep and gives a counter-definition of hegemonic conduct.[24] The position in the property space of the case/cases selected always implies a relationship with other cases, and this defines as relational the features that make a case eloquent. The relational idea of eloquence informs selection design in all the following four cases, specifically: i) the critical-case design, formulated through the argument of double hierarchy; ii) the most-different-systems design, formulated through the argument from irrelevant difference; iii) the most-similar-system design, formulated through the argument from relevant difference; iv) the extreme-case design, formulated through the argument from radical otherness.

In critical-case design, the property space is partitioned into two sections between which a theory establishes a direct or indirect proportionality relation (Perelman and Olbrechts-Tyteca 1958, English translation 1969, § 76). One area of this space is inhabited by the case (or cases) studied, the observation of which allows a claim on the totality of cases considered, guaranteed by the plausibility of the assumed hierarchy. The roots of this argument can be found in the *Rhetoric* of Aristotle, where we can read: "that if the harder of two things is possible, so is the easier" (Aristotle II (b) 19, English translation 2015: 107). If an athlete can jump two meters, he or she can – for sure – jump one meter. The gist of this procedure is based on the observation of a case (or a small set of cases) characterized by the highest or lowest probability to have some characteristics. If what we observe contradicts our expectations, we can maintain that those expectations – *a fortiori*, with greater reason – will be infringed where their infringement is easier.

In the most-different-systems design, we have two cases, or two small sets of cases, that occupy two reciprocally very distant positions in the property space. This distance should reduce similarities between them, so we focus on the persisting similarities, that plausibly we assume to be present among the unobserved cases less reciprocally distant than those observed.

In the most-similar-systems design, we have two cases, or two small sets of cases, that occupy two very close positions in the property space. This nearness should reduce dissimilarities between them, so we focus on the persisting

76 *The qualitative research design*

differences, that plausibly we assume to exist among the unobserved cases less reciprocally close than those observed.

Continuing with the geometrical metaphor adopted, Figure 4.4 illustrates the four strategies described earlier (which will be elaborated on in the following sections) to get information-rich cases for our research. To make possible a graphical representation of this aspect of the research design, compatible with the Flatland geometry of a printed page, the dimensions of the property space have been reduced to two. Obviously, in real research contexts, the dimensionality of this property space can be bigger (in the psychiatric ward example, by the way, the property space is a three-dimensional one).

These four case-selection designs can be understood – according to Diane Vaughan – as tools to develop "analogical theorizing" through comparison, sometimes direct, sometimes implicit, of different cases (Vaughan 2014: 64, 84). So, to conclude, the eloquence of a case, its capacity to convey information, rests

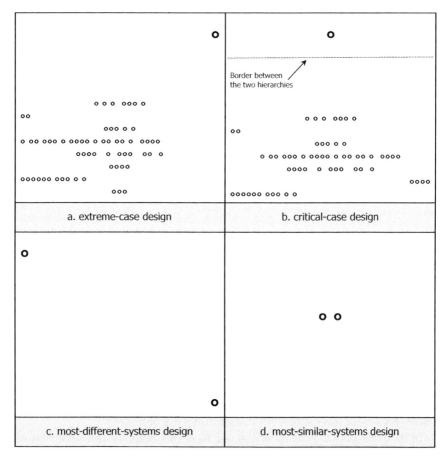

Figure 4.4 Four strategies to obtain information-rich cases

The qualitative research design 77

upon its position in a theoretical field. After this overview, we can go in depth into the illustration of the arguments that guide the selection of the observed cases.

The tool that the theory of argumentation offers for the selection of cases from whose observation an answer to our research questions can be distilled is the argument by example. In the chapter dedicated to the relations establishing the structure of reality, Perelman and Olbrechts-Tyteca (1958; Eng. tr. 1969, § 78 and 79) attribute to this argument three main functions: to generalize a rule, to illustrate it, or to offer a model to be imitated. This last function, a normative one, is not pertinent for our purposes so, in what follows, I will focus only on first two functions of the argument by example, rephrased, in accordance with Stefan Willer, Jens Ruchatz and Nicolas Pethes, as "knowledge constructing" and "knowledge representing" (Willer, Ruchatz and Pethes 2007, cited in Šorm 2010: 123–128).[25]

In its *knowledge construction* function, the example offers new information on the topic at hand. The observation of a set of cases – usually a small one – is carried out to qualify a superset of unobserved cases that share with the observed ones some relevant properties. The information transfer from observed to unobserved cases can be thought of as a diminished version of the synecdoche, where the part studied is *not* meant to represent the whole (*pars pro toto*), but it speaks eloquently only for a bigger part with which it shares a set of relevant properties (*pars pro pars*)[26] The logical tool that underpins the information transfer is the argument from analogy (see Section 3.3), with which the similarity between observed and unobserved cases is adequately defended as relevant to authorize the information's extension of scope. Moving from the extended version of the argument from analogy, presented in Section 3.3, the defence of the analogical extension from observed to unobserved cases implies an effort to persuade the reader that:

1   The similarity or the planned dissimilarity between observed cases and the superset of unobserved cases can be considered relevant for further similarities or dissimilarities that are in question;
2   The unplanned similarity or dissimilarity between observed cases and the superset of unobserved cases is not so relevant as to constitute a strong enough reason to dismiss the analogical extension;
3   No counter-analogies are known, no cases with the expected similarity or dissimilarity are known for which the analogical extension is inappropriate.

The critical questions with which every argumentation schemes presented in the next pages will be equipped will consider all the conditions for the analogical extension outlined. To this general frame, other assumptions are added, that are specific to the version of the argument by example employed. In what follows, four versions of the argument by example will be illustrated: the argument from double hierarchy, those of irrelevant and relevant differences and the argument from the radical otherness. Each of these arguments rests on specific assumptions (for instance, that of the plausibility of hierarchy) that delimit the soundness of the information's extension from observed to unobserved cases. Assumptions about the relevance of what we can call bridging similarities between observed

78   *The qualitative research design*

and unobserved cases and those specific to each version of the argument from the example define the conditional plausibility of the information's scope extension. Or, putting it in other words, these assumptions define the authenticity range of the empirical material collected, defining the set of questions about the unobserved cases to which the sample analysed can offer an eloquent answer. Each argumentation scheme here proposed will be equipped with critical questions to improve its soundness.

The *knowledge-representing* version of the argument from example shares with the knowledge construing version some formal similarities, but with a different goal. The purpose of the knowledge-representing version of the argument from the example is to illustrate, through one or few cases, the information grounded in the collected data. This definition of the knowledge-representing example qualifies it as nothing more than a textualization tool, as an instrument with which the results of a piece of research are offered to the reader.[27] I used this rhetorical tool in my work on mental distress (Cardano 2010) where I asked four people, viewed as flesh-and-blood ideal types, to illustrate as much as possible typical strategies of mental distress sense-making that emerged from the analysis of 60 discursive interviews, carried out a few years before the publication of the essay.

In the following sections, the four sampling designs thematized will be illustrated through a concise presentation of one or two pieces of qualitative research based on them. We start with the most promising design, that of the critical case going through two different forms of madness, that of the patients and the staff of a therapeutic community, and that of the temperate *folie à deux* of married life.

4.2.1 *The critical-case design: the argument of double hierarchy*

The first study convened for the illustration of the critical-case design was carried out by Victor Sharp in the 1970s. Sharp tried to test the so-called social control hypothesis, germinated from the radical psychiatry movement. The social control hypothesis maintains that all the institutions for psychiatric patients combine the mission of cure with that of custody and control. This disposition – in Sharp reflection – is so rooted in psychiatric institutions that it can also be recognized in contexts where should be substitute by that of rehabilitation, where the therapeutic relationship is planned to be as balanced and democratic as possible. To test this hypothesis, Sharp decided to carry out an ethnographic study of a British halfway community for ex-psychiatric patients (part of the Richmond Fellowship), whose staff declared a strong anti-institutional orientation, and an open orientation to flattening the authority pyramid. Sharp, so to speak, bet on the presence of a staff control attitude in the context where it was less probable. If he had won the bet, he would have been able to maintain – more convincingly – that the control disposition of the staff that operates in psychiatric institutions with a shallower vocation toward the patients' empowerment would be stronger. Through his fieldwork, Sharp was able to document a specific way in which the staff relates with the community's residents that he named "interpretive work" (1975). The patients' requests and claims were both individualized and read as a symptom of

The qualitative research design 79

their (presumed) residual pathology. For instance, the request of a patient to get a note changed to use the public telephone was commonly interpreted as a sign of his continuous dependence upon the personnel. This practice allows the staff to deflect the criticisms of residents on their control dispositions and carry on believing on their open, dialogical attitudes. The evidence collected authorized Sharp to conclude that if the disposition toward manipulative control emerges even in the psychiatric institutions where the commitment to ban it is strongest and rooted in an explicit critical ideology, all the more does this disposition permeate all psychiatric institutions.

The second study called to illustrate the critical case design was carried out by the Canadian sociologist Andrea Doucet (2000). The "intellectual puzzle" that guided the Doucet study focusses on the gender division of domestic responsibilities. She asks herself: "Why is there a persistent link between women and domestic responsibility?" (Doucet 2000: 165). To answer this question, Doucet carried out a study, explicitly inspired to the critical case design, by interviewing 23 British heterosexual couples with dependent children who identify "themselves as consciously attempting to share the work and responsibility for housework and childcare" (166).[28] The couples were selected through a combination of criterion and snowball sample (see what follows). Doucet analysed a middle class sample composed of individuals with a high level of education and a good income. Most of the men in the sample (21/23) had full-time paid work; the women were almost evenly divided between part-time and full-time paid work. The research, carried out between 1992 and 1994, was based on a very interesting declination of the interview methodology named "Household Portrait" (167; Doucet 1996). In each couple, the partners were interviewed separately and jointly.[29]

The hypothesis that guided the Doucet study assigns particular relevance to the community norms that have a decisive impact on the actual division of domestic responsibilities, independently of the will of the couples. These norms attribute to women the responsibility for most social and relational activities, like participating in a child's birthday party and speaking to the children's paediatrician or teacher. Undertaking the same activities, men undergo the uncomfortable experience of being viewed as "sissies" and becoming the target of jokes by other men, employed in more traditionally male occupations (174). Like Sharp, Doucet betted on a specific empirical result, testing her hypothesis – the persistency of an unbalanced division of domestic responsibilities – in a context where the possibility of being disproved was highest, and – alluding to the double hierarchy argument – she maintains:

> My view was that if these couples were unable to create new patterns of household labour, less defined and restricted by gender, then it would be apparent how deep rooted these processes were in the wider population.
>
> (Doucet 2000: 167)

Doucet won the bet (her work being published) and concludes by recognizing – even in the social context where it was least probable – the persistence of "norms

80   *The qualitative research design*

that privileged women as primary carers and men as primary earners within the sites of family, work and communities" (178).

The case selection procedure guided by the argument of the double hierarchy is the most promising in qualitative research. Borrowing from a methodological context quite far from that proposed here, we can say that this design is the one that guarantees the higher "leverage", understood by Gary King, Robert Kehoane, and Sidney Verba as the greatest capacity to explain "as much as possible with as little as possible" (King, Keohane and Verba 1994: 29). Moreover, the critical-case design plastically illustrates the conditions under which the qualitative research gives the best proof of itself when theory offers a strong contribution to the carrying out of a piece of research (cf. Tavory and Timmermans 2014: *passim*). There are not so many qualitative studies guided by critical case design, a fact that harmonizes with the very notion of critical study.[30] Nevertheless, it is worth noting that the logic that informs the double hierarchy argument can be adopted, not only for the research design phase but also during the analysis and textualization procedures. Moving from the actual configuration of the empirical materials, we can adopt the argument from double hierarchy to make our research conclusions more sound – every time we can establish a hierarchy in our data, for instance, working with an extreme or deviant case.

On the logical plane, the argument of double hierarchy moves from a specific assumption on the structure of the social phenomenon studied. Specifically, this assumption – part of the propositional commitments that delimit the assertibility conditions of our claims – establishes the existence of two distinct hierarchies for the phenomenon under study. Using the geometrical metaphor (see Figure 4.4), this assumption partitions the property space that frame the research into two sections between which a theory establishes a direct or indirect proportionality relationship, which allows us to say something about the wider hierarchy by observing the smaller one, and in doing so, counting on significant leverage.

In Sharp study, the double hierarchy is established by distinguishing among the more democratic psychiatric institutions, with the highest propensity to flattening the authority pyramid, represented by the therapeutic communities and all the other psychiatric institutions. In the Doucet research, the double hierarchy opposes the small minority of couples that tenaciously attempt to share the responsibilities for housework and childcare to many couples whose family life is organized by gendered rules that give women the heaviest burden of responsibilities.

The assumption on the structure of the phenomenon studied – framed in two hierarchies – is accompanied by another one that establishes the shape of the relationship between the properties considered. This assumption, again part of the propositional commitment of the reasoning, institutes a linear, or at least monotone, relationship between the position of the cases in the hierarchy and their status on the properties considered. To reach his conclusions, Sharp assumed a linear relation between the degree of authoritarian control and the level of democratic organization of the relations between care-givers and cared-for, between staff and patients. Similarly, the conclusion of the Doucet study is underpinned by the assumption of a linear relationship between the public commitment to share

The qualitative research design 81

household responsibilities and correspondent practices in daily life. To explain better the meaning of these linearity assumptions, let us consider a hypothetical situation in which the linearity condition is violated. Hypothetically, we can have a couple where the husband is a very champion of machismo, who maintains that women have to take care of the house and the children, and the man is exempted from all this sissy stuff. This man is married to a woman who agrees with his view. Having the gift of invisibility, a researcher spends a couple of months observing what really happens in the home of this apparently happy family. The researcher discovers that it is the husband who takes care of the children, who cleans the house and prepares unusual kickshaws for the whole family. The husband's behaviour – in this case – may be due to a deep mistrust of his wife's ability to take care of the family. If we want to adopt the conclusions offered to us by Doucet in the study analysed, we must be able to exclude this kind of "non-linearity". For instance, maintaining that a macho man of that kind is probably condemned to going mad trying to reconcile his rooted refusal of sissy stuff and his abnegation in doing them.[31]

The singling out of a critical case is underpinned by assumptions about hierarchies and the (linear) relationship between the properties that organize them: the therapeutic community for Sharp; the 23 couples publicly committed to a balanced division of the household responsibilities for Doucet. Moving from these assumptions, Sharp and Doucet can pronounce their *a fortiori* argument. In the Sharp case, this argument would sound like: if even in the therapeutic community there is manipulative control over patients, all the more reason that it will characterize all psychiatric institutions with a lower propensity to flatten the authority pyramid. Doucet's version of this argument would sound like: if even among couples publicly committed toward a balanced division of household responsibilities, women have a greater burden of care, all the more reason that the division of household responsibilities will be more unbalanced where there is lower or no commitment in that direction.

The cogency of the argument of the double hierarchy can be dialectically improved through the use of some specific critical questions (see Section 3.1):

1   Is the assumption of a hierarchy in the context studied plausible?
2   Is the position of the selected case/cases in the hierarchy appropriate to confer on it/them the status of critical case/cases?
3   (For studies based on more than one critical case) Are the number of selected cases and the heterogeneity among them appropriate to express their critical condition?
4   Is it appropriate to assume a linear, or at least monotone, relationship between the property that defines the hierarchy and the others related to it?[32]
5   Is it plausible to exclude deviant cases from the linear relation assumed?

For the two studies selected to illustrate the critical-case design, all the answers to the five critical questions are positive. In this fact we can recognize the first function of the critical questions, to authorize the use of the double hierarchy for the

82   *The qualitative research design*

research question at hand. The second function, already shown for the argument-from-analogy scheme (see Section 3.3), is to contribute to the specification of the propositional commitment of the proponent, including the answers to critical questions among the premises of the reasoning. In doing so, the full expression (with the critical question embedded in) of the argument of the double hierarchy delimits the conditional plausibility (see Section 3.2) of the reasoning.[33]

In the Sharp study, this means that the conclusion about the ubiquity of social control in psychiatric institutions is subordinated:

1   to the plausibility of the hierarchy proposed;
2   to the suitability of the position of the case selected in the hierarchy of democratic psychiatric institutions, a position that qualifies the community studied as a proper critical case;
3   to the plausibility of the assumption of a linear relationship between commitment toward the empowerment of people cared-for and actual practices in that direction;
4   to the plausibility of the exclusion of deviant cases, in which, despite the explicit authoritarian intentions of the staff, the relationship between staff and cared-for people is shaped by a power equilibrium.

For the Doucet study, the plausibility of the conclusions is subordinated to the plausibility of the equivalent statements expressed earlier – having changed what needs to be changed – plus an additional one:

5   to the suitability of the sampling procedure adopted that selected the 23 couples interviewed.

Doucet resorted to a combination of criterion and snowball sample (Doucet 2000: 167) which seems totally appropriate and, by the way, offers the opportunity to illustrate the idea of context-sensitivity of the qualitative research. It is quite common to consider snowball sampling as a biased procedure that does not deliver enough heterogeneity, being influenced by the nature of the network of the case zero who triggers the avalanche. In the Doucet study, the low heterogeneity of the cases selected, their belonging to a strict social network, becomes an advantage for the research design, conferring more sharply the status of critical on the cases selected.

Before moving to the next argument scheme, a reflection on the general eloquence of the argument of the double hierarchy could be worthwhile. Both Sharp and Doucet betted on a specific outcome of their empirical immersion. What would happen if they had lost the bet? As I said incidentally earlier about the Doucet study, the results of research based on the critical case design in which the authors lost their bet would not be so interesting for publication in a scientific journal. Let us consider Doucet's study and imagine that she had discovered a perfectly balanced division between partners of the domestic responsibilities. Would such a result be interesting enough to be published? Probably not. The reviewers'

The qualitative research design   83

comments might sound something like: "Bloody hell! You have analysed the champions of the balanced division of domestic responsibilities, and – surprise, surprise! – you obtained a balanced division indeed". The eloquence of the argument of the double hierarchy is, therefore, dependent on the results. This asymmetry of the expendability of the research results can create specific problems when this research design is adopted. If I have invested time, resources and maybe reputation in a study where only one kind of result is worth publishing, my reading of the data can be biased by a sort of scientific wishful thinking. In my interpretation of the data, I could be induced involuntary to frame the analysis in a way that confirms my theoretical expectations. For this design, the reflexive attitude of the scientific community seems decisive, maybe more than for another kind of research design.

4.2.2 The most-different-systems design: the argument from irrelevant difference

One of the most effective illustrations of the most-different-systems design can be found in the comparative ethnography carried out by Walter Powell in the 1970s, before he become the founder, with Paul Dimaggio, of the new institutionalism approach. The puzzle that inspired the Powell study refers to the process through which scholarly publishing houses decide which book to publish. To answer this question, Powell compared two academic publishing houses based in the New York metropolitan area. He did not frame his study according to the most-different-system design; nor had he planned a comparative case study from the beginning (Powell 1985: xxvi–xxx). The American sociologist perfected the design of his study through a successive contingent decision that gave him a chance to observe in depth two academic houses, owned by a parent publishing corporation (85).[34] As usual, to protect the privacy of the participants involved, the two publishing houses acquired invented names, becoming Apple Press and Plum Press.

Apple Press was a small house, employing some 30 people, that published not more than 100 books per year. Apple Press is organized in a quite informal way, and its editorial search methods – observes Powell – resemble a garbage can process. Plum Press is a much larger and more formal company. It had twelve times more employees than Apple Press and published about six times more books. Despite their massive scale differences the decision-making process through which a book was published presents, in the two houses, close similarities.

Powell recognized the resemblances between the Apple and Plum through a "learning curve" (129) typical of qualitative research. At first sight, he was surprised by the great autonomy of the editors in both companies in deciding on the books for which to sign a contract. Continuing his ethnographic observation, Powell realized that the editors' discretion was more apparent than real. The huge flow of books in both houses imposed a common queue discipline that separated the over-the-transom materials from those arriving – sometimes solicited – from already-published authors. In both houses the organizational procedure was governed by an unobtrusive control process defined by their managers. The

84   *The qualitative research design*

editors made decisions based on cognitive premises established by the managers. The "premise-setting" was underpinned by different procedures; among them the most incisive was the idea of complementarity between published and as-yet-unpublished books. In Powell's words: "Editors select manuscripts that are appealingly compatible with previously published books" (154). The editors' socialization process, in both houses, made these premises or, in other words, these scripts, guidebooks selection practices. This organizational practice created a peculiar "Matthew Effect" (178) that gave more and more chances of getting into print to known scholars, penalizing the young and unknown. This initial process was still further strengthened by the extra-organizational ties between editors – again in both houses – and the authors already acquired. Editors and authors had reciprocal bonds and moral obligations. Satisfied (published) authors continue submitting their books to their editors who become their friends. Editors reciprocated with a favourable queue policy and with benevolent attention to the new authors proposed by the authors, so to speak, of the stable. There emerges from the results of the study a clear presence of an organizational isomorphism unifying the two houses despite their organizational differences (formality *versus* informality and scale) which can be considered irrelevant.[35]

The strength of this research design and the eloquence of the selected cases are supported by the theoretical frame that defines the properties' space within which the cases appear greatly distant. In the Powell study, the property space that defines the reciprocal distance between Apple and Plum is settled by the economic potential (scale) of the two publishing houses and by their organizational style: formal vs informal. The positions in the property space of the cases are considered as being bound to another relevant property from which heterogeneity is not expected, although highly probable.[36] In the study of the scholarly publishing houses, this relevant property consists of the decision-making processes through which a book getting into print. What the results of the Powell study document is the absence of a relevant heterogeneity between Apple and Plum in the complex process that leads toward the publication of a book. The argument from irrelevant difference, in more general terms, assigns a special solidity to the traits that the most distant cases share.

As for the critical-case design, the most different systems design soundness is rooted in some specific assumptions about the relevance of the properties that structure the property space and on the relation that they have with the connected property – in Powell's example, the process of getting into print. These assumptions are parts of the propositional commitments that delimit the assertibility conditions of our claims on the irrelevance of some crucial properties: scale and degree of formality of the organization in Powell's ethnography.

With regard to the relevance of the properties that mark as most-different the cases considered, this design assumes that they possibly have the highest impact on the connected property where we observe the level of heterogeneity between cases. In Powell's study, this assumption relates to the potentially high causal impact of the scale and the organizational mode – formal vs informal – on the process of getting a book into print. This propositional commitment implies the weakening of the causal relevance of any other properties that, with good reason, can mark a distinction between the cases in the study. For instance, this assumption maintains that in the academic market, the theoretical or ideological orientation of the publishing houses has a lower causal impact on publication compared with the scale and degree of formalization of the publishing houses. Together with the definition of the two sets of properties (relevant the ones observed; irrelevant the others), goes another assumption on the inter-contextual stability of causal mechanisms. In the Powell study, this assumption relates to the fact that what makes the two publishing houses converge in the getting-into-print process is not different between the two presses. What, for instance, has to be excluded with good reason is that the decision-making process that leads to the publication of a book is only unobtrusive managers' control in Plum Press and is a moral obligation or something else in Apple Press.

The last very important assumption relates to the form of relations between the properties that mark cases as different and the property causally connected to them. This relation must be linear, or at least monotone. I try to clarify this point in Figure 4.5 which illustrates the linearity assumption and what can challenge it.[37] The figure still further simplifies the relationship between the profiles of the two publishing houses and the process of getting into print. The profile of the companies is represented solely by their dimension or scale. The getting into print process is stylized in terms of organizational complexity.

The dotted line represents a linear relationship between the organizational complexity of the getting-into-print process and the dimensions of the two publishing houses. The results of the Powell study contest this relationship by

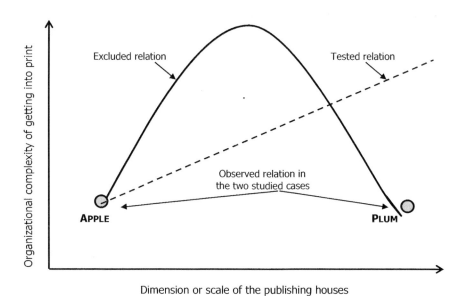

Figure 4.5 Assumption of linearity in the most different systems design

86   *The qualitative research design*

maintaining an equal level of organizational complexity in Apple and Plum. The study findings are sound if we can exclude – for good reasons – a bell-shaped relationship, like the one represented in Figure 4.5, for which the same organizational complexity of the getting-into-print process for the most distant cases is accompanied by a high level of organizational complexity for companies with dimensions between the two extreme here considered. It seems quite difficult to imagine how a hypothetical Orange Press, with a dimension intermediate between Apple and Plum, can show a totally different queue discipline, informal control of the editors, and relational style with the authors acquired. In any case, to dispel doubt about the possible bell-shaped relationship, it is possible to add to the original two cases design a third one, namely the Orange Press or any other company with an intermediate dimension.[38]

The cogency of argument from the irrelevant difference can be dialectically improved through the use of specific critical questions (see Section 3.1):

1   Are there good reasons to assume a strict relationship between the properties that define the case considered as maximally different and the property related to them?[39]
2   Are the properties singled out to mark as maximally distant the cases studied those that plausibly have a substantial impact on the property on which we focus our attention? Specifically, is it plausible to assume that the properties from which the studied cases are maximally distant are among those that have the highest impact on the properties that we bet have uniform values in the cases studied?
3   Can we reasonably exclude that other properties (not considered in the research design) have a high impact on the property (or properties) we expect to be unvarying throughout the cases studied?
4   Are the cases studied really maximally distant in the property space laid out for the research design at issue?
5   Can we exclude that the homogeneity observed in the compared cases is due to a different mixture of the properties that make them maximally distant, or to other properties not thematized in the research design?
6   Is it appropriate to assume a linear or a monotone relationship between the properties that makes cases maximally distant and the other property/properties related to them?
7   Given the type of empirical analysis planned, are the numbers of cases considered and the mutual distance between them adequate to claim the irrelevance of the differences considered?

For the Powell study, the answers to all these critical questions might be considered as tentatively positive, although the author does not thematize them explicitly. As I said before, the study of the American sociologist was not framed from its beginning as most-different-system design, but the claims the author makes for his findings and the rich dialogue he carried out with the pertinent theoretical frames authorizes my reading of *Getting Into Print*.

The qualitative research design   87

As for the double hierarchy argument, the answers to the critical questions have to be considered as part of the premises that underpin the conclusion reached. Being part of the propositional commitment of the proponent of the argument from the irrelevant difference, the answers to the critical questions contribute to delimiting the conditional plausibility of the argument itself.

To conclude on this argumentation scheme, two points seem worthy of mention. The first refers to the way in which the successful results of this research design can be interpreted. We can adopt different – more or less conservative – registers. In the more conservative register, the homogeneity observed between cases – in the Powell study, between Apple and Plum Press – is read as the sign of the causal irrelevance of the factors that mark the distance between the observed cases. In this reading – not seconded by Powell – we do not exclude some heterogeneity in the process of getting into print in the academic market, but we exclude that it can be due to the scale or to the degree of formalization of the publishing houses. In the less conservative register, the same homogeneity is read as evidence of a deep trans-contextual regularity. The evidence collected is considered enough to claim it as a steady feature of the scholarly publishing houses. In this last register, it is possible to sense a nested use of the argument from the double hierarchy. If there are no differences between the two extreme cases considered, with greater reason, that homogeneity in the organizational practices will characterize all the publishing houses with intermediate features between the two extremes.[40] This last argument, again, implies a linearity assumption whose plausibility must be defended.

The last point refers to the eloquence of the most-different-systems design when the differences expected to be absent are actually observable. As for the double hierarchy argument, if we lose our bet on the expected results, the relevance of our research is deeply weakened. If Powell observed relevant differences in the decision-making processes of Apple and Plum, he could simply confirm the well-known relationship between company scales and organizational processes: nothing new under the sky. So as for the argument from double hierarchy, the eloquence of the argument from irrelevant differences depends on the empirical results obtained, with all the extra-epistemic traps recognized in the critical-case design (see Section 4.2.1).

4.2.3   *The most-similar-system design: the argument from the relevant difference*

The illustration of the most-similar-system design and, through it, of the argument from the relevant difference is entrusted to two interesting qualitative studies, with different levels of design complexity. The first study, with the soberer design, is a comparative ethnography focussed on two choirs based in a small North American city. Carla Eastis carried out this study to assess the solidity of what in the 1990s became a sort of sociological common sense, according to which the higher the participation in voluntary associations, the higher will be the level of social capital and, consequently, the functioning of democratic institutions (Eastis 1998: 66). The expectation for this sort of automatism was supported by the simplified reception of Robert Putnam's theory of social capital,

88 *The qualitative research design*

germinated in a study of Italian voluntary associations (Putnam, Leonardi and Nanetti 1993). To challenge this conjecture, Eastis compared two very similar voluntary associations, both choirs.[41]

The choice of this kind of voluntary association responds to specific theoretical requirements: these are associations mostly characterized by horizontal links which offer their members frequent occasions for face-to-face interactions. These features, in Putnam's theory, are recognized as particularly effective in generating social capital. The two associations, similar in their localization and the type of activity proposed, choral singing, showed relevant differences that the author framed into the theory of organizational contingencies. Eastis – previously a choir singer – followed, in parallel and for four months, the activities of the choirs renamed, for the sake of confidentiality, Collegium Musicum and Community Chorus. The Collegium Musicum was the Department of Music's ensemble, part of the local university by which it is financed. Directed by an academic, the Collegium Musicum had 20 white members, most of whom had some connection with the university as graduate students, faculty or staff members. The repertoire, prepared in the rehearsals, and performed under Eastis's observation, was taken from a fifteenth-century Flemish composer, with passages in Latin and French. The Community Chorus is a nonprofit association, founded by a local radio in 1963, to become economically independent eight years later, counting only on the fund-raising capacities of its members. The Community Chorus numbered 80 members with a blend of whites, African Americans, and Hispanics, bonded by their love for singing, although less well-trained in music compared with the academic choir. The repertoire of this more popular chorus had the theme "Broadway tonight!" and consisted of medleys and solo pieces from musicals such as Camelot and My Fair Lady, performed exclusively in English (69).

Eastis focussed her analysis on three theoretical dimensions, crucial for the production of social capital: i) the recruitment styles of chorus' members; ii) the norms and values built through participation in musical activities; iii) the choirs' development of the organizational skills required to keep the voluntary associations alive. For each of the three dimensions considered, Eastis found relevant differences between the two voluntary associations. Their recruitment styles emerged as deeply different. The catchment area of the Collegium Musicum was strictly confined to the university, where it looked for experienced singers. The case of the Community Chorus – where everybody can "come and join" (71) and where no particular competences such as the capacity to sight-read a musical score were required – is different. The differences that separate the two choirs as to access barriers – high for the Collegium, low for the Chorus – are reflected in the extension and nature of the network of social relations activated by participation in artistic activity. The network is extended for Community Chorus, limited for those of the Collegium. As for norms and values, Eastis through observation of rehearsal process, recognized important differences in how musicians assessed the relative ability of their peers, with the opposition between talent, having a wide vocal range, for Collegium, and skill, being able to sight-read a score, for Community. Differences also emerged in the level of the involvement of the choirs in rehearsals, with a high and low commitment, respectively, for Collegium Musicum and Community Chorus members, and so with a different basis for the creation of cooperation and trust among musicians. With regard to the last dimension, the acquisition of organizational skills transferrable to contexts other than that of the choirs, Eastis detected relevant differences between the two voluntary associations. The Community Chorus, not being funded by any public institutions, needed to collect money for its activities, developing through the commitment to fund-raising activities organizational skills that, according to Putnam, are most important for the development of active citizenship. Being funded by the local university, the Collegium Musicum members were not compelled to weave social relationships in order to keep the choir alive or forced to develop organizational skills spendable in a wider social context.

On the basis of these empirical results, Eastis concluded that the impact on social capital and the functioning of democratic institutions deriving from participation in voluntary associations is anything but homogeneous, that there are relevant differences on this issue between the two choirs. Some associations – but not all – promote the extension of social networks; others nurture the rooting of values among their adherents, but these deep-seated values do not necessarily offer support to democratic institutions or promote forms of active citizenship. Eastis concluded:

> General statements about the consequences for American democracy that are gleaned from examining membership rates in broad categories of voluntary associations are at best simplistic. At worst, they distract us from the basis of the debate: What is social capital, anyway?
>
> (76)

The second – more sophisticated – study, aimed at illustrating the argument from relevant differences, was carried out more recently, tackling an issue not so common in sociological research. The research, conducted by Annegret Kuhn, a scholar in global and area studies, moves from a very specific question: "Why, and through which causal mechanisms, should natural resource exploitation lead to the increased contentious mobilisation of ethnic minorities?" (Kuhn 2018: 389). To answer this question, the German scholar explicitly resorted to a most-similar-systems design based on the comparison of three local indigenous communities in Bolivia.[42] The scenario of the study was the peripheral regions of Bolivia with a strong presence of ethnic minorities, an area considered as "a prime example of the increasing trend of a new extractivism or 'extractive boom' in Latin America" (388). Bolivia is also relevant for its particular ethnic heterogeneity, due to the presence of 36 different ethnic groups (392). Natural resources extraction – natural gas in the case at hand – frequently creates conflicts, or at least grievances, among the resident communities, that do not share with the extraction companies the economic benefits of this business.

Starting from the results of a quantitative analysis of conflict events at the provincial level, Kuhn selected three indigenous communities, with a very similar ethnic, economic and cultural profile, but different as to two relevant dimensions: the

90 *The qualitative research design*

presence of a gas extraction plant and the expression of collective grievance and social mobilization. The first case studied was that of the *capitania* – a supracommunal form of indigenous organization (405) – Yaku Igua of the Guarani people in the Gran Chaco province, named as the "Yaku Igua case".[43] In the Yaku Igua *capitania* operated the Planta de Separacíon de Líquidos de Gran Chaco (Gran Chaco Gas Plant) whose construction triggered social mobilizations, ethnic conflicts that made this case a "typical case" (392) of the social mobilization triggered by natural resources exploitation. This core case has been compared to the Chiquitano communities – henceforth, "Chiquitano case" – where there was no natural gas extraction, social grievances, or mobilization. The third case considered is that of the Guaraní community members of the Consejo de Capitanes Guara de Chuquisaca, from the provinces of Hernando Siles and the neighbouring province of Luis Calvo, department of Chuquisaca (henceforth "Monteagudo case") (393). The Montegaudo case was characterized by the presence of a gas extraction plant which did not trigger grievances and social mobilization. To compare the three cases, Kuhn carried out about 130 "semi-structured as well as standardised interviews with indigenous community members" (393). The profiles of the three cases, as emerged from the interviews, is schematically – perhaps too didactically – illustrated in the following figure (Figure 4.6).

The first three properties in the figure define the similarity between the cases compared: all were small communities with a relevant presence of ethnic minorities, based in a peripheral region and characterized by a historical experience of a weak state, not oriented to advocating minorities' rights. The fourth and fifth properties define the core of the causal analysis, focussed on the relationship between natural resources exploitation and social conflicts. The other properties considered in the study (from 6 to 12) were used to explain the processes or causal mechanisms that could explain "how things work in (those) particular contexts" (Mason 2002: 1).

The comparison between the three cases showed important differences, particularly between the Yaku Igua and the Monteguado cases, both characterized by the presence of a natural gas extraction plant but tackled in a very different way. Both Yaku Igua and Monteguado cases complained about the economic implications of the presence of a gas extraction plant either because of the direct consequences on the environment (Property 6) or because of the exclusion of the local communities from the wealth associated with the natural resources extraction (Properties 7, 8, 9). Comparison with the Chiquitano case on the economic profile of the three communities clearly expresses the idea of a relative impoverishment associated with the presence of a gas plant, in the area of unemployment and land tenure. The common impoverishment of Yaku Igua and Monteaudo cases suggested that something is missing to trigger social mobilization in Monteaudo context. To explain the persisting difference between Yaku Igua and Monteaudo cases, Kuhn drew relevant resources from two different theoretical frames: the opportunity approach, that considers the organizational resources available, and the framing process that focusses on the attribution of responsibility for damages complained about (390). From these perspectives emerged relevant differences between Yaku Igua e Montegaudo cases. The Yaku Igua community counted on

The qualitative research design   91

Properties	Cases		
	Yaku Igua	*Chiquitano*	*Montegaudo*
1. Small community with a relevant presence of ethnic minorities	Yes	Yes	Yes
2. Peripheral region	Yes	Yes	Yes
3. Historical experience of a weak state	Yes	Yes	Yes
4. Natural gas extraction	Yes	No	Yes
5. Conflicts and Social Mobilization	Yes	No	No
6. Grievances for environmental degradation	Yes	Not applicable	Yes
7. Presence of collective grievances for lack of general infrastructural endowments for housing and adequate electricity and water supply	Yes	Yes	Yes
8. Grievances for unemployment	Yes	No	Yes
9. Grievances for lacking land tenure	Yes	No	Yes
10. Organizational capacities of indigenous organizations and leader	Strong	Weak	Weak
11. Framing of the natural resources extraction	Implying government discrimination	Not applicable	Not framed in a critical way
12. Previous experience of servitude/forced labour	No	No	Yes

Figure 4.6 Profile of the three cases compared in the Kuhn study on Ethnic Mobilization against Resource Extraction

appropriate organizational resources and on a framing process that attributed the responsibilities of poverty and environmental degradation to a "government discriminating against the Guaraní people" (398). Neither strong organizational resources nor a critical interpretive frame was present in the discourses of the indigenous community members in Monteguado. Kuhn's essay takes another step toward the explanation of the differences between the Yaku Igua and Montegaudo cases, perhaps in an abductive momentum.

Kuhn, surprised by the absence of social mobilization against the gas plant in Montegaudo, directed her gaze to the past history of the community. The results – in my reading – can be explained with the Stouffer theory of relative deprivation, more analytically developed by Walter Garrison Runciman in his work *Relative Deprivation and Social Justice* (1967).[44] The gist of the argument developed by Runciman is that the relative deprivation experience is related to the reference group that each

92 *The qualitative research design*

individual adopts. In the Montegaudo case, the community members compared their situation with that of their ancestors subjugated by servitude, forced labour, that no longer survived. Adopting their ancestors as a "reference group", the members of the Monteguado community considered their current living conditions good enough, or at least not authorizing social mobilization. On this last point, the words of Kuhn are eloquent.

> It can be assumed that this issue of servitude, on the one hand, contributes to explaining the less powerful organizational capacity of the Guaraní communities and representatives in the Monteagudo case: these communities had less time to build up strong organizational structures and to gather leadership experiences as the build-up of such local organizational capacities was substantially hampered by phenomenon of forced labor. On the other hand, the collective memory of periods of forced labor has apparently also influenced the perspective that local indigenous people take both on their own situation and on the government of Evo Morales for doing something about these adverse living conditions.
>
> (400)

The results of the Kuhn study sketch a web of relations that connect natural gas extraction and the emergence of the collective mobilization of ethnic minorities, in which the conditions of life, organizational resources, and cultural framing perform a specific role whose definition was possible through close observation.

The main purpose of the most-similar-system design is to challenge the plausibility of relation – identified through a specific theoretical sensitivity – between two or more properties. In the Eastis study, the relationship whose plausibility is challenged assumes a deterministic shape and connects the spreading of voluntary associations with the production of social capital. In the Kuhn study, the relationship confronted associates natural resource exploitation with the development of contentious mobilization of ethnic minorities. The scope of the argument from the relevant differences, therefore, is not confined to stating a counter-analogical claim (see Section 3.3), maintaining that not all the cases that share some more-or-less close family resemblances also share a specific state on a property at the centre of the analogical reasoning. In other words, the scope of the argument from the relevant difference is not narrowed to the falsification of a statement – in Popper's meaning – through the production of "strictly or purely existential statements" (Popper 1935, English translation 2002: 47) as "there is a voluntary association that does not produce social capital", that authorize claiming that "not all the voluntary associations produce social capital". Applied to the context of qualitative research, which has in its DNA focalization on details, the application of the argument from relevant difference implies the elucidation of the social mechanisms that sometimes associate and sometimes separate the causes to the effects, for instance, the natural gas extraction and the mobilization of ethnic minorities.

What makes selected cases information-rich is, again (see Sections 4.2.1 and 4.2.2), the soundness of the theoretical frame constitutive of the properties' space

The qualitative research design 93

in which the compared cases appear as most similar. The theory to be challenged with the argument from relevant differences must be sound because it is from its plausibility that the relevance of the results acquired derives. In adopting this kind of research design, we have to pay particular attention in avoiding the so-called "straw men fallacy", avoiding challenging a claim that has some similarities with our polemical target but is considerably weaker.[45] Kuhn would have fallen into this fallacy if in order to attack the thesis that binds natural resources exploitation with ethnic mobilization, she had expressed the communities' reaction only through actions labelled terrorist. As in the critical-case design and in the most-different-system design, also in the most-similar-systems design whoever chooses it bets on a specific result, in this case on the heterogeneity of a relevant property between the cases compared. Eastis betted on the different capacity of the two choirs to produce social capital. Kuhn bet on the different propensity of the cases compared to react to their poor living conditions with social mobilization.

The plausibility of argument from relevant difference conclusions rests on some specific assumptions that must be considered part of the propositional commitments that define the outline of the conditional plausibility (see Section 3.2) of the scope extension for the research results. The scope extension of the results acquired – again – is plausible if the claim for the relevance of the criteria adopted for the case-selection is adequately defended. More specifically, we have to assume and defend the relevance of the properties that make the cases studied maximally similar for the property causally connected to them. In the Eastis study, this effort means maintaining that the social features of a voluntary musical association like a choirs can authorize expectation of a high production of social capital. For this purpose, Eastis underlines that choirs are associations characterized mostly by horizontal links that offer their members frequent occasions for face-to-face interactions and that this feature seems promising enough for the production of social capital.

Among the assumptions that delimit the assertibility conditions of the results acquired must be included the one that, with good reason, excludes that the heterogeneity observed must be attributed to the intervention of some hypothetical properties not considered in the design. In the Kuhn study, we need good reasons to exclude that the heterogeneity observed is due not to the property observed but to another one responsible, so to speak, for the suppression of the homogeneity. This unobserved property can be the occurrence of a severe or fatal workplace accident in one of the communities studied (perhaps the Iaku Igua Community), without which (counterfactual reasoning) we wouldn't have observed the heterogeneity between the compared cases. To focus on all these aspects of our reasoning, five critical questions can help:

1   Are there good reasons to suppose a close relationship between the properties that define the case considered as maximally similar and the property related to them?[46]

2   Are the properties singled out to mark the cases studied as maximally similar those that plausibly have a relevant causal impact on the property on which we focus our attention? Specifically, is it plausible to assume that the properties

94 *The qualitative research design*

on which the studied cases are maximally similar are among those that have the highest casual impact on the property that we bet have different values in the cases studied?

3 Can we reasonably exclude that other properties (not considered in the research design) have a high causal impact on the property (or properties) we expect with different states throughout the cases studied?

4 Are the cases studied really maximally similar to the property space laid out for the research design at issue?

5 Given the type of empirical analysis planned, are the numbers of cases considered, and the degree of similarity between them, adequate to make claims for the persisting difference among them?

For both the Eastis and Kuhn studies, the answers to all these critical questions can be considered as positive, although the authors do not thematize them explicitly.[47] As for the previously presented arguments, the answers to the critical questions have to be considered as part of the premises that underpin the conclusion reached. Being part of the propositional commitment of the proponent of the argument from the relevant difference, the answers to the critical questions contribute to delimit the conditional plausibility of the argument itself.

Analogously with the previous argumentation scheme, also for the argument of the relevant difference, its eloquence is related to the results acquired, which is to say the outcome of the bet. If both Eastis and Kuhn had lost their bets for not documenting any relevant difference between the compared cases, the added values of their contribution would be deeply reduced. This asymmetry between the eloquence of the two possible outcomes of the study – finding or not finding differences between the cases studied – recreates all the extra-epistemic traps recognized in critical-case design (see Section 4.2.1).

4.2.4 *Extreme-case design: the argument from radical otherness*

The classical and controversial Garfinkel work on Agnes, *Passing and the Managed Achievement of Sex Status in an "Intersexed" Person* (Garfinkel 1967: Chapter 5), can be efficaciously used to illustrate the extreme case design. Harold Garfinkel met Agnes at the Department of Psychiatry of the University of California Los Angeles, in October 1958. Agnes was a 19-year-old girl raised as a boy until she was seventeen but, by the time she was interviewed, her "appearance was convincingly female" (119). Despite her feminine aspect, Agnes had the normal external genitalia of a male, and she managed to pass as an intersex person to fulfil her dream of becoming a "natural, normal female" through a surgical operation (121). She wanted the operation done by "competent hands at minimum or no cost" (161), remunerating the involved research team with her willingness to participate in study on her unusual biological condition and biographical trajectory. Garfinkel was part of the research team with some other psychiatrists and carried out a long tape-recorded interview lasting 35 hours which underpinned his seminal contribution.

The qualitative research design 95

The controversial aspect of the Agnes study emerged eight years after the conclusion of the research, with the publication of its main findings in Chapter 5 of *Studies in Ethnomethodology*. In the Appendix of the book, Garfinkel revealed a final twist in the already fascinating story of Agnes.

> In February, 1967, after this volume was in press, I learned from my collaborator, Robert J. Stoller M.D., that Agnes in October, 1966, had disclosed to him that she was not a biologically defective male.
>
> (285)

In the Appendix, reading a long quotation from a book published by Stoller, we learn that Agnes had been taking oestrogens since age 12, stealing her mother's medications (her mother was recovering from a pan-hysterectomy) and continuing in this way by buying the pills at the chemist's, telling the pharmacist she was picking up the hormone for the mother and paying with money stolen from the latter's purse (287). This disclosure, which changed the status of Agnes from intersex to transgender, provoked diverse reactions in our community of inquiry. The most critical was that of James Coleman, who maintained that the Garfinkel essay was a "colossal deception" (Coleman 1968: 128) that testifies to "not only an ethnomethodological disaster in itself but also evidence of the more general inadequacies of ethnomethodology" (129). Having chosen to illustrate the extreme case design with the Garfinkel's study, my view of this contribution does not parallel that of Coleman. The final twist in the Agnes story gives more strength to the main idea of Garfinkel's essay, that of the managed achievement of gender as an interactive social process, which is the gist of the essay – analysed here – by the founder of ethnomethodology.[48] Agnes's capacity to perform her sought-after gender role was so efficient as to persuade the researchers themselves and also showing the interactive dimension of "the 'managed achievement' of gender" (Stryker and Whittle 2006: 58).

Through his long tape-recorded interview with Agnes, from November 1958 to August 1959, before and after the surgical operation, Garfinkel address his attention toward the process with which Agnes created her identity of a natural, normal female, learning to be competent as a female person, "to act like a lady" (Garfinkel 1967: 146). In Garfinkel's analysis, Agnes plays the role of Schütz's figure of the stranger (Sassatelli 2007: 14). The Schütz definition of the figure of stranger fits perfectly with the *dramatis personae*, with the character of Agnes.

> For our present purposes, the term 'stranger' shall mean an adult individual of our times and civilization who tries to be permanently accepted or at least tolerated by the group which he approaches.
>
> (Schütz 1964: 91)

Agnes was an adult individual who tried to be permanently accepted as a natural, normal female – before the biographical turning point of the surgical operation, despite her masculine genitalia, and after the surgical operation, despite her

96   *The qualitative research design*

artificial vagina. The cultural otherness of the stranger, plastically represented by the Montesquieu character of the Usbek prince, allows him/her to "place in question nearly everything that seems to be unquestionable to the members of the approached group" (96).[49] Garfinkel defined Agnes as a "practical methodologist" (Garfinkel 1967: 180), making observable what is usually unquestioned: the naturalness of sex and gender.

> Agnes' practices accord to the displays of normal sexuality in ordinary activities a "perspective by incongruity." They do so by making observable *that* and *how* normal sexuality is accomplished through witnessable displays of talk and conduct, as standing processes of practical recognition, which are done in singular and particular occasions as a matter of course, with the use by members of "seen but unnoticed" backgrounds of commonplace events, and such that the situated question, "What kind of phenomenon is normal sexuality?" – a member's question – accompanies that accomplishment as a reflexive feature of it, which reflexivity the member uses, depends upon, and glosses in order to assess and demonstrate the rational adequacy for all practical purposes of the indexical question and its indexical answers.
>
> (180)

Garfinkel's study illustrates one of the most sophisticated uses of the extreme-case design consisting of recognizing the rules that govern social phenomena through the analysis of their patent violation. Through this research design, being aware of all the epistemic traps – well illustrated by Garfinkel – which it implies, it is possible to see the world otherwise, to prudently walk in other shoes to guess what it can mean. It goes without saying that the eloquence of an extreme or deviant case does not rest upon the representativeness of the whole set of cases on which the focus is concentrated. Agnes is all but a "normal person" (obviously, not in a derogatory meaning), but it is her radical otherness that allows recognizing the features of the "the relative natural conception of the world" (Schütz 1964: 228).

Another less sophisticated use of the argument from radical otherness is based on the assertibility that the extreme expression described does exist. In Jennifer Platt's words:

> A single case can undoubtedly demonstrate that its features are possible and, hence, may also exist in other cases and, even if they do not, must be taken into account in the formulation of a general proposition.
>
> (Platt 1988: 11)

This is, for instance, the purpose of the study of Fredrik Sivertsson and Christoffer Carlsson on a sample of juvenile offenders focussed on people who, having grown into adulthood, did not show a clear criminal risk (Sivertsson and Carlsson 2015). This use of the extreme or deviant cases (in Sivertsson and Carlsson the deviants were the ones who renounced deviance), does not lead to the positivist goal of falsifying a theory but more modestly to articulating its contents to fit better with

The qualitative research design 97

the new – deviant – evidence. Quoting the Swedish scholars: "a deviant case analysis does not necessarily invalidate theories, but they may call for greater attention to contingencies and conditional effects" (391).

As for the previous case selection design, also the one based on the extreme or deviant case is underpinned by a set of assumptions related to the condition of being extreme ascribed to the case or cases observed. These assumptions can be clarified through a set of critical questions in the case at issue:

1 Are the properties that define the space in which the observed case occupies an extreme position theoretically or pragmatically relevant?
2 Are there good reasons to exclude that the otherness of the case studied is fortuitous or transitory?
3 Does the otherness of the case studied offer a good interpretive or explicative key for common run of the things (Schütz's critical "stranger" question)?
4 Can the simple statement of the existence of the case inhabited by radical otherness observed offer a theoretical or pragmatic contribution?

To plausibly employ the argument from radical otherness we must answer "Yes" to the first two critical questions and again "Yes" to the third – the Schütz's critical "stranger" question – or at least to the fourth. The answers to these critical questions become parts of our propositional commitment and delimit the assertibility conditions of our claims.

The four research designs and the arguments connected to them presented here (Sections 4.2.1, 4.2.2, 4.2.3, 4.2.4) are the ones that guarantee the highest level of eloquence, based on the richest information cases. It is not always possible to frame our research on one of these argumentative schemes, but when it is not possible, the general idea expressed in these designs can be preserved by using another argumentative tool, proleptic argument (Walton 2009). As already said in Section 3.2, in the proleptic argument the sequences of dialectical moves constitutive of a persuasive dialogue are advanced by one interlocutor only, who makes a claim, considers the possible objections to it, and reshapes his/her reasoning to defuse the objections considered.

A first instance of the use of proleptic argumentation in the area of case selection was introduced earlier, through the description of the selection of nurses to be interviewed in the study of psychiatric wards. In the following Section, a new example will be proposed, adopting, in exposition style, the dialectical posture proper to proleptic argumentation, that of dialogue.

4.2.5 Selecting cases by means of proleptic argumentation

To illustrate this sampling strategy I will use one of my most recent works, also in the area of otherness, but in this case, the otherness analysed is not that of madness, but that of New Religious Movements (hereafter NMRs). This study, carried out with my colleague Nicola Pannofino, end at analysing an aspect of religious behaviour that has remained in the shadows, both in the scientific

98 The qualitative research design

literature and in public discourse: deconversion from NMRs (Cardano and Pannofino 2015).[50]

The idea of researching deconversion emerged after the publication of a critical pamphlet written by some ex-members of the spiritual community of Damanhur – one of case studied for my PhD thesis. The authors of this limited-edition book, entitled *Damanhur alla rovescia* (*Damanhur Inside Out*) asked me to read it and express an expert opinion. The book was composed of a selection of posts published in two online anti-cult forums and depicts a most critical image of the spiritual community. The request for my opinion of their book was interwoven with an indirect invitation to carry out a scientific study into their experience of leaving Damanhur and consequently advancing their grievances against the community leader. Being assured of the collaboration of my colleague for this enterprise, I agreed to the project of a study of deconversion from Damanhur, but without promising a partisan representation of it. Counting on the help of ex-members of the community (some of whom I had met about 20 years earlier during the preparation of my PhD thesis), Nicola Pannofino and I planned to carry out in-depth interviews with an eloquent sample of "small apostates" (7, 9–11). Pannofino and I recognized the theoretical relevance of the study of the biographical trajectories of individuals who had experienced two dramatic turning points in their lives: conversion to an unconventional religious organization and, after a while, deconversion from it. Twice in their lives these people had swum against a very strong current, and this makes their stories particularly interesting. Having acquired the cooperation of Damanhur ex-members, we immediately realized – partly assisted by the advice of the editor of the publishing house with which we planned to publish our nascent book – that we needed some other leave-taker cases to compare with those of Damanhur. The final research design was based on the comparison of four NMRs that we identified through a cognitive path that can be framed in the following dialogue, illustrating the logical structure of a case selection procedure based on proleptic argumentation. The dialogue represented in Figure 4.7 can be read as a dialectical confrontation between the two authors (Nicola Pannofino and I), in the role of *proponent* (as a one-man) and a hypothetical critical and reflexive expression of the "community of inquiry" (Tavory and Timmermans 2014: Chapter 7), in the role of *respondent*, before whom we intended to defend research results that we planned to acquire.

The sample design defined through this exhausting confrontation is illustrated in the following figure (Figure 4.8) and leads to the identification of four NRMs. For each of the four formal configurations defined by the combination of the two dichotomies (high vs low in rejection of the world; presence vs absence of an initiatory structure), an NMR was identified with the obligation to represent the four types of doctrinal orientation. What we got was not a microcosmos of the NMR field, but a diminished version of the synecdoche, where the part studied is *not* meant to represent the whole but to speak – possibly eloquently – on some relevant aspects of the phenomenon studied.[51] Case selection guided by proleptic argumentation shares with the designs previously proposed the attribution of a decisive role in the theory defining the property space in which the cases are positioned. It is through theory that we commit ourselves to the attribution of relevance to the dimensions that constitute the property space defined. Theoretical choices

PROPONENT	It is difficult to reach apostates willing to cooperate in social research, so I mean to interview all the ex-believers that I can reach. That of apostates is a hidden population, for which the best solution is to use a convenience sample.
RESPONDENT	The sampling procedure you suggest has undoubtedly the quality of feasibility, but to have a better idea of the experience of deconversion, it is important to consider the type of cults from which the ex-believers come. Following the Weberian lesson, it is important to consider attitudes toward the world, particularly the degree of rejection of the world.
PROPONENT	I see your point, theory matters! I will re-design the sample considering the issue of the degree of rejection of the world, although, at this moment I have not a very clear idea how.
RESPONDENT	A good start; but analysing the leave-taking from religious organizations, don't you think that you have to pay attention to the cults' internal organization?
PROPONENT	I see, but don't you think that this information can emerge from the field?
RESPONDENT	That is possible, but I think that there is enough research on this topic to obtain the necessary heterogeneity in advance.
PROPONENT	So tell me how.
RESPONDENT	An interesting feature of the NMRs is the presence in their organization of an initiatory structure. Some cults, for instance, the Damanhur that you well know, distinguish different spiritual levels that represent the degree of devotees' participation in the knowledge of salvation and their more material power in the organization.
PROPONENT	This seems relevant. I have two properties, how to resist the temptation of cross-tabling them. This means considering four kinds of NMRs: s high degree of separation from the world with an initiatory structure; a high degree of separation from the world without initiatory structure; a low degree of separation from the with an initiatory structure; and a low degree of separation from the world without an initiatory structure. That's the formula for the perfect sample!
RESPONDENT	This sounds good, but till now you have only considered the formal attributes of the NMRs. Don't you think that the doctrine's contents matter?
PROPONENT	Ok, pain in the neck, I will also consider doctrine, focussing on the most relevant cleavage between NMRs, the ones inspired by Oriental doctrines and those inspired by Western doctrines.
RESPONDENT	This dichotomy perhaps can work for the main Churches (although I have some doubts also in this area), but for sure it doesn't work for NMRs, where we have broader heterogeneity. A look at the most recent theories on NMRs can be good medicine.
PROPONENT	Again theory! Tell me what you have in your mind.
RESPONDENT	Among the most convincing classifications of NMRs, those proposed by Lorne Dawson and Steven Tipton seem the most suitable for the study you plan to carry out. These scholars use different criteria to classify NMRs, but looking for the common points between these two authoritative proposals, we can distinguish four doctrinal fields: Neo-Oriental groups, human-potential movements, conservative Christian groups, Magical-esoteric groups[*].
PROPONENT	So, in the end, you have proposed three criteria, saying nothing about how to combine them. Have you an idea on this point?
RESPONDENT	What seems to me most suitable is a hierarchical order, with which we give priority to formal criteria, then looking for doctrinal heterogeneity in the formal pattern.
PROPONENT	Ok, I see your point, have a look at this final sample design and tell me if it is suitable for you. If it isn't, I think that I have to abandon this theory-of-argumentation sect!

[1] The classifications of the NMRs evoke in the dialogue can be found in Dawson (1998) and Tipton (1982).

Figure 4.7 Sample design for a study of deconversion from Italian New Religious Movements: an example of proleptic argumentation application

100 *The qualitative research design*

		Degree of rejection from the world	
		Low	High
Initiatory structure	Absent	**Soka Gakkai** *Neo-Oriental groups*	**Jehovah's Witnesses** *Conservative Christian groups*
	Present	**Church of Scientology** *Human-potential movements*	**Damanhur** *Magical-esoteric groups*

Figure 4.8 Sample design for a study of deconversion from Italian New Religious Movements

in the case at issue the consideration as relevance criteria of the degree of rejection of the world, the presence of an initiatory structure and the partition of the doctrinal proposals in the four families serve the acquisition of as much "potential for comparison" (Barbour 2007: 53) as possible. Meanwhile, theoretical choices the plea for the relevance of the criteria adopted consist of propositional commitments that delimit the assertibility conditions of our claims about leaving NMRs in a broader meaning. The theoretical choices that orient the case selection define the "authenticity range" (Topolski 1977: 434) of the empirical material acquired. It defines the set of questions that can be addressed to the cases observed, expecting to receive a plausible answer. Here the rule is expressed by the last sentence of Wittgenstein's *Tractatus*: "What we cannot speak about we must pass over in silence" (Wittgenstein 2002: 89, original edition 1921). This means that, in the case of NMRs, if for the definition of the property space conferring relevance on the case selected, we do not consider the theoretical dimensions related to, for instance, the political contiguity of the NMRs, or to relation with hegemonic religions, we must pass over in silence the impact of these aspects on the leave-taking. The last point expresses – I hope clearly – the idea of conditional plausibility, a plausibility conditioned by the relevance of the theoretical criteria adopted in case selection to guarantee valid insight into the phenomenon studied.

For this kind of argumentative reasoning, the functions carried out by the critical question are performed by the dialectical interventions of the respondent. The respondent, so to speak, plays the role of the Devil's advocate, by criticizing the claim of the proponent and inviting him/her to think otherwise about the issues tackled.

Having defended the relevance of the research question and the eloquence of the selected empirical contexts, what is missing to conclude the topic of the research design is the defence of the suitability of the planned methodological path, to which the next section is dedicated.

4.3 Defending the suitability of method

The defence of the suitability of the methodological path goes through all the phases of qualitative research. It is, so to speak, a symphony in four movements: i) planning (part of the research design definition); ii) the field; iii) data

The qualitative research design 101

analysis; iv) reconstruction (part of the textualization process). In each of the four movements, the defence of method appropriateness assumes a specific form, and it is triggered by different figures of respondents: the community of inquiry for the first and the last movements; the participants for the second and third movements.

In this section, I will focus on the first movement, that of planning the methodological path, leaving the discussion of the last movement, that of reconstruction, to the last chapter of the book. In the middle, between the first and the last movements, what happens necessitates the presence of two different argumentative lines relating to *before* and *after* immersion in the participants' lives. During the field and data analysis phases, as pointed out in previous chapters, one of the distinctive features of qualitative research, context-sensitivity, finds its wider expression. Thus, in these phases, we observe the pacing of the method to the empirical context studies, first in its flesh-and-blood expression, then in its representations in a heteroclite set of texts.[52] The openness of qualitative research implies that the defence of the suitability of method can reach, so to speak, its full maturity only when we decide to conclude our work to be submitted to the evaluation of our peers (or tutors for students). It is when everything has been done that we can give the last paintbrush stroke to our representation of their lives. This last discourse on the methodological path followed answers the need for accountability (see Section 1.2) and in a broader sense aims to persuade the reader of the plausibility of our research results.

Focussing on the planning phase, which pertains to the research design, the defence of the suitability of method aims to reach two objectives: one epistemic, the other practical. The epistemic goal relates to the fittingness of method with, on one hand, the research question that inspires the study and on the other, to the empirical context singled out to solve our intellectual puzzle. If our research question refers to the health practices in a psychiatric ward, and we have access to one or more of these sites, the most suitable method is participant observation. We then have to decide whether to go there as pseudo-patients, observing the medical practices with the lowest degree of perturbation (see Section 5.1), or whether it is more appropriate, perhaps also from the ethical point of view, adopting an uncover observation role.[53] If the last is the choice, we have to choose between conventional solo-ethnography or team ethnography (Erickson and Stull 1998). Defending the suitability of method in the case at issue means considering all the pros and cons of the possible alternatives and having good reasons to defend the ones chosen. The defence of the suitability of method, again from the epistemic point of view, implies a meditated reflection on the level of participants' cooperation requested and on the reasonable cooperation that we can get from them. Remaining with the psychiatric ward example, if we plan to carry out in-depth interviews with inmates or ex-patients, we have to consider whether the prospect respondents have sufficient insight capacities and if they can emotionally afford the discussion of themes like physical restraint or violence, which may have crossed their biographical trajectories and their bodies.[54] Within this frame, we also have to consider the opportunity to combine different qualitative methods, if their integration can improve the soundness of the research results. The combination of methods, particularly in the trendy version of mixed

102 *The qualitative research design*

methods, is not a guarantee of better results. The catchy slogan "more methods, more evidence" does not seem very convincing to me.

From the pragmatical point of view, the first criterion against which to evaluate the suitability of the method is that of feasibility. We can move from a very interesting question, on paper, and we can identify the most convenient empirical context and the best qualitative method to apply, but the combination of all these ingredients presents some difficulties. The idea of simulating a psychotic crisis seems – on paper – very promising for the study, using the ethnographic method, of coercion in psychiatric cure. Before starting to act the role of a schizophrenic person in front of our bathroom mirror, to be prepared for the field experiment, we have to ask ourselves if we have enough courage to do so, if we are prepared to receive, maybe for some days, heavy medication that we really do not need and will affect our future wellbeing in unpredictable ways for an unpredictable length of time. You must also ask yourself if you are ready to take the risk of being accused of interrupting the public service, in case someone should discover your deception. The ethical aspects of our research (see Section 4.1) also falls within the area of pragmatical considerations: the research can be performed only if we can guarantee respect for the ethical principle of minimization of harm, autonomy, and confidentiality (Hammersley and Traianou 2012: 52–55).

Concluding what I have metaphorically defined as a virtual court trial, in which the relevance of the research question, the eloquence of the cases selected, and the suitability of the method have been defended, all the arguments developed compose an object usually named a research project. Sometimes the research project simply inhabits our mind, propped up by some jotted notes on a sheet of paper or in a double copy file in our computer. The main function of this informal version of the research project is to guide us – with all the flexibility needed – in our scientific enterprise. Frequently the research project assumes a more formal shape, becoming the document with which we answer a call for competitive research funding, or with which, at the beginning our academic careers, we present our research proposal to a PhD jury. In this case, we can see the second function of a research project, that of safe conduct for what we like most: doing qualitative research! Having completed our discussion on the research design, we can jump to the other desk work in qualitative research, that of data analysis (see Chapter 5).

Notes

1 The idea of qualitative research as the making of an argument has been advanced, among others, by Marshall and Rossman (1999: 10); Mason (2002: 193); Schwartz-Shea and Yanow (2012: 339). The same notion, referred to the wider context of social sciences, has been convincingly maintained by Wentzel (2018: xiii). About the audience to be persuaded, beside the common situation described in the text and identified in the scientific community, there is also the case in which the audience coincides with the community studied, as in the case of collaborative ethnography (Lassiter 2005).

2 The ban of the theory is not strict in the most recent versions of the grounded theory. In the essay written by Ansel Strauss and Julian Corbin, published in the first version of the famous Handbook of Qualitative Research, the authors shyly admit the possibility of using a theory not directly generated by data, but only on condition of meticulously playing the collected data against it (Strauss and Corbin 1994: 273). Greater space for

The qualitative research design   103

theory seems to be recognized by Susan Leigh Star who, combining grounded theory tenets with the pragmatist philosophy, comes to recognized the legitimacy of abduction (Star 2007: 81), and more systematically by Jo Reichertz (2007) who recognizes an abductive heart in grounded theory. According to Iddo Tavory and Stefan Timmermans (2014: 136), the revaluation of theory in all versions of grounded theory continues to be lukewarm.

3   The word method came from the Greek and is composed of the noun οδός (road) and the proposition μετά (with which). Therefore, the term method signifies the road with – along – which.

4   Aristotle maintained that nature abhors a vacuum, namely, a void is impossible. This belief survived until the seventeenth century, contested by the results of Evangelista Torricelli's experiments. I hope that the *horror doctrinae* doesn't last for such a long time.

5   The use of the law as a model for argumentation in scientific practices is coherent with the Stephen Toulmin approach (Toulmin 1958).

6   One of the core ideas in the grounded theory approach is rather that the research question must emerge from the field.

7   Abbott's position is paralleled by Janice Morse who maintains: "All qualitative research should be constructed around an intellectual puzzle of some kind, and should attempt to produce some kind of explanation of that puzzle, or an argument" (Mason 2002: 18). On the necessity of having something to say – possibly interesting – as a starting point for the research process, see also Wentzel (2018: 1).

8   The position expressed in the text is coherent with the pragmatist approach toward the research process expressed in the previous chapters. Charles Sanders Peirce, in the essay *The Fixation of Belief*, published in 1878, assigns to scientific research the task of establish a belief through the dissolution of a doubt (Peirce 1935–1966: § 5.358–5.387; Gallie 1952: 85–93). This point is better expressed by John Dewy with the notion of "problematic situation" as the start of scientific research (Dewey 1938: Chapter vi).

9   I have taken this distinction from Arnaldo Bagnasco, who used it during a seminar in my department about 15 years ago. It may be that, in the meantime, Bagnasco wrote down this thesis, but unfortunately I haven't been able to find it. The society/sociology dichotomy expresses, in a more compact way, the relevance sources identified by Catherine Marshall and Gretchen Rossman (the authors use the word "significance" instead of "relevance"), that distinguish four different relevance sources: for theory, for policy, for practice, for social issues, and for action (Marshall and Rossman 1999: 35–38). The first source, theory, can be assimilated to what I define as relevant for sociology. The other three sources can be assimilated to what I define as relevant for society.

10   The relevance issue can be considered as one of the applications in qualitative research of the Peircean pragmatic maxim, that invites us to consider the products of research activities – in the words of Tavory and Timmermans – "for their potential practical effects – their ability to lead practical commitments or consequences" (2014: 115). We can consider the practical consequences both for sociology and for society.

11   The sociologists with me in the field are Raffaella Ferrero Camoletto, Luigi Gariglio, and Eleonora Rossero. The largest group in which the research results have been discussed also includes Marta Caredda (jurist), Claudio Carezana (psychiatrist), Maria Grazia Imperato (psychiatric nurse), Cristina Pardini (jurist), and Valeria Quaglia (sociologist).

12   For the promotion of the originality of our research questions the "argument heuristics" proposed by Andrew Abbott could be useful (Abbott 2004: Chapter 4). The American sociologist proposes four heuristics: i) problematizing the obvious; ii) making a reversal: expressing a research question that assumes something opposite to the received view of our disciplinary field; iii) making an assumption: namely making a hazardous hypothesis as a base of the research question; iv) reconceptualizing: reframing a problematic situation in an uncommon frame. For this, but not only for this last

104 *The qualitative research design*

purpose, the use of the argument from analogy seems promising, being, in Abbott's words, "the queen of heuristics" (118).

13 Respect of these ethical principles is usually checked by specific Ethical Committees, not always aware of the specificity of qualitative research. This, sometimes, becomes a sort of formal gatekeeping that creates obstacles which are not always surmountable.

14 The classical trope of synecdoche hardly works in qualitative research, where not always a part stands for the whole (cf. Becker 1998: 67–68).

15 In the "prehistory" of quantitative sampling strategies, the two procedures here considered, random and purposive selections, were considered equally valid for the construction of a representative sample. This was the position of the head of Denmark's statistical bureau, Adolph Jensen, presented in the conference of the International Statistical Institute in Rome in 1925. The exclusion of purposive selection from the set of valid tools for the production of a representative sample dated 1934, with the publication of the seminal contribution of Jerzy Neyman's "On the Two Different Aspects of the Representative Method: The Method of Stratified Sampling and the Method of Purposive Selection". In this paper, presented before the Royal Statistical Society in 1934, Neyman identified in the stratified random sample the only method that can guarantee the representativeness of the sample (see Prevost and Beaud 2016: Chapter 8).

16 In the interesting work of Tuija Virkki, a piece of qualitative research on nurses and social workers in Finland, the emotional habitus concept is defined as follows. "Emotional habitus can be conceptualized as the embodiment of the feeling rules that enable the subject to utilize emotional skills in preventing violence. . . . Emotional habitus enables care workers to prevent violence and at the same time, to secure their own position as competent professionals who are able to carry out their tasks according to their professional ideals of caring and emotional management" (Virkki 2008: 76, 85).

17 The difficulty of the nurse's work in psychiatry is increased in the Italian context, where the educational system produces only a generic profile of nursing, without any specific training in psychiatry.

18 In a literature review, Morse and Colleagues estimate the quota of mental health workers who had experienced a high level of burnout as between 21% and 67% (Morse, Salyers, Rollins et al. 2012: 342).

19 For the sake of accuracy, the third criterion, that of "being there", combines theoretical and empirical information.

20 The relevance of the defence of the selection criteria adopted can be framed within the proleptic argumentation structure (see Section 3.2).

21 In the text, I assumed that with non-inclusion among the criteria of sample design of properties like religion or political attitudes, the chances of getting enough "potential for comparison" (Barbour 2007: 53) on these dimensions is low. If I don't plan in advance to have a good quota of non-Catholics in my sample, in a cultural context where the Catholic religion is hegemonic, it is very difficult to be able to compare their attitude toward physical restraint of Catholic and non-Catholic nurses. Nevertheless, we cannot exclude that on some properties not considered relevant for the sample design we can get enough heterogeneity, the range of authenticity of a sample can be defined only on an empirical basis, considering the potential of comparison in fact acquired.

22 Transparency is what is missing in the grounded theory procedure for the extension of the research's results from observed to unobserved cases, the "theoretical saturation" notion (Glaser and Strauss 1967: 61–62).

23 In the example of psychiatric nurses, the coordinates that define the property space (three-dimensional) are sex, seniority, and being involved in a contested or contestable physical restraint procedure witnessed by the ethnographer.

24 The analysis of deviant practices has a long history in sociology, starting from the Durkheim study of suicide (Durkheim 1897), the Garfinkel study on the passing of Agnes, a transsexual woman (Garfinkel 1967), until the more recent contribution of Edgar Morin

The qualitative research design 105

on *La Rumeur d'Orléans* oriented to seeing in the extraordinary clues to the ordinary ("*à voir dans l'extraordinaire le dénonciateur de l'ordinaire*" Morin 1969: 9–10).

25 In Western culture, the normative function of the example was emblematically represented by the literary genre of hagiography, where a story of a saint was told to urge Catholic believers to introduce some aspects, if not of sainthood, at least of deep devotion into their daily lives. The two functions of the example analysed in the text show relevant similarities with the notions of strategic and illustrative sampling proposed by Jennifer Mason (2002: 123–127).

26 The reader can recognize here some resemblances, at least on a linguistic level, with the notion of transferability elaborated by Egon Guba and Yvonna Lincoln (Guba and Lincoln 1979: 110–127; Guba 1981; Guba and Lincoln 1982). In this methodological frame, the transfer between observed cases (sending context) and unobserved cases (receiving context) is underpinned by the analogy (fittingness) between them. Following that path, I try to make the analogical reasoning explicit and more articulated, to avoid what – in my view – can be considered as the main problem of the transferability notion, the attribution to the reader the burden of proof of the "fittingness" that authorizes the analogical extension. As I said previously (see Section 1.2), Guba and Lincoln define the extension from the observed case/s to other analogous case/s through the communication metaphor. So we have a sending context, the one studied, and a receiving context, the target of analogical extension. What authorizes the passage from the sending and receiving contexts is the "thick description" (Geertz 1973: Chapter 1) of both. The sending context's thick description is the duty of the author of the research, the thick description of the receiving context is the responsibility of the reader or, in a wider sense, the scientific community which identifies the similarity between the two objects of the argument from analogy.

27 The definition of the knowledge representing the examples presented here differs both from the quite essential sketch of the illustrative or evocative sample offered by Mason (2002: 126–127) and from my previous systematic reflection on this topic (Cardano 2011: 72–76). Here I moved – I hope with a fairly convincing argument – the knowledge representing example from the area of research design to that of textualization.

28 The reference to critical-case design was not so explicit for the Sharp study (Bloor 1986: 320).

29 The joint interview allows observing, in a sort of experimental perspective, the relations between partners through turn-taking and through how topics are tackled and shared between the two interviewees.

30 Moving from qualitative to quantitative studies (or toward what we can define, ahead of one's time, mixed methods) we find a quite famous and relevant example of critical-case design in the study carried out by John Goldthorpe, David Lockwood, Frank Bechhofer, and Jennifer Platt: *The Affluent Worker* (1968, 1969). Goldthorpe and colleagues designed a study aimed to test a hypothesis; at that time, it was worked out to explain the reduction of political consent toward the Labour Party in working-class areas of the country meant as a symptom of a radical ideological change. To explain this surprising fact, some scholars introduced the hypothesis of a bourgeoisification of the blue collar workers. Goldthorpe and Colleagues betted against this interpretation of ideological change and decided to test their alternative hypothesis in a social context where, following the directions of the advocates if the theory they wanted to contrast, the working-class- bourgeoisification theory had the highest probability of being corroborated. The study was carried out in Luton, a social and industrial context where everything conspired toward working-class bourgeoisification. The study did not confirm this ideological change, so Goldthorpe and colleagues concluded that – *a fortiori*, with greater reason – in the other areas of the country, where the premonitory symptoms of the bourgeoisification syndrome were less marked. The double hierarchy argument can be used gently, adopting its logic to define "conservative" conditions for our research results (see Uzzi 1997: 38). I owe this last biographical reference to Sheen Levine.

106 *The qualitative research design*

31 Thinking about these kinds of nonlinearity can be considered as a situated exercise of proleptic argumentation.

32 I deliberately avoided wording the fourth critical question in the causal lexicon, by naming the properties involved as dependent and independent variables, to authorize the use of the argument of the double hierarchy also in a descriptive way.

33 As I said in Chapter 3, conditional plausibility can be thought of as the analogical equivalent, in the area of argumentative reasoning, of the conditional probability proper to statistical inference. In statistics, the conditional probability of an event B is the probability that the event will occur given the knowledge that an event A has already occurred. It is normally expressed by the notation $P(B|A)$. In the argumentative version of this kind of thought, conditional plausibility, we have statements instead of events.

34 The remark in the text on the originally unplanned feature of the research design allows me to underline that what really matters is the final configuration of the methodological structure, to which it is possible to come following the typical flexible pace of qualitative research. This also means that it is always possible to reframe our research design to increase the eloquence of the collected data.

35 The Powell study will be employed here with some philological liberty, to make the methodological aspects of the most-different-systems design as clear as possible.

36 As in critical-case design, in most-different-systems design we have to bet on an empirical result that, at first sight, seems improbable.

37 A similar assumption underpins the double hierarchy argument (see Section 4.2.1).

38 The necessity of further addition of study cases: a hypothetical Chestnut Press, with an intermediate dimension between Apple and Orange, and a hypothetical Strawberry Press, with an intermediate dimension between Orange and Plum, and going on at this rate, only means that the theoretical frame which orients the study is not solid enough.

39 Also for this argument I deliberately avoided wording the critical questions in the causal lexicon by naming the properties involved as dependent and independent variables, to authorize the use of the argument from irrelevant differences too in a descriptive way.

40 This reading of the Powell study is coherent with the more authoritative one developed by Jennifer Platt who, about *Getting Into Print* wrote: "It seems to rest on the *a fortiori* argument that if such cases can be encompassed by the same general proposition, it must follow that those with other (perhaps less extreme) values on the same variable are also covered by it" (Platt 1988: 16).

41 Eastis didn't frame her study as a most-similar-system design, but this was really the logical structure of her study, and the argument of the relevant differences is the gist of her work.

42 Annegret Kuhn presents her study as a combination of most similar systems design and deviant case analysis (Kuhn 2018: 388). In my view, research design as a whole can be framed as a most-similar-systems design, based on three cases. The proposed reading of the method that leads this very elegant piece of research makes it more suitable for didactic purposes and, in the meantime, eloquently shows the advantages of a comparison based on more than two cases.

43 Interestingly enough, the borders of the case studied was defined by Kuhn adopting the space categories of the native population.

44 Actually Kuhn did not refer to Runciman, but her argument seems to evoke this seminal book. On the theory of reference groups see also N. 10, Chapter 1.

45 "The straw man fallacy occurs where an arguer's position is misrepresented, by being misquoted, exaggerated, or otherwise distorted, and then this incorrect version is used to attack his argument and try to refute it" (Walton 2008: 21).

46 The relation considered in critical question 1 must be tested against the straw man fallacy.

47 Comparing the critical questions developed from the most-different-systems design and the most-similar-systems design we can realise that these two designs are not perfectly specular. The critical questions 5 and 6 developed for the most-different-systems

The qualitative research design   107

designs do not have an equivalent in the most-similar-systems design. The issue of inter-contextual stability of the causal mechanism (critical question 5 for the most-different-systems design), in the most-similar-systems design is controlled by the similarity of the cases compared. Linearity assumption for the most-similar-system design is unnecessary. In this last design (most-similar-systems design) the argument *a fortiori* is not used because it is quite obvious to maintain that if similar cases are different, less similar cases will be even more different.

48 On this point, see Sassatelli (2007) and the introduction to *Passing* in the reader edited by Susan Stryker and Stephen Whittle (2006: 58).

49 The Usbek prince was the author of the imaginary epistolary *Persian Letters*, published by Montesquieu in 1721. Montesquieu used an effective narrative expedient which consists of imagining a Persian prince in eighteenth-century Paris whose otherness allows him to grasp the aspects of French culture hidden under the surface of daily life. Usbek constitutes an hyperbole of Schütz's figure of the stranger, capable, by his radical extraneousness to French culture, of noticing what the "natives" take for granted.

50 The monograph that illustrates the main results of our study on the deconversion from NMRs was published in Italian, but a good synthesis of the research can be found in two subsequently published papers in English: Pannofino and Cardano (2017); Cardano and Pannofino (2018).

51 For a more analytical description of our cases' selection, see Cardano and Pannofino (2015: 19–22).

52 Things are simpler in quantitative research, where the relation between the planned method and the one actually applied is defined in terms of correct application (I planned to collect – through a random sample – 1000 interviews, and I got them), or in terms of errors (unfortunately 50 individuals refused the interview, so the sample is clouded by a bias).

53 In the text, I allude to the David Rosenhan ethnographic experiment. Rosenhan was convinced that the psychiatric diagnoses were all but well founded. To test this hypothesis, Rosenhan projected a singular field experiment, through which eight sane people gained secret admission to 12 hospitals in United States. To be admitted, they claimed to hear voices in their head. The eight brave experimenters, all except one, were admitted to the mental hospital as patients, and although once they arrived in the ward, they immediately stopped acting, they were held for a long time (from a minimum of 7 days to a maximum of 52), then discharged with the diagnosis of "schizophrenia 'in remission'" (Rosenhan 1973: 251).

54 The emotional echo of our research activities into participants' bodies is obviously an ethical issue on which I said less than the essential in Section 4.1, where I presented three general ethical principles; minimization of harm, respect of autonomy, and that of confidentiality. The principle to be considered here is that of the minimization of harm.

References

Abbott A. 2004 *Methods of Discovery: Heuristics for the Social Sciences*, New York, W.W. Norton & Company.

Aristotle. 2015 *Rhetoric*, English translation by W. Rhys Roberts, Fairhope, AL, Mockingbird Publishing.

Barbour R.S. 2007 *Introducing Qualitative Research: A Student's Guide to the Craft of Doing Qualitative Research*, Los Angeles, London, New Delhi and Singapore, Sage Publications.

Becker H.S. 1998 *Tricks of the Trade: How to Think about Your Research While You're Doing It*, Chicago and London, The University of Chicago Press.

Bloor M.J. 1986 *Social Control in the Therapeutic Community: Re-Examination of a Critical Case*, in "Sociology of Health and Illness", Vol. 8, No. 4, pp. 305–324.

108 *The qualitative research design*

Bregar B., Skela-Savic B., Kores Plesničar B. 2018 *Cross-Sectional Study on Nurses' Attitudes Regarding Coercive Measures: The Importance of Socio-Demographic Characteristics, Job Satisfaction, and Strategies for Coping with Stress*, in "BMC Psychiatry", Vol. 18, No. 171, pp. 1–10.

Cardano M. 2010 *Mental Distress: Strategies of Sense-Making*, in "Health: An Interdisciplinary Journal for the Social Study of Health, Illness and Medicine", Vol. 14, No. 3, pp. 253–271.

———. 2011 *La ricerca qualitativa*, Bologna, Il Mulino.

Cardano M., Pannofino N. 2015 *Piccole apostasie. Il congedo dai nuovi movimenti religiosi*, Bologna, Il Mulino.

———. 2018 *Taking Leave of Damanhur: Deconversion from a Magico-Esoteric Community*, in "Social Compass", Vol. 65, No. 3, pp. 433–450.

Coleman J.S. 1968 *Reviewed Work(s): Studies in Ethnomethodology: By Harold Garfinkel*, in "American Sociological Review", Vol. 33, No. 1, pp. 126–130.

———. 1993 *The Rational Reconstruction of Society*, in "American Sociological Review", Vol. 58, No. 1, pp. 1–15.

Dahan S., Levi G., Behrbalk P., Bronstein I., Hirschmann S., Lev-Ran S. 2018 *The Impact of 'Being There': Psychiatric Staff Attitudes on the Use of Restraint*, in "Psychiatric Quarterly", Vol. 89, No. 1, pp. 191–199.

Dawson L. 1998 *Comprehending Cults: The Sociology of New Religious Movements*, Oxford, Oxford University Press.

Dewey J. 1938 *Logic: The Theory of Inquiry*, New York, Henry Holt and Company.

Doucet A. 1996 *Encouraging Voices: Towards More Creative Methods for Collecting Data on Gender and Household Labour*, in L. Morris and S. Lyon (eds.), *Gender Relations in the Public and the Private*, London, Macmillan, pp. 165–175.

———. 2000 *There's a Huge Gulf between Me as a Male Carer and Women: Gender, Domestic Responsibility, and the Community as an Institutional Arena*, in "Community, Work & Family", Vol. 3, No. 2, pp. 163–184.

Durkheim E. 1897 *Le suicide. Étude sociologique*, Paris, Alcan.

Eastis C. 1998 *Organizational Diversity and the Production of Social Capital: One of These Groups Is Not Like the Other*, in "American Behavioral Scientist", Vol. 4, No. 1, pp. 66–77.

Ellis C., Bochner A.P., Denzin N.K., Goodall H.L., Pelias R., Richardson L. 2008 *Let's Get Personal: First-Generation Autoethnographers Reflect on Writing Personal Narratives*, in N.K. Denzin and M.D. Giardina (eds.), *Qualitative Inquiry and the Politics of Evidence*, Walnut Creek, CA, Left Coast Press, pp. 309–333.

Erickson K., Stull D. 1998 *Doing Team Ethnography: Warnings and Advices*, London, Sage Publishing.

Gallie W.B. 1952 *Peirce and Pragmatism*, Harmondsworth and Middlesex, Penguin Books.

Garfinkel H. 1967 *Studies in Ethnomethodology*, Englewood Cliffs, Prentice-Hall.

Geertz C. 1973 *The Interpretation of Cultures: Selected Essays*, New York, Basic Books.

———. 1983 *Local Knowledge: Further Essays in Interpretive Anthropology*, New York, Basic Books.

Glaser B.G., Strauss A.L. 1967 *The Discovery of Grounded Theory: Strategies for Qualitative Research*, New Brunswick and London, Aldine Transaction, A Division of Transaction Publishers.

Goldthorpe J.H. 2000 *On Sociology: Numbers, Narratives, and the Integration of Research and Theory*, Oxford, Oxford University Press.

Goldthorpe J.H., Lockwood D., Bechhofer F., Platt J. 1968 *The Affluent Worker: Industrial Attitudes and Behaviour*, Cambridge, Cambridge University Press.

The qualitative research design   109

————. 1969 *The Affluent Worker in the Class Structure*, Cambridge, Cambridge University Press.

Guba E.G. 1981 *Criteria for Assessing the Trustworthiness of Naturalistic Inquiries*, in "Educational Communication & Technology Journal", Vol. 29, No. 2, pp. 75–91.

Guba E.G., Lincoln Y.S. 1979 *Naturalistic Inquiry*, Beverly Hills, London and New Delhi, Sage Publications.

————. 1982 *Epistemological and Methodological Bases of Naturalistic Inquiry*, in "Educational Communication & Technology Journal", Vol. 30, No. 4, pp. 233–252.

Hammersley M., Traianou A. 2012 *Ethics in Qualitative Research*, London, Sage Publications.

King G., Keohane R.O., Verba S. 1994 *Designing Social Inquiry: Scientific Inference in Qualitative Research*, Princeton, Princeton University Press.

Kuhn A. 2018 *Explaining Ethnic Mobilization against Resource Extraction: How Collective Action Frames, Motives, and Opportunities Interact*, in "Studies in Conflict & Terrorism", Vol. 41, No. 5, pp. 388–407.

Lassiter L.E. 2005 *The Chicago Guide to Collaborative Ethnography*, Chicago and London, The University of Chicago Press.

Laudan L. 1977 *Progress and Its Problems: Toward a Theory of Scientific Growth*, Berkeley and Los Angeles, University of California Press.

Lincoln Y.S., Guba E.G. 1985 *Naturalistic Inquiry*, Beverly Hills, CA, Sage Publications.

Madison G.B. 1988 *The Hermeneutics of Postmodernity*, Bloomington, Indiana University Press.

Marshall C., Rossman G.B. 1999 *Designing Qualitative Research*, Third Edition, Thousand Oaks, London and New Delhi, Sage Publications.

Mason J. 2002 *Qualitative Researching*, Second Edition, London, Sage Publications.

Mills C.W. 2000 *The Sociological Imagination*, Fortieth Anniversary Edition, Oxford and New York, Oxford University Press (original edition 1959).

Morin E. 1969 *La Rumeur d'Orleans*, Paris, Édition de Seuil.

Morse G., Salyers M.P., Rollins A.L., Monroe-DeVita M., Pfahler C. 2012 *Burnout in Mental Health Services: A Review of the Problem and Its Remediation*, in "Administration and Policy in Mental Health and Mental Health Services Research", Vol. 39, No. 5, pp. 341–352.

Morse J.M. 1994 *Designing Funded Qualitative Research*, in Denzin N.K., Lincoln Y.S. (eds), *Handbook of Qualitative Research*, Thousand Oaks – London – New Delhi, Sage Publications, pp. 220–235.

———— 2009 *Tussles, Tensions, and Resolutions*, in J.M. Morse, P.N. Stern, J. Corbin, B. Bowers, K. Charmaz, E. Adele and A.E. Clarke (eds.), *Developing Grounded Theory: The Second Generation*, pp. 13–19.

Moscovici S. 1961 *La psychanalyse, son image et son public*, Paris, PUF.

Pannofino N., Cardano M. 2017 *Exes Speak Out, Narratives of Apostasy: Jehovah's Witnesses, Scientology and Soka Gakkai*, in "International Journal for the Study of New Religions", Vol. 8, No. 1, pp. 1–26.

Patton M.Q. 2015 *Qualitative Research & Evaluation Methods*, Fourth Edition, Thousand Oaks, CA, Sage Publications.

Peirce C.S. 1935–1966 *Collected Papers of Charles Sanders Peirce*, in C. Hartshorne, P. Weiss, and A.W. Burks (eds.), 8 vols. Cambridge, MA, Harvard University Press.

Perelman C., Olbrechts-Tyteca L. 1969 *The New Rhetoric: A Treatise on Argumentation*, London, University of Notre Dame Press (original edition 1958).

Platt J. 1988 *What Can Case Studies Do?*, in R.G. Burgess (eds.), *Studies in Qualitative Methodology: Conducting Qualitative Research*, Greenwich and London, JAI Press, pp. 1–23.

Popper K.R. 2002 *The Logic of Scientific Discovery*, London and New York, Routledge (original edition 1935).

110 *The qualitative research design*

Powell W. 1985 *Getting Into Print: The Decision-Making Process in Scholarly Publishing*, Chicago, IL, The University of Chicago Press.

Prevost J.G., Beaud J.P. 2016 *Statistics, Public Debate and the State, 1800–1945. A Social, Political and Intellectual History of Numbers*, New York and London, Routledge.

Putnam R.D., Leonardi R., Nanetti R.Y. 1993 *Making Democracy Work: Civic Traditions in Modern Italy*, Princeton, NJ, Princeton University Press.

Reichertz J. 2007 *Abduction: The Logic of Discovery of Grounded Theory*, in A. Bryant and K. Charmaz (eds.), *The Sage Handbook of Grounded Theory*, Los Angeles, London, New Delhi and Singapore, Sage Publications, pp. 214–228.

Rosenhan D.L. 1973 *On Being Sane in Insane Places*, in "Science", Vol. 179, No. 4070, pp. 250–258.

Runciman W.G. 1967 *Relative Deprivation and Social Justice: A Study of Attitudes to Social Inequality in Twentieth-Century England*, London, Routledge and Kegan.

Sassatelli R. 2007 *When Coleman Read Garfinkel . . . !*, in "Sociologica", Vol. 12, No. 3, pp. 1–24.

Schütz A. 1964 *Collected Papers II: Studies in Social Theory*, The Hague, Martinus Nijhoff.

Schwartz H., Jacobs J. 1979 *Qualitative Sociology: A Method to Madness*, New York, The Free Press.

Schwartz-Shea P., Yanow D. 2012 *Interpretive Research Design: Concepts and Processes*, New York and London, Routledge.

Sharp V. 1975 *Social Control in the Therapeutic Community*, Farnborough, Saxon House.

Silverman D., Marvasti A. 2008 *Doing Qualitative Research: A Comprehensive Guide*, Los Angeles, London, New Delhi and Singapore, Sage Publications.

Sivertsson F., Carlsson C. 2015 *Continuity, Change, and Contradictions: Risk and Agency in Criminal Careers to Age 59*, in "Criminal Justice and Behavior", Vol. 42, No. 4, pp. 382–411.

Šorm E. 2010 *The Good, the Bad and the Persuasive, Normative Quality and Actual Persuasiveness of Arguments from Authority, Arguments from Cause to Effect and Arguments from Example*, Utrecht, Lot.

Star S.L. 2007 *Living Grounded Theory: Cognitive and Emotional Forms of Pragmatism*, in A. Bryant and K. Charmaz (eds.), *The Sage Handbook of Grounded Theory*, Los Angeles, London, New Delhi and Singapore, Sage Publications, pp. 75–93.

Strauss A., Corbin J. 1994 *Grounded Theory Methodology: An Overview*, in N.K. Denzin and Y.S. Lincoln (eds.), *Handbook of Qualitative Research*, Thousand Oaks, London and New Delhi, Sage Publications, pp. 273–285.

Stryker S., Whittle S. (eds.). 2006 *The Transgender Studies Reader*, New York and London, Routledge.

Tavory I., Timmermans S. 2014 *Abductive Analysis: Theorizing Qualitative Research*, Chicago and London, The University of Chicago Press.

Tipton S. 1982 *Getting Saved from the Sixties: Moral Meaning in Conversion and Cultural Change*, Berkeley, University of California Press.

Topolski J. 1977 *Methodology of History*, Dordrecht and Boston, D. Reidel Publishing Company (original edition 1973).

Toulmin S.E. 1958 *The Uses of Argument*, Cambridge, Cambridge University Press.

Uzzi B. 1997 *Social Structure and Competition in Interfirm Networks: The Paradox of Embeddedness*, in "Administrative Science Quarterly", Vol. 42, No. 1, pp. 35–67.

Vaughan D. 2014 *Analogy, Cases, and Comparative Social Organization*, in R. Swedberg (ed.), *Theorizing in Social Science: The Context of Discovery*, Stanford, Stanford University Press, pp. 61–84.

The qualitative research design 111

Virkki T. 2008 *The Art of Pacifying an Aggressive Client: 'Feminine' Skills and Preventing Violence in Caring Work*, in "Gender, Work and Organization", Vol. 15, No. 1, pp. 72–87.

Walton D. 2008 *Informal Logic: A Pragmatic Approach*, Cambridge, Cambridge University Press.

————. 2009 *Anticipating Objections in Argumentation*, in H.J. Ribeiro (ed.), *Rhetoric and Argumentation in the Beginning of the XXIst Century*, Coimbra, University of Coimbra Press, pp. 87–109.

Wentzel A. 2018 *A Guide to Argumentative Research Writing and Thinking: Overcoming Challenges*, London and New York, Routledge.

Willer S., Ruchatz J., Pethes N. 2007 *Zur Systematik des Beispiels*, in J. Ruchatz, S. Willer and N. Pethes (eds.), *Das Beispiel: Epistemologie des Exemplarischen*, Berlin, Kulturverlag Kadmos, pp. 7–59.

Wittgenstein L. 2002 *Tractatus Logico-Philosophicus*, London and New York, Routledge (original edition 1921).

5 On qualitative data analysis

In qualitative research, as a rule, data analysis starts a millisecond after the beginning of data collection. The two-times approach, typical of quantitative research, does not apply to qualitative research. Having renounced, for the sake of accuracy, a predefined script for data collection procedures, we must analyse, moment by moment, how each single observational practice works, to progressively improve the suitability of data collection. Let us consider one of the simplest data collection procedures, the in-depth interview. Apart from the corrupted version of this procedure, which the French sociologists Didier Demazière and Claude Dubar call "disguised questionnaire" (1997), in the proper use of this dialogical tool the interviewer has to invent the right question as s/he goes along.[1] In the words of another French sociologist, Jean-Claude Kaufmann, "the best question is not that prompted by the interview guide: it must be found from what has been said by the respondent" (Kaufmann 2006: 48, my translation). In doing so, in inventing at the moment the right question or the right ethnographic practice, the researcher must analyse the empirical materials s/he acquires while s/he is in the field, to learn from them the best way to perform the study.

Besides this need for reactive harmonization in the field, there is another typical situation in which data analysis follows closely upon data collection. For all qualitative methods based on direct observation of social interactions, namely naturalistic or participant observation, field experiment, shadowing, and autoethnography (see Chapter 2), immersion in the field is usually followed by the desk activity of writing.[2] The activity of writing about our field experiences, which all methodological handbooks invite us to do daily, is another instance of analysis *during* data collection. The writing of fieldnotes is eminently an activity of analysis, through which we give form to our experiences. As is well-known to anybody who has carried out ethnographic work, the writing of fieldnotes is anything but a transference of our memories onto paper (or our laptop screen). Writing fieldnotes means analysing our experience and memories, prompted by brief notes jotted down in the field and taking advantage of a moment of less intense activity. Writing, from many points of view, is an instrument of discovery triggered by analogical thought (Vaughan 2014) and abductive inference typical of qualitative research.

During the data collection phase, not only do we write our fieldnotes and transcribe our tape-recorded interviews, but we also *read* these materials. The reading offers a guide on how to continue our study, namely, to realize what to focus on

On qualitative data analysis   113

next, or what additional questions we must present to the respondents-to-be, or what participants' voices are missing and must be introduced through a "second stage sampling" (Barbour 2007: 73). Before moving toward the discussion on how to analyse collected data, a short reflection on the nature of qualitative data seems appropriate.

5.1 The nature of qualitative data

What we analyse in qualitative research are texts sometimes complemented with some "humanly produced artefacts" (Tilley 2001: 258). Strictly speaking, artefacts embody the nonverbal aspects of human culture. Starting from Lévi-Strauss's reflections, a tendency to consider artefacts as language with a "silent grammar" emerged (258). On this point, I agree with the anthropologist Christopher Tilley for whom "things are not texts or words" (259).[3] I do not want to erect a wall between artefacts and texts built on the shaky opposition between subjects and objects, but I think that for the sake of clarity, the distinction between them is necessary.[4] Qualitative analysis applies both to artefacts and texts, the latter expressed in words, in sounds and on still or moving images. The heterogeneity of empirical materials is the cypher of qualitative data analysis.[5]

There are three different sources of heterogeneity. The first is represented by a quite common combination – in a single study – of data stemming from different data-collection techniques. This is the typical situation in ethnographic research where we have to tackle fieldnotes, interview transcripts, naturalistic data, and sometimes artefacts too. In my ongoing team ethnography about psychiatric wards, the team must manage the fieldnotes written daily in order to represent staff-patient interactions, the simplified representation of these interactions in the medical records (naturalist data), the transcripts of interviews carried out with the medical staff and with the patients, and the artefacts encountered during the fieldwork, the constraints – whose images are impressed in the memory or in a photograph – which patients are bound to their beds. The second source emerges in qualitative team research, where every member of the team interprets his/her role in the field with the liberty that qualitative data collection imposes. The organization of the team ethnography obsessively evoked on so many occasions in these pages, provides for some periods in which two ethnographers are simultaneously present in the same ward. Comparison of the fieldnotes written on these occasions delivers an obvious, and happy, result: each of us, in the same situations, observes and takes notes in a personal way that allows an interesting form of contrast and complementation: heterogeneity again. The third heterogeneity source is the main features of qualitative research, the context-sensitivity of the data collection procedures (see Chapter 2). It could be useful to quote again Rapley's words on how to perform in-depth interviews, to trigger a double-hierarchy argument: if we have high heterogeneity in one of the simplest data collection procedures, *a fortiori* we shall have still more heterogeneity in the more complex ones.

> You don't have to ask the same question in the same way in each interaction. You often cover the same broad themes in different interviews – either

114　*On qualitative data analysis*

through the interviewee or you raising it as a subject for talk. This is a central rationale of qualitative interviewing – *that it enables you to gather contrasting and complementary talk on the same theme or issue.*

(Rapley 2004: 18, italics in the original)

Following this advice, as we should, at the end of a study based on, or including, in-depth interviews, we have a set of interviews carried out by the same interviewer (the heterogeneity increases when more than one interviewer is involved), with a diverse *wording* for the questions addressed to respondents, and with relevant differences in the *themes* tackled case by case. To illustrate the specificity of qualitative research on this point, comparison with the equivalent situation in quantitative research can be instructive. Let us imagine a situation in which we want to collect information on the cultural profile of a group of people, for instance leave-takers from a New Religious Movement, using both a questionnaire and an in-depth interview. If we focus, both through questionnaires and in depth-interviews, on three properties (variables in quantitative lingo): the motives of the conversion, the emergence of discomfort as a member of the religious organization and the taking leave from it. The following figure (Figure 5.1) guides us to a comparison between the two interlocution games.

Figure 5.1 takes Rapley's advice perhaps too literally and deliberately dramatizes the heterogeneity of qualitative data-collection procedures. Sometimes things go smoothly. It happens that all the themes in the interview guide are explored with all the respondents (with all of them we go through the themes A, B and C), and possibly with a narrower range of variation in the wording too, but qualitative research never shows the data collection uniformity that we find in the quantitative. As I said earlier, the heterogeneity further increases when there is a combination of different data-collection procedures (for instance, observation plus interviews) and when we move from a solo to tandem or team research. The true miracle of qualitative data analysis – which takes place every day – is that even in the midst of such confusion we can reliably read and interpret our data. How is this possible?

We – qualitative researchers – recognize similarities in our empirical materials, despite their not being as uniform as they are in the quantitative field. We achieve this result through a – mostly tacit – use of the argument from sign and the argument from analogy (see Chapter 3). If, through some variations on the theme of the emergence of discomfort ("How did things change after what you defined as the honeymoon period?"; "What do you mean by difficult relations with the leader?"; "You have told me something about self-esteem; could you elaborate on this?"), we collect answers like those reproduced in what follows, managed through a combination of the argument from sign and that from analogy.

NADIA:　After the early honeymoon period . . . I started – unconsciously – to notice the contradictions. Because in this film [alluding to The Truman Show] there were a number of gaps. But the incredible thing was that these things I had felt on the rational level I had set aside. Because the power of this film was so

Quantitative research: standardized questionnaire

Property A Conversion motivation	Operational definition a
Property B Emergence of discomfort	Operational definition b
Property C Departure from the religious organization	Operational definition c
Synthetic representation	Cultural trait: a combination of (a, b, c) with the same "formula" for all the respondents

Qualitative research: in-depth interviews study

Property A Conversion motivation	Expressed through the wording a_1
	Expressed through the wording a_2
	Expressed through the wording a_3
	$\vdots$
	Expressed through the wording a_n
Property B Emergence of discomfort	Expressed through the wording b_1
	Expressed through the wording b_2
	Expressed through the wording b_3
	$\vdots$
	Expressed through the wording b_n
Property C Departure from the religious organization	Expressed through the wording c_1
	Expressed through the wording c_2
	Expressed through the wording c_3
	$\vdots$
	Expressed through the wording c_n
Synthetic representation	Cultural trait: a combination of one to three from among a_n, b_n, c_n with a possible different "formula" for respondents, for instance:
	Nadia: a_1, a_3, a_7, b_1, c_4, c_6
	Valeria: a_5, a_9, b_1, b_2, b_7
	Ezio: a_1, a_6, a_9, c_1, c_4, c_7
	Stefano: b_1, b_9, b_{11}, c_1, c_7, c_9
	Osvaldo: a_1, a_3, a_6, a_9, a_{11}, a_{13}
	Luca: b_1, b_2, b_4, b_{11}
	Irene: c_1, c_2, c_4, c_9, c_{11}

Figure 5.1 Comparison between two stylized versions of asking questions relates to three
properties, in quantitative and qualitative research

116 *On qualitative data analysis*

great that it overcame everything that could call it into question. I would say: "it can't be that way! I'm the one that doesn't understand"

(Cardano and Pannofino 2015: 98, 2018: 439).

VALERIA: There has always been – continuously for twenty years – this idea of having to live up to something he [the community leader] expected and that you could never give him because there was always a new one [demand], something that you couldn't be or couldn't reach. Obviously, you were always one step behind him. It was a heavy burden, a heavy inner burden because he constantly made you feel like a defective person

(Cardano and Pannofino 2015: 98).

Luca: Living in a social environment of this type, your self-esteem – from my point of view – is more and more diminished because you are always less than what you should be and give, and therefore you always feel indebted and your self-esteem sinks lower and lower and lower . . . I have always felt – because of this mechanism of lowering self-esteem – always insufficient even with respect to my ability to be happy with what I had had achieved.

(Cardano and Pannofino 2015: 99)

We can plausibly conclude that for all three respondents the roots of their discomfort are mainly emotional and relate to a sense of inadequacy that emerged in order to reduce the cognitive dissonance between the dream of Damanhur that led them to conversion and the lived experience of their initiatory path (Cardano and Pannofino 2015: 96–103). This reasoning can be framed into the argument-from-analogy scheme presented in Section 3.3 and reproduced here.

In the situation at issue, three rather than two cases are being considered, but the logical structure of the reasoning is the same. In the publications cited on

THE ARGUMENT-FROM-ANALOGY SCHEME – EXTENDED VERSION

Major premise:	Generally, case C_1 is similar to case C_2.
Similarity basis premise	The similarity between C_1 and C_2 is evident for the features $f_1, f_2, f_3, \ldots f_n$.
Relevant similarity premise	The similarity between C_1 and C_2 observed so far is relevant to the further similarity that is being examined.
Irrelevance of differences premise	The differences between C_1 and C_2 observed so far do not constitute a strong enough reason to dismiss the idea of their similarity.
No known counter-analogy premise	No C_3 cases is known so far that shares with C_1 the features $f_1, f_2, f_3, \ldots f_n$, but for which A is false.
Minor premise:	Proposition A is true in case C_1.
Stability of feature premise	The observation of a theoretically relevant set of C_1 instances for a wide enough time span so far allows us to say that proposition A is true in C_1.
Conclusion:	Proposition A is true in case C_2.

On qualitative data analysis   117

deconversion from the community of Damanhur, Pannofino and I also focussed on the counter-analogy argument, that considered some devotees excluded from the category of "vague and confused discomfort" as a first step in the deconversion process (Cardano and Pannofino 2015: 96–97).

The argument from sign comes in handy when we have to move from specific time-and-space-bounded instances to more abstract and general "rules", or when, using the so-called "evidential paradigm" (Ginzburg 1978; English translation 2013), we recognize in some clues from either participants' words or their actions the sign of something unexpected or at least relevant. For instance – returning to psychiatry – in the recurrent staff worries about the leaking of information about the use of physical restraint, we can recognize the germ of an ethical doubt about its legitimacy, and also – to be cynical – the fear of undeserved social denunciation of a practice that staff consider ethically and legally right. As I said in Chapter 1, the argument from sign is the most acute tool to tackle the thorny issue of invisibility. We use it both in quantitative and qualitative research but with the important difference previously underlined. If in quantitative research the argument from sign – embedded in the operational definitions – precedes data collection, in qualitative research it is developed during and after data collection (see Section 1.2).

Both the argument from sign and that from analogy deliver conjectural conclusions that assign to a category every piece of data with a membership function that cannot be harnessed into classical bimodal logic, with 0 or 1 membership values, but with a multimodal or fuzzy logic (Zadeh 1965).[6] In quantitative research, with few exceptions, classification procedures are rooted in binary logic for which, as in the Diagnostic Statistics Manual – the "bible" of biological approach to mental distress – you are or are not mad, in zero-one logic. Returning to deconversion, we can subsume the three respondents' answers under the broad category of "feeling of inadequacy", assigning them a differentiated membership value, for instance 0.6 for Nadia, 0.7 for Valeria, and 0.8 for Luca. The numerical values in this example are not so relevant; what matters is the idea of fuzziness in the membership of the target category, to which we return in the following.

United by this comfortable flexibility and openness, qualitative data are diverse in some important respects, about which it is possible to introduce some distinctions. I propose to distinguish three broad sets of data: representations, reproductions, and naturalistic data (cf. Cardano 2011: 241–247).[7] The distinction between these three types of data can be outlined by considering the agency of the researcher involved in their production from two distinct points of view: the impact of the researcher on the action observed, and that on their portrayal in the text to be analysed.

The first kind of researcher agency can be expressed through the degree of perturbation introduced into the field, an aspect also known in the methodological literature as "reactivity". By the term perturbation, I mean any kind of modification of the context observed due to the researcher's intervention. We can distinguish three situations: the absence of perturbation, interactive perturbation,

118 *On qualitative data analysis*

and observational perturbation. We have observational perturbation whenever the participants involved in our study are aware of the attention paid to them by the researcher and, for this reason, they can (possibly, not always necessarily) modify their behaviour to "save their face" (Goffman 1956) or simply to please the researcher.[8] This is the typical situation of uncover participant observation where participants – not necessarily all of them – are aware of our role and can modify, at least for a while, their daily activity (cf. Figure 2.1).[9] We also encounter observational perturbation in all of data-collection procedures based on the interlocution between a researcher and one or more respondents (in-depth interview) or a larger group (in either a group interview or a focus group). We meet interactive perturbation when the researcher is immersed in any social context as a bona fide member where nobody knows the identity or purposes of the scholar. In this situation, the perturbation of the context is simply due to the fact that an extra person entered the scene. This is the typical situation of naturalistic observation, covert participant observation and field experiments, from which we cannot exclude perturbation. In the third area, that of the absence of perturbation, includes all the data-gathering procedures for which the influence of the researcher is inexistent, in which the researcher agency is confined to the data analysis of data whose existence does not depend on him/her.

The impact of researchers in the first steps of the transformation of their lives in our works (Geertz 1988), their agency in the portrayal of the social phenomena focussed on, can be categorized in three states: passivity, mimetic intervention, and selective intervention. We have a selective intervention when the researcher choses both what to represent and how to do it. This is the typical situation when writing fieldnotes. Immerged in a social context, ethnographers must choose the direction of their gaze, decide what to describe, and then choose how to describe and interpret the facts observed.[10] The mimetic kind of portrayal of observed actions is based on the use of specific technology for tape- or video-recording. Moving from a tape-recorded interaction, for instance an in-depth interview, we get a text through the orthographic transcription based on the transformation – one-to-one – of sounds into words. The portrayal of the interaction in which the researchers were immerged does not imply either selection (all that was tape-recorded must be transcribed verbatim) or interpretation (we just transcribe, saving for later the interpretation of the text).[11]

The researcher's agency in portraying participants' actions becomes passivity when the researcher simply collects the texts or the artefacts to be analysed, without any kind of intervention in their construction. Documentary analysis works this way. A good example in the area of mental health is Peter Conrad's study of on the impact that genetic discourses had in the social representation of serious mental illness (bipolar disorder and schizophrenia). Conrad analysed 110 news stories published in five major American newspapers and in three news magazines over a 25-year period (Conrad 2001). In the field of artefacts analysis, an interesting example is the study carried out by William Rathje and Cullen Murphy on consumption behaviours, analysed through the observation of the stratification of rubbish in a public garbage dump (Rathje and Murphy 2001).

On qualitative data analysis 119

Combining the two dimensions of the researcher agency impact considered earlier on the action and its portrayal, we obtain the properties' space illustrated in the figure that follows (Figure 5.2).

Logical and empirical reasons imposed a reduction of the dimensionality of the property space, with the exclusion of four out of nine configurations, the ones crossed out in the table, for which it is difficult – at least for me – to imagine a kind of empirical material and a data-collection procedure which delivers it.

Naturalistic data, as depicted in Figure 5.2, are characterized by the lowest level of researcher agency. One of the most effectual definitions of naturalistic data comes from Jonathan Potter through his macabre "dead social scientist test" (Potter 2002). To separate the naturalistic data from the research-provoked ones, the scholar invites us, for any piece of data, to ask ourselves if it can be available for the analysis "if the researcher got run over on the way to work" (541). If, for instance, I plan to perform an interview with a newly enrolled nurse in one of my psychiatric wards, and to do so I leave home early in the morning, after having walked my 17-year-old dog Pippo, but on the way to the railway station a meteorite fell on my head, it is impossible that posterity will ever benefit from the transcript of the planned interview. The transcript of an interview – like all researcher-generated data – does not pass the dead-social-scientist test. Interviews, focus group transcripts, any kind of fieldnotes (inspired by natural or participant observation, by a field experiment, autoethnography, or shadowing), as well as any texts produced by participants at the request of the researcher, do not pass the dead-social-scientist test; therefore, according to Potter, they are research-provoked data. Naturalistic data are all of the texts and artefacts whose production is independent from the researcher's agency. On the contrary, other empirical material would satisfy this request; for example, the spontaneous diary of a teenager from the past century, accidentally found in the cellar of a rural house, all the Facebook posts that we read as "lurkers", the published biography of cancer survivors, the Shoah memorial under the central railway station in

Impact on the action: perturbation

		Absent	Interactive	Observational
	Passive	Naturalistic Data		
Impact on the action's portrayal	Mimetic	Reproductions *Sub-type 2*		Reproductions *Sub-type 1*
	Selective		Representations *Sub-type 2*	Representations *Sub-type 1*

Figure 5.2 Researcher agency impact on the action observed and on its portrayal

120 *On qualitative data analysis*

Milan, the prosaic furniture of a bank meeting room, or a mountain of garbage analysed with archaeological sensitivity by William Rathje and Cullen Murphy (Rathje and Murphy 2001).

Reproductions and representations are the outcome of two different processes, depending on the degree of perturbation that accompanies their generation. Let us start with the reproductions, Sub-type 1, gathered through data-collection methods that imply observational perturbation. These kinds of reproductions are the most common; they are the outcome of all those data-collection procedures based on a dialogue between researchers and participants: two typical examples are the in-depth interview and focus groups. Sub-type 2 of reproductions, generated by data-collection methods that do not imply any kind of perturbation, is very rare. I was inclined to exclude that configuration from the typology in Figure 5.2 when I recalled a most peculiar study, perhaps even ethically questionable, carried out by a young graduate student I met in my university about 20 years ago, Giovanna Resta. Giovanna prepared her master's degree dissertation on gossip, choosing as a case study the nursery school where her mother then worked. In order to justify her presence, Giovanna invented a fake research project on children's learning, but her real research interest was schoolteachers' gossiping. After failing to collect gossip through overt participant observation, she decided to covertly tape-record the schoolteachers' chatting at the coffee machine, a strategic site in every Italian workplace. She left her purse near the coffee machine, with the tape-recorder switched on inside. In a sort of confession of her field experience, written with two other young scholars for one of the most prestigious Italian sociological journal, she wrote:[12]

> The tape recordings revealed to me so many aspects of the interactions between the schoolteachers that I could not have grasped otherwise: if in my presence the use of obscene language was very limited, once "among themselves" the schoolteachers permitted themselves vulgar comments, caustic comments and double meanings that I would never have suspected. Furthermore, my absence allowed them to gossip about me and my mother too.
>
> (Bobbio, Resta and Venturini 2001: 313, translation mine)

The distinction between naturalistic data and Sub-type 2 of reproduction is blurred, in the addition to the very relevant ethical difference between these two kinds of data. A strict application of the "dead social scientist test" (Potter 2002) allows the distinction: without Giovanna's perfidious and ethically debatable stratagem, the transcript of the schoolteachers' gossip would not exist, even though researcher perturbation was absent in the generation of this material.

In the table row of researcher selective intervention (see Figure 5.2) we find the two last kinds of data, representations Sub-type 1 and Sub-type 2, separated by the kind of perturbation that accompanies their construction, observational, or interactive. As I said earlier, the selective construction of this kind of data is an intertwined two-step procedure. First, researchers select what to describe, the direction of their gaze; second, they transform their lived experiences into words,

On qualitative data analysis 121

adopting the rhetorical, narrative style which is part of their repertoire. The first step, addressing their gaze depends only partly on the researcher. What I had the opportunity to observe in an acute psychiatric ward was always the product of a negotiation among me, the staff, the patients and, sometimes, the care-givers.[13] The second step, that of distilling words from our lived experiences, implies the choice of how to combine of direct and indirect discourses. In describing a clinical colloquium, I must choose between:

Indirect discourse

Doctor Venice received Daisy, a 23-year-old patient with the nurse Carolyn.[14] Doctor Venice told the patient that she could not stay at home with her mother because they quarrelled continuously; nor could she live on the street because she would be in danger of being raped or beaten and she would probably start taking drugs again, further jeopardizing her mental health.

Direct discourse

DOCTOR VENICE sees the 23-year-old patient Daisy, accompanied by the nurse Carolyn. This was the tone of the colloquium.

DOCTOR VENICE: "You can't go home to your mother; you have to go back into the therapeutic community. With your mother, you can't stay, because after half a day you fight and she throws you out of the house. And you can't be alone outside the house. You would have sex with the first person you met. You have already had – I don't know – six or seven abortions; you have taken every kind of drug, you have been beaten up many times on the street".

It seems quite obvious that, for the scrap of social interaction described, direct speech works better to illustrate the rough approach of Doctor Venice. But not always can we choose between direct and indirect forms of speech because the information we have is not rich enough to allow a precise reconstruction of who said what. Not all of us can boast the memory capacities of the novelist Truman Capote who was able to "get within 95 percent of absolute accuracy" of a conversation without the help of a tape recorder (Plimpton 1966). Moreover, what happens in the field is not exclusively a set of linguistic acts; nonverbal language is relevant too. How participants use their bodies, how they handle objects, and the objects' agency (cf. Latour 1993) cannot be represented only through a sequence of turn-taking. So, in the end, fieldnotes, the empirical material that best illustrates the features of representations, are a blend of descriptive and interpretive statements, direct and indirect discourses, related sometimes to the social interactions among the participants, and sometimes to our relationship with them. The formula in which all these ingredients are combined depends on the opportunity that the field offers the researcher, and on his/her choice in the fieldnotes writing. Representations are the texts that embody to the greatest

122 *On qualitative data analysis*

extent the personal characteristics of the researchers and their way of being in the world, both as scholars and as people. The differences between the two sub-types of representations – Sub-type 1 and Sub-type 2 – relates to their "range of authenticity" (Topolski 1977: 434, original edition 1973), a feature that allows tracing in a more general way the differences among the five kinds of qualitative data described. The historian Jerzy Topolski - as already said in the previous chapters - defines the range of authenticity of a historical document as the "the sum of those questions (problems) to which a given source can provide true answers" (1977: 434, original edition 1973). To harmonize the notion of authenticity range with the epistemological frame adopted in this book (see Section 4.2) which proposes substituting the notion of true with the less demanding one of plausibility. In this perspective, any kind of empirical material can be characterized by a specific face-authenticity range that assumes a specific value considering the substantive content of data. In broad terms, it is possible to say that for the study of the linguistic aspects of a culture, reproductions give more accurate information. Studying the language in which a community of practices, like that of nurses, defines its ordinary activities, representations acquired through in-depth interviews or through focus groups offer precious elements. For the study of social interaction and what people do (not only what they say they do), reproductions offer richer data. Related to the contents of actions, for instance, routine activities vs deviant behaviour, representations Sub-type 1 or Sub-type 2 offers a different contribution. Among representations, Sub-type 2 (burdened by interactive perturbation) can be more appropriate for the study of deviant behaviours, compared with Sub-type 1 (burdened by observational perturbation). Anyway, there is not a general rule, a formula, to evaluate whether one kind of data is more promising than others.[15] For each concrete situation, the researcher must consider the specific nature of the acquired data and define the questions to which it can give a plausible answer.

The last issue of the nature of qualitative data relates to the conditions in which they are shareable in a team of researchers involved in the same study or the wider community of research, for meta-analysis or, more simply, for re-use (cf. Heaton 2004). Speaking of re-use for naturalistic data does not seem appropriate. For naturalistic data, any analysis is always a primary analysis; what can change is the researcher who analyses this empirical material or the time in which the same researcher carries out his/her analysis. The sharing and the re-use of representations and reproductions are a different matter. The sharing of reproductions, usually verbatim transcripts of in-depth interviews or focus groups, does not create any particular problem. It requires a detailed system of annotation for verbal and nonverbal interactions between speakers and a clear agreement among the research group on the protection of respondents' privacy. Representations – no matter of which Sub-type – are the empirical materials that create the most serious sharing difficulties.[16] Sharing fieldnotes among team-mates requires fixing some general rules on note-taking, not so strict as to shackle the team's research practices. If the study is carried out in more than one site and there is a division of work assigning different sites to different researchers, a period of simultaneous presence of the team members in all the studied sites is essential. Having been in the site of one's

On qualitative data analysis 123

teammate allows deeper comprehension of his/her fieldnotes. Last and most important is a continuous critical and reflexive discussion of the data acquired week by week. The secondary analysis of fieldnotes, strictly speaking, is a very difficult enterprise. Fieldnotes unfold their full meaning only to those who wrote them, evoking experiences of the field through their words. This makes it quite difficult to carry out an analysis of fieldnotes drawn up by someone who has not collected them. The number of secondary analyses of fieldnotes (representations in the proposed classification) can be counted on the fingers of one hand. One of the most interesting exercises in this direction was performed by Anna Weaver on the Julius Roth's fieldnotes from a TB sanatorium (Weaver 1994).

Having clarified the data features that we can use for our analysis, what seems urgent now is the illustration of the logic of qualitative data analysis.

5.2 The logic of qualitative data analysis

From the logical point of view, qualitative data analysis can be thought of as a sequence of categorization procedures. We usually start from the categorization of our data aspects one at a time; then we connect the categories applied to our textual corpus to observe the relations among them, getting more complex categorization forms, namely some fuzzy versions of taxonomies and typologies. This process embodies what Wright Mills named the "grammar" of sociological imagination (Mills 2000: 213, original edition 1959).[17] In the study of the deconversion process which saw as characters the ex-members of the Damanhur community, I analysed the deconverts' biographical trajectories, trying to categorize each relevant step.[18] Placing the applied categories side by side, I recognized some relationships among the stages of this journey into magic. Focussing on the last part of the voyage, and combining different categories applied to the textual corpus, I defined an ideal type of the deconversion process that includes four steps, through which the participants passed in different ways. In the fuzzy sets jargon, this means that the deconversion narratives collected show a different degree of membership in the ideal type proposed and this is in tune with Weber's original notion of the concept, on which I will elaborate in what follows.

The process of categorization is all but specific to qualitative research; it is the cognitive cypher of human beings' way of being in the world, as has been poetically expressed by Douglas Hofstadter and Emmanuel Sander: "Nonstop categorization is every bit as indispensable to our survival in the world as is the nonstop beating of our hearts" (Hofstadter and Sander 2013: 15). The elegant analogy proposed by Hofstadter and Sander allows me to clarify my idea of qualitative research's relationship with common-sense practices. The received – positivist – view of science depicts it as a linguistic game totally different from that played by lay people, totally alien to common sense. The view of qualitative research that inspires this book goes in the opposite direction. Qualitative research is the highbrow continuation of common sense with only one added ingredient: reflexivity, which implies critically observing how we empirically back our claims. Moving from the categorization that I daily perform in my activities, for instance,

124 *On qualitative data analysis*

those of husband, father, Occitan dancer, dog owner, and to those I perform as a sociologist, I have to add to the process the critical observation of my cognitive activities, a persistent tendency to dialectically doubting my way of carving out representations of the phenomena I am studying. Returning to the categorization process, the Hofstadter and Sander definition is a necessary starting point for my argument.

> The act of categorization is the tentative and gradated, gray-shaded linking of an entity or a situation to a prior category in one's mind. . . . The tentative and non-black-and-white nature of categorization is inevitable, and yet the act of categorization often feels perfectly definite and absolute to the categorizer, since many of our most familiar categories seem on first glance to have precise and sharp boundaries, and this naïve impression is encouraged by the fact that people's everyday run-of-the mill use of words is seldom questioned; in fact, every culture constantly, although tacitly, reinforces the impression that words are simply automatic labels that come naturally to mind and that belong intrinsically to things and entities.
>
> (14)

What seems very important to me in this definition is the open reminder of the fuzziness of our process of categorization, which cannot be represented as organizing the things of the world in "different drawers of a chest of drawers" (13). This deliberate vagueness is the red thread of all qualitative research practices, starting from the formulation of "sensitizing concepts" (Blumer 1969) to the representation of our research findings through metaphors, analogies and ideal types. The engine of the categorization process is – continuing with Hofstadter and Sander – the analogy opposed to the classification "which aims to put all things into fixed and rigid mental boxes" (20).[19]

Putting together all the elements of the puzzle, the qualitative data-analysis process can be defined as a process of "categorization through analogy-making" (20), which best fits – in my view – with the context-sensitivity of qualitative data-collection procedures and with the very nature of qualitative data. After all this "philosophy" some "how to do" indications – to which I shall dedicate the rest of this chapter – would seem necessary.

The essentials of qualitative data analysis can be abridged in a lean, so to speak, version of the Template Analysis proposed by Nigel King (King 2012), in whose words: "Template Analysis is a style of thematic analysis that balances a relatively high degree of structure in the process of analysing textual data with the flexibility to adapt it to the needs of a particular study" (426). What makes the version of Template Analysis proposed here lean is the renunciation of a "high degree of structure in the process of analysing" which, more explicitly, means renouncing a (necessary) "hierarchical organisation" (431) of the categorization process proposed by the British psychologist ("coding", in King's words). King presents Template Analysis as a procedure that combines theory- and data-driven procedures (430), characterized by specific flexibility that allows "researchers

On qualitative data analysis 125

to tailor it to suit their own style toward qualitative data analysis" (447). Here I will take all the flexible aspects of King's proposal, including the underlined freedom from any theoretical or epistemological frames, leaving to the user of this version of Template Analysis the choice of whether or not to use the technical paraphernalia of coding procedures such as the hierarchical or lateral coding which characterizes the full version of this approach.

In a nutshell, the analysis procedure proposed starts with the definition of a set of categories to analyse the textual corpus. These categories come mainly from our research questions and from the theoretical frame in which the research questions have germinated. The categories that compose the initial version of the template should be defined as "sensitizing concepts" (Blumer 1969: 148) to allow the "categorization through analogy" (Hofstadter and Sander 2013: 20), defined earlier as central in qualitative data analysis. The initial template can be applied to the whole textual corpus or, following King's advice (2012: 435), to a subset of our data for a preliminary assessment. The application of the first nucleus of the categorization tool produces three outcomes:

- Some initial categories will be expunged due to their incapacity to recognize relevant aspects in the textual corpus;
- Some initial categories will be modified to better fit in with the empirical materials analysed;
- Some new categories will be created, perhaps invented through an abductive *élan*, urged by the necessity of making sense of some surprising facts (see Chapter 3).

This process, according to King, progresses "through an iterative process of applying, modifying and re-applying the initial template" (430).

It is important to underline here that, due to the heterogeneity of qualitative data (see Section 5.1), all the pieces of the textual corpus assigned to a category, has fuzzy-membership relation with it. Moreover, any single piece of data, for instance, any extract of an interview of an ethnographic diary, can be assigned to more than one category, in the same thematic area or different ones.

Earlier (Section 5.1) I introduced three extracts from as many interviews of ex-members of the Damanhur community: Nadia, Valeria, and Luca. Through a combination of the arguments from sign and from analogy, they were categorized as instances of a feeling of inadequacy expressed with varying intensity (for illustrative purposes, I assigned to this category the three cases with a membership function ranging from 0.6 to 0.8). All the three extracts can be categorized, for instance, as the kind of metaphor used to express this feeling, a visual metaphor for Nadia (the film reference), and two different versions of a physical/mechanical one for Luca (a mechanism), and one for Valeria (the idea of burden). A multiple, fuzzy categorization can be applied to the Doctor Venice extract too (see earlier). It seems reasonable to recognize an assertive style: the expression "you can't" was used three times, united with a roughness that – considering other interactions with patients – seems the very key to Doctor Venice. Both categories detected

126 *On qualitative data analysis*

can be applied to the short text considered as a fuzzy register, or in other words, through an analogical assignment that respects the nature of available data.

The categorization process can be guided both by the contents of the textual corpus and by its formal attributes. With regard to the substantive aspects of the texts, the best source for category germination are the theories that guided the research design definition as well as all the theories that the encounter, sometimes the clash (Gadamer 1960, English translation 2004: 270) with empirical data can make necessary.[20] In the content analysis of a text, we can consider both presence and absence. Risking evaluation of Doctor Venice's clinical style through the analysis of an 81-word text – a liberty taken for the sake of brevity – what is missing in the interlocution with Daisy seems to be interest in her version of the story. The detection of the absences in a text must be guided by a specific theoretical frame to avoid recognizing irrelevant absence. Doctor Venice did not tackle the issue of the invasion of Earth by aliens or the topic of the centrality of argumentation theory in qualitative research practice (although this last can be considered a most bizarre, if not crazy, thought). Generally speaking, the detection of one absence implies a comparison with a text – real or virtual – whose relevance must be defended. Counting on a longer textual expression of Doctor Venice's interaction with patients, we can compare these texts with an ideal type of clinical interview carried out by a phenomenologist psychiatrist (for instance Ludwig Binswanger, Eugène Minkowski, or the father of Italian psychiatric system reform, Franco Basaglia). We can also take as a benchmark the clinical interviews carried out by some of Doctor Venice's colleagues working in either the same or in other wards.

Analysis of the formal aspects of textual corpus can take into account the narrative or argumentative structure of the discourses analysed. This kind of analysis is obviously indebted to specific theories from which it borrowed the necessary categorization tools. In one of my first encounters with madness (Cardano 2007), I analysed the illness narratives of mental health patients using a basic version of the narrative scheme proposed by Algirdas Julien Greimas (1987). The "basic" connotation of the version of the scheme used allows me to introduce a more general remark on the use of theory and theoretical tools. I think that we must *employ* these tools with all the liberty that their creative use demands. Orthodoxy in an empirical science can become a limitation that impedes us from realizing a fruitful dialogue with our data (cf. Czarniawska 2004: 80–81). To return to the Lithuanian semiologist, Greimas proposes a semiotics scheme meant to analyse every narrative discourse through the definition of the narrative mechanisms which give the story its meaning. The core of each narrative is the relationship between a subject – usually the protagonist/hero – and an object of value. The task of the subject is to conquer or defend the object. In the complex forms of narratives, the subject has to confront with an opponent who hinders the hero's actions through a sequence of vicissitudes that Greimas organizes into four phases: contract, competence, performance, and sanction. Let us consider a typical fairy-tale that starts with a princess promised in marriage to a prince, the hero of the story. During the wedding preparation, out of the blue, an evil dragon

On qualitative data analysis   127

arrives and kidnaps the princess. So the subject, the prince, and his "object of value", the princess, are separated by the opponent, the evil dragon. The prince undertakes to rescue the princess held captive by the dragon in a high, apparently inaccessible tower. This is the contract phase. Princes, despite their training in the art of war, commonly are not prepared to combat dragons. So the prince decides to learn the demanding art of dracomachia, the art of fighting dragons. This is the competence phase. When the prince is ready, he goes to the evil dragon's castle to challenge the green, slimy, fire-spitting opponent to a duel. The duel is the performance phase. The duel lasts for some time, but in the end the dragon is defeated, and the prince can finally kiss the princess. This is the sanction phase. During this phase, considering performance outcomes, it is possible to evaluate the degree of fulfilment of the contract. In the case at issue, with the head of the evil dragon rolling down the hill, the sanction is positive.

Analysing a set of narrative texts with the Greimas scheme implies, first of all, the individuation in each text of the portion that embodies the four canonical phases: contract, competence, performance, and sanction, and then to categorize the shape assumed, case by case, by each of them. These narrative phases are not necessarily in order: the storyteller can start the narrative from the end, the sanction phase, or from the middle, the performance depicting herself/himself fully immerged in the action. Any of the narrative phases, moreover, can be spread out to different places of the text. It is possible to find the contract phase partly in the incipit of the text, partly in its middle and partly at the end. For any phase, after having recognized where – in the narrative – it is recounted, the analyst has to qualify its form. For instance, considering the contract stage of the prince's vicissitudes, the analyst must evaluate whether it was extorted or was the expression of the hero's free will. Was the prince really in love with the princess and did he decide freely to challenge the evil dragon to a duel? Was the prince not rather in love with a beautiful servant girl and forced by the father of the princess, the king, to rescue his pimply, obnoxious daughter girl?

My use of the Greimas scheme in the analysis of mental distress narratives required a preliminary articulation of the original model. To the four canonical phases, I added another one, performing the same function as the arrival of the evil dragon, i.e., to trigger the story. In the case at issue I called this phase "health theft". This was my creative or spoiling articulation of the original scheme. Before the health theft, the heroes of my stories lived a happy life, unconsciously united with their object of value, mental health. Something went wrong, and they started to be afflicted by mental distress. The contract phase in these stories coincides with the hero's commitment to reconquer his/her condition of health. Competence is the phase in which the hero tries to identify who/what is responsible for his/her distress, then (through diagnosis) gives it a name. With this task, the hero goes through the performance phase, seeking remedies for his/her mental suffering. The last phase, that of sanction, decrees the degree of the hero's success in the recovery enterprise, in re-taking control of one's life.

Some extracts from the illness narratives analysed can illustrate the process of qualification of the five (four plus one) phases of the illness narratives. First,

128   *On qualitative data analysis*

let us consider two instances of the health-theft phase, the background event that generates the biographical disruption (Bury 1982) typical of illness narratives. Bianca and Lucia (all names invented) describe the theft of their health as the irruption of voices in their heads (verbal hallucinations, in psychiatric jargon).

> That morning, it was Sunday, besides the fact that I kept hearing voices and the voices told me that something bad would happened to my dad or that something bad would happened to me and that I had to do everything possible to kill myself, they said stuff like that. So I took a scissors and in a fit of . . . I don't know what it was, if it was a fit of madness or what . . . and I stuck the scissors into my throat. They were long ones, tailor's scissors, and then I felt I was suffocating. I went out on the stair landing, and I covered the landing with my blood. My father arrived to remove the scissors and bring a towel, and he said to me: "Why are you doing this to me? Why are you doing this to me?" That's all.
>
> BIANCA

> In practice, having struck my brain [in a car accident], led me to hear voices: negative voices and positive voices. The voices consisted . . . I don't know how I can give an example . . . if I was looking over the balcony they said to me: "Throw yourself down! What good are you? You are useless, throw yourself down!". So they were an offensive kind of voices, weren't they? But other voices were reassuring: "What a good girl, how well you have done this job!". Reassuring, no? I mean, there was always this mixture of voices that bothered me and I still suffer from it because it still bothers me. . . . The first time I had the first symptom, my mom was in the mountains . . . my brother was coming back, and I had the first symptom at my mom's house. What happened? I started hearing voices, and I tried to silence them. I started slamming the doors loudly, and I turned up the volume on the radio, so as to not to hear them . . . So all the neighbours were worried because it was ten o'clock in the evening and they said: "What the hell is she doing in there, something strange must have happened! Who knows what has happened in that house?". My mother was a very respected person by everybody. Something must have happened, so they called the priest, they called the police . . . they called everybody, they even called my doctor, who looked after me!
>
> LUCIA

A quick comparison between these two narratives allows a differential qualification of the health theft phase from four vantage points. In Bianca's narrative, the presence of voices is associated with a violent event, dramatically evoked by images of the tailor's scissors stuck in the throat and that of the blood covering the house landing. Lucia was attacked by her voice, but she held out. She did not throw herself over the balcony, which is saying a lot. Connected with this aspect, it is possible to recognize differences in the more general features of the voices heard by Bianca and Lucia. The voices that Bianca heard were only malignant.

On qualitative data analysis 129

Lucia told us that she lived with both malignant and benign voices. The good voices told her that she was a nice girl, that she worked well, and this cheered her up. Bianca's drama has a secondary character, the father who deeply blames his daughter for what she has done to him (not to herself). Lucia's action is performed in front of an audience made up of neighbours, and the issue was the family's losing face. Finally, in Lucia's health-theft phase, an embryo of explanation of the beginning of the voices. In Lucia's narrative, the voices arrived after a car accident that produced brain damage.

The illness narratives analysed distinguish themselves as to the relevance annexed to each of the five phases considered and principally because of the narrative closure expressed by the sanction phase. Through consideration of the succession of the phases, and the type of sanction, in agreement with Kenneth Gergen I defined three main types of narratives: tragedy, comedy-romance and heroic saga (Gergen 1994: 197), considering the judgement of the storytellers of the end – at the time of the interviews – of their stories; considering whether or not the hero comes to term with mental distress. On the qualification of the narratives' last phase, reading Noemi's and Giacomo's stories add some useful elements.

I also had six months of hospitalisation at Peony Villa, so I was really . . . really in a bad state, so that even a doctor there told me: "It's over for you, you will stay like this forever!". Hearing this stuff . . . which unfortunately I heard – I didn't invent them because I was fairly lucid . . . Then, luckily for me, I was admitted to Villa Orchid too. It was my salvation because I met Rossi, the head of the hospital. He was an exceptional doctor, and I told him: "Help me to come back, to find my life; I don't believe that any human being deserves all this!". In short, my luck was to find Rossi, who helped me to understand.

Noemi

It's not like I am going to change between today and tomorrow, change and become a more confident person, a calmer, happier person. I am always going to be a bit unhappy, let's say, always a bit like that, with this sadness in me. I don't think that anybody can take this sadness away . . . Instead of leading an independent life, I am always . . . let's say bound by . . . I mean dependent on the goodwill of others, the kindness of others; I'm not . . . not autonomous and independent, I'm dependent on the kindness of others. If others are kind to me, I can get along; if they really don't care about me, I can't go forward.

Giacomo

Seen from their end, the sanction phase, these two stories present decisive differences which allow categorizing the genre of the two narratives. That of Giacomo is undoubtedly a tragedy where, after the biographical disruption due to the onset of mental distress, the protagonist was unable to reconquer control of his life and confidence in his abilities. Noemi's story is different; she descended into the underworld, having her self-esteem wounded by the insensitivity of the first

130 *On qualitative data analysis*

doctor she met (in the role of the opponent) but then showed that she was able to recover, under the guidance of doctor Rossi (in the role of the helper), endowing her the capacity to understand and command her otherness.

Focussing on the formal aspect of a text, besides the analysis of its narrative structure, it is possible – and sometimes remunerative – to consider its argumentative structure. All the texts meant to persuade an audience can be analysed using some of the tools introduced in Chapter 3, mainly for methodological purposes.

Two fine pieces of qualitative research illustrate how the categorization process can include concepts deriving from the field of the theory of argumentation. The most eloquent example to my knowledge is the study by Ineke Van der Valk of right-wing parliamentary discourses on immigration in France (Van der Valk 2003). The study was triggered by the surprising exploits of the extremist right-wing candidate Jean-Marie le Pen of the Front National, during France's 2002 presidential election. The success of Madame le Pen was a result of her immigration policy based on the principle of "national preference", which gave priority to French people – seeing immigrants, "the other", as a threat. Van der Valk asked herself if the anti-migration repertoire was equally rooted in the mainstream French Right. Thus, she analysed the parliamentary speeches of two less radical French right-wing political formations, the Union for French Democracy and Rally for the Republic. The Dutch scholar examined the political speeches delivered in 1996 and 1997 by two members of parliament, one each from the two mainstream right-wing parties.

Van der Valk suggested that political discourses have mainly a persuasive function and that their argumentative structure can profitably be analysed. The essay analyses the commonplaces (*topoi*) that innervates political discourses, the argumentative fallacies into which the two speakers fell when using their rhetorical devices. In one commonplace, defined as "a discursive resource in which one may find arguments for sustaining a conclusion" (319), Van der Valk encountered the typical paraphernalia of the burden: immigrants are a burden on social expenditure, that of unemployment: immigrants cause unemployment; that of exploiting: immigrants take advantage of the receiving society by disobeying laws and rules (324). Closer to the formal aspects of the texts was the analysis of argumentative fallacies, e.g., that of the straw man and the ad-hominem arguments. Straw-man fallacy emerges when a "fictitious standpoint is ascribed to the government in order to make opposition easier" (325). The very common (abusive) ad-hominem argument arose to discredit political opponents, to contest left-wing politicians, not because of contents of their proposals but because of their credibility, "by pointing to inconsistencies between standpoints and former practices" (328), thus reproducing the typical *tu quoque* variant of the ad-hominem fallacy. In her analysis Van der Valk also consider the rhetorical dimension of political discourses, focussing on the metaphors used to represent migration processes, among which those of war and aggression dominate.

Another interesting application of the theory of argumentation instruments can be found in the study carried out by Gilbert Ramsay on the on-line discussion about Al-Qaeda (Ramsay 2012). Ramsay analysed Muslm.net, an Arabic-language web

On qualitative data analysis 131

forum specifically devoted to the discussion of Islamic issues, where the positions of Al-Qaeda are usually criticized but still encounter some advocates. The main issue relates to the conditions which make possible the development of on-line counter-narratives against the terrorist organization. As an initial exploratory study, Ramsay followed the posts of a forum member, Ibn al-Badiya, from late 2009 to early 2010. Ibn al-Badiya, involved in a sort of virtual shadowing, was chosen for his clear position against Al-Qaeda's claims, and also for his capacity to catalyze discussions on the topic at hand.[21] The scholar focussed mainly on the logical structure of the discussion triggered by Ibn al-Badiya, observing how his critical positions against Al-Qaeda were backed or criticized. Analysis of the logical structure of the argumentations was carried out assuming, as an ideal-typical model "critical discussion" defined, according to Frans van Eeemeren and Rob Grootendorst as "an exchange of views in which the parties involved in a difference of opinion systematically try to determine whether the standpoint or standpoints at issue are defensible in the light of critical doubt or objections" (Van Eemeren and Grootendorst 2004: 52). Due to the topic – Al-Qaeda – attention was focussed on deviations from the critical discussion with special attention to fallacies. To perform the analysis, Ramsey introduced some transformations in the texts considered which allow them to fit in better with the analytical model. The dialectical confrontation triggered by Ibn al-Badiya's posts passed through a four-steps process: i) the removal of those elements irrelevant to the analysis; ii) the integration of texts with aspects implicit to the argument; iii) the substitution of ambiguous formulations with clearer ones; iv) the rearranging of the claims to underline their role in the dialectical confrontation (Ramsay 2012: 57; Van Eemeren and Grootendorst 2004: 103–104). This passage can be important in the analysis of not-so-meditated texts as can be those prepared for a parliamentary debate (cf. Van der Valk 2003).

The defence of the Al-Qaeda claims, the attempt to deconstruct counter-narratives, rested mainly on two fallacious strategies: an evasive attitude and the advance of the ad-hominem argument.

> In every case assessed, attempts to criticize Al-Qaeda were met with at least some responses which were either ad hominem or evasive. Members of the forum's self-described 'jihadi' community appeared to assume more or less automatically that consistent critics of Al-Qaeda were paid employees of governments or affiliated organisations.
>
> (58)

Making our template sensitive to the narrative and argumentative aspects implies considering, among categorization procedures, the formal aspects complementing attention toward the substantive aspects of the texts.

The application to the textual corpus of our growing template produces a set of categorizations of which it is necessary to keep track as a preliminary step toward analysis of their relations. There are many ways to keep track efficiently of the categorizations applied to our data. We move from the most primitive based

132 *On qualitative data analysis*

on manual annotation on the paper-printed version of our texts of the categories assigned one by one to more technological use of the computer-aided-qualitative-data-analysis software (known by the acronym CAQDAS). Exploration of the qualitative research results in the literature which I had the opportunity to consult persuaded me that there is no relationship between the degree of informatics sophistication of the categorization (better known as coding) and the quality of the results achieved. Erving Goffman's unsystematic and, somehow rhapsodic, way of doing data analysis is well known, but this does not jeopardize the relevance of the Canadian sociologist's contributions.[22] Symmetrically, the use of the more sophisticated CAQDAS and reference to any of the possible methodological approaches including that proposed here does not guarantee quality or soundness to research findings. Reading in the abstract of a paper that the author used Nvivo, Atlas.ti, or Ethnograph in analysing data and that his/her analysis was carried out under the methodological auspices of Grounded Theory, IPA, or theory of argumentation does not sufficiently convince me of the relevance of the results presented. What convinces me is the quality of the dialogue between data and theories allowed by the methodological path followed. So what we need in keeping track of our categorizations and analysing the relationships among them is the procedure that fits best with our mindset and guarantees the highest level of accuracy that we can manage.

The simplest version of this procedure, at the roots of the algorithms of the most sophisticated CAQDAS, is the organization of the categorization assigned in a matrix such as that proposed by Matthew Miles and Michel Huberman in their 1980s handbook and recently republished in an updated version enriched by Johnny Saldaña's contribution (Miles and Huberman 1985; Miles, Huberman and Saldaña 2014). Huberman, Miles, and Saldaña assign to the matrices primarily the role of displaying compactly the cumbersome data produced by qualitative research. Starting from this miniaturization, through the organization of data in a matrix it is possible to analyse the relationships among categorization forms assigned to the relevant portions of our texts. A matrix is a tool originally developed by political scientists to compare countries, mainly in qualitative perspectives. The common layout of a matrix sees the organization of cases in rows and that of properties in columns. In the intersection between a case and a column, we find the result of a categorization process. An example of a matrix is illustrated in Figure 5.3. The matrix presents some hypothetical psychiatric clinical interviews carried out by Doctor Venice (whom we met earlier, along with Daisy).

The examples represent, in a quasi-fictional way, six clinical colloquiums categorized into a set of five properties constitutive of the template guiding the categorization process. The matrix in Figure 5.3 is open, both with regard to cases and properties, and must be imagined as containing – in its complete version – all Doctor Venice's psychiatric interviews observed, and all the properties that could possibly constitute the template used in the data analysis. Among the rows we can see the six patients' profiles and in the columns the property used for the categorization process. With the exceptions of the cells defined by the intersection between the patients' names and the two socio-demographic properties, gender

Properties / Cases	Gender	Nationality	Clinical colloquium focus	Emotional climate	Patient's behaviour	...
Daisy	Female	Italian	The organization of the patient's life after discharge from hospital. *Venice: You can't go home to your mother; you have to go back into the therapeutic community (Fieldnotes pp. 17–19).*	Atmosphere very tense and harsh.	Deep embarrassment and submission.	...
Mike	Male	Italian	Physical condition: urological problems. *Venice: In the afternoon, we'll take out the catheter, and you'll feel better (Fieldnotes p. 32).*	Sympathetic.	Worried, but eventually trustful.	...
Saif	Male	Sudanese	Trauma experienced during Libyan detention before rubber-dinghy landing in Italy. *Saif: I dream of the prison in Libya all the time. I can't sleep!* *Venice: Tonight the staff will give you something to sleep, don't worry (Fieldnotes pp. 41–45).*	Sympathetic, with a prevailing orientation toward the contrasting of symptoms.	Deeply disoriented.	...
Tracy	Female	French	Delusional contents and medical treatment. *Tracy: I have the power to heal people. I received this gift from the aliens of Zodiac.* *Venice: Are the aliens green or another colour? (Fieldnotes pp. 47–8)*	Humorous. Doctor Venice and the nurse make fun of Tracy.	It is not clear if Tracy understands the situation. She passes from enjoying the playful climate to the suspicion of being teased. *Tracy: Are you serious?*	...
Ella	Female	Italian	Drug abuse as a psychotic crisis evolves. *Ella: I haven't smoked for ages.* *Venice: Are you sure? The urine text show the opposite! (Fieldnotes pp. 53).*	Very harsh. Doctor Venice underlines that he doesn't like being teased by patients.	Slight embarrassment mixed with verbal aggressiveness. *Ella: You fucking cops!*	...
Arthur	Male	Italian	Interruption of physical restraint and requiring more "appropriate" behaviour from the patient for the remaining days in hospital. *Venice: If we remove the restraint, you have to behave yourself. Do you understand what I mean?* *Arthur: Yes, I have to behave like a normal person and take the medicines (Fieldnotes p. 67).*	Harsh. The dimension of implicit menace appears: "If you don't behave yourself, you will be tied up again".	Docility and fear.	...
...	...	...	...	...	...	...

Figure 5.3 Hypothetical matrix on Doctor Venice's psychiatric clinical interviews

134 *On qualitative data analysis*

and nationality, witnessed through direct observation, the other cells are characterized by two features: the qualification of the case for the considered property and a fragment of the textual corpus that – partly – justify the categorization. Let us consider the categorization of Daisy's clinical colloquium focus:

> The organization of the patient's life after hospital discharge.

> *VENICE*: *You can't go home to your mother; you have to go back into the therapeutic community.*

The matrix illustrates that the focus of the colloquium was the patient's living arrangements after discharge; yet this was not the only focus. In the longer extract of the interaction between the doctor and the patient (see earlier, page 121), we can also recognize the doctor's surprisingly harsh attack on Daisy's self-esteem. For three of the invented psychiatric interviews, those of Daisy, Ella, and Arthur, the emotional climate is characterized by a particular harshness. The three clinical scenes are not uniform, nor are the patients' profiles, so the categorization proposed depends necessarily on analogical reasoning. In addition to the specificity of the three patient-doctor interactions, we see some similarities, some family resemblances that authorize assigning them to the category of a "harsh emotional climate". The membership (belonging) of the three empirical instances at issue to the category "harsh emotional climate" is fuzzy. Doctor Venice was harsher (we have to imagine this judgement backed by extensive fieldnotes) with Ella, perceived as a deceiver, than with Arthur, due to his forced docility. The doctor was even less hash – but still sour – with Daisy. The text in italics offers an item of empirical materials which authorizes the categorization applied. To find all the elements that underpin the categorization proposed we have to consider the complete interaction between Doctor Venice and Daisy whose location in the fieldnotes is indicated in the cell: (for instance, *Fieldnotes pp. 17–19*). All this shows up an important difference between the matrices used in qualitative and quantitative research spelt out in N. 23.[23]

The matrix is the open starting point of the detection of relationships among the categorizations applied to textual corpuses. The matrices are open because we can change any categorizations assigned through a reshaping of our argument from analogy. They are also open because we can add new rows or new columns at every step of the data analysis, through the enrichment of our analytical template, or through – again assisted by the argument from analogy – acknowledgment of similarities between the cases analysed and some new ones (cf. Miles, Huberman and Saldaña 2014: 114).

In analysing our data, the first task is to check for the relationship postulated as relevant in the research design. This move is usually accompanied by an explorative approach in which the "surprising fact" detected becomes – through an abductive inference (see Chapter 3) – a matter of course. For this purpose, close observation of deviant cases can be illuminating. As for the exploratory approach, it is difficult even to give "friendly advice" (114), but the general suggestion of Miles, Huberman, and Saldaña seems appropriate:

On qualitative data analysis 135

It's always helpful to *start with a quick scan* – a "squint analysis" or "eyeballing" down columns and across rows and through network pathways to see what jumps out. Then, verify, revise, or disconfirm that impression through a more careful review.

(117).

In this exploration we can take as a guide the most promising categorizations, the "sensitizing concepts" of our analytical template that seems most theoretically relevant, to observe how the other categories (or properties) relate to them. For instance, we can focus on what is associated with a dialogical attitude during psychiatric interview, perhaps the theoretical frame adopted by the doctor, perhaps be his/her experience of mental distress – consistent with the commonplace of the wounded healer. We can also take as a guide the cases that, for theoretical or empirical reasons, attracted our attention and observe what properties define their profiles, and which – among the other cases – show some family resemblances. We can, for instance, focus on the nurse who fought against unreasonable physical restraint and won the battle, in order to observe his/her profile and the relationship that s/he entertains with the other members of staff. The matrix display allows detection possible constellation of relationships whose empirical consistence must be checked against the complete textual materials (117). It is only by going back to the original data that we can plausibly maintain the existence of a relationship between the categories assigned to our data. As I said earlier, the information stored in a qualitative matrix does not substitute the contents of our textual data (see N. 23).

Having first recognized some relevant relationships among the categorizations applied to our textual corpus and, second, having identified some constellations of properties, it is now time to represent them. In doing so, we have to bear in mind the very nature of the data we are managing: their intrinsic fuzziness due to both the data collection procedures adopted and the epistemic profile of the categorization process.

The most appropriate tool to represent the constellation of properties identified through the analysis of the relationships between the categorizations applied to our data is – in my view – the Weberian ideal type. Max Weber defined this conceptual instrument in a frame distant from our reflections on the analogical nature of the categorization process and the context sensitivity of the qualitative data collection procedures but the methodological proposal of the German sociologist fits perfectly our discourse.[24] I again quote the Weberian definition of an ideal type as a launching-pad for our reflection.

An ideal type is formed by the one-sided *accentuation* of one or more points of view and by the synthesis of a great many diffuse, discrete, more or less present and occasionally absent *concrete individual* phenomena, which are arranged according to those one-sidedly emphasised viewpoints into a unified *analytical* construct. In its conceptual purity, this mental construct *cannot* be found empirically anywhere in reality.

(Weber 1949: 90, original edition 1904)

136 *On qualitative data analysis*

Weber clearly underlines the anti-realistic nature of the ideal-type concept that can be thought of an instrument, according to Wittgenstein "to see something *as something*" (Wittgenstein 1958: 213). The two "somethings" connected in the empirical use of the ideal type, empirical data and their representation, are programmatically different. In Weber's reflection, we do not meet the idea of structural isomorphism which, on the contrary, characterizes Levi-Strauss's anthropology, to give but one example. The Weberian ideal type is not isomorphic with the phenomena represented; it is their programmed hyperbole guiding our gaze toward the particular aspects deserving most attention of the phenomena examined. With further analogical *élan*, we can frame this cross-eyed attitude in the activity of inventing metaphors. My point here is that the Weberian ideal type has an intrinsic metaphorical structure that makes its use promising in qualitative research.

To recognize the analogical correspondences between the Weberian ideal type and metaphor, the reflection of the analytical philosopher Max Black can be helpful. In his influential book *Models and Metaphors* (1962), Black offers the example of the use of the ferine metaphor of a wolf to describe a man:

> The effect, then, of (metaphorically) calling a man a "wolf" is to evoke the wolf-system of related commonplaces. If the man is a wolf, he preys upon other animals, is fierce, hungry, engaged in constant struggle, a scavenger, and so on. Each of these implied assertions has now to be made to fit the principal subject (the man) either in normal or in abnormal senses. If the metaphor is at all appropriate, this can be done – up to a point at least. . . . The wolf-metaphor suppresses some details, emphasizes others – in short, *organizes* our view of man.
>
> (Black 1962: 41)

The last sentence is the perfect calque of Weber's definition of the ideal type based on the one-sided emphasis of some aspects of the phenomenon represented. A few pages later, Black introduces the idea of seeing something as something, which is the second aspect that the ideal type shares with the metaphor.

> A memorable metaphor has the power to bring two separate domains into cognitive and emotional relation by using language directly appropriate to the one as a lens for seeing the other; the implications, suggestions, and supporting values entwined with the literal use of the metaphorical expression enable us to see a new subject matter in a new way.
>
> (236–237)

The Weberian tool, due to its logical properties, allows representing the relationships among the properties analysed and organized through the categorization process authorizing fuzzy membership of the phenomena subsumed under the ideal type. This conceptual instrument takes into account the heterogeneity of the data collection procedures and respects the fuzziness of the categorization process. The ideal type can be used to represent any topic. We can create ideal types of individuals, moving from the analysis of the transcripts of their interviews. We

On qualitative data analysis   137

can define ideal types of organizations, of social processes (Vaughan proposed some ideal types of "organizational deviance" 2014: 80), of events and of any other object that can be contemplated in sociological research. The elaboration of ideal types allows us to consider simultaneously and systematically a set of features of the social phenomena studied, avoiding the tedious sequence of description of the phenomenon studied one property at a time ("univariate analysis" in the quantitative jargon). Finally, the use of ideal types gives due importance to theory in the analysis of qualitative data.

The production of a set of ideal types, obviously, does not exclude any other way of representing the research findings, including the simplest description of the cases studied in an analytical mode, considering a less complex constellation of properties. The emphasis I placed on the construction of ideal types relates to its metaphorical status. My view is that metaphors, in qualitative research, play the same role as models play in quantitative research, perhaps in a more creative way as a result of the intrinsic openness of this representation tool.

A leading example of creative use of metaphorical tools is the study carried out by Stuart Wright on leave-taking from New Religious Movements (Wright 1991). For the study of this process of role-exiting, Wright proposed the substitution of the metaphor of escape from a prison – usually advanced by anti-cult movements – with the less dramatic one of divorce.[25] In doing so, Wright institutes an analogical correspondence between New Religious Movements (in his words "non-traditional religious movements") and marriage. The two social contexts compared require a burdensome commitment from those who decide to join, consisting of loyalty, devotion, and sacrifice. According to Lewis Coser, both are "greedy institutions" (Coser 1974). Taking leave from either marriage or New Religious Movement implies intense emotional involvement and takes place in an interactive context. The proposed metaphor allows recognizing the processual dimension of the deconversion, focussing on the actions of both the devotee and the organization "to save the union".

Each metaphorical dispositive has a blind spot, something that is not properly seen or is distorted, and in the use of these conceptual tools it is essential to consider the biases and limitations introduced by our conceptual choices.[26]

Notes

1 According to Demazière and Dubar, an in-depth interview becomes a "disguised questionnaire" (in French, *questionnaires déguisés*) if the interviewer is guided by a long list of questions that leave the respondent a short time to answer, thus obstructing the production of discourses.
2 As will be clear in what follows, the kind of data that we acquire using naturalistic or participant observation, field experiment, shadowing, and autoethnography are "representations". All these field methods can enrich their data through the use of video technology, but in my view these additional materials do not exempt the writer from responsibility. In other words, they are "another way of telling" (Berger and Mohr 1982) in which both visual texts and written texts can coexist.
3 Luigi Gariglio attracted my attention to some products of our material culture, such as framed photographs, which are both artefacts and texts. That is the case of the framed photo of my wedding day which stands on my office desk, an object which not only

138 *On qualitative data analysis*

reminds me to return home after a long day of teaching, red-tape, and scientific meetings in a Plexiglas piece of art, but is also a text telling the story of my wife Carla and me, elegantly dressed and happy because our informal cohabitation has been officially transformed into an institutional bond. This example suggests that the distinction between texts and artefacts must be considered as a fuzzy one (see Section 1.2).

4 Through the challenging works of Bruno Latour, we have learnt that it is possible to attribute to artefacts the quality of agency, while avoiding the anthropomorphism which endows them with a mind and intentions (Latour 1993).

5 The situation is decidedly simpler in the quantitative field where, thanks to the operational definition, all the information is represented by numbers. The complexity of quantitative data analysis rests on the statistical models applied to the data, not in the information representation itself.

6 On fuzzy logic see Section 1.2.

7 The idea of distinguishing between representations and reproductions germinates from reading Dan Sperber's essay, "On Anthropological Knowledge" (1982, English translation 1985). Moving from an epistemological frame quite distant from that proposed here, Sperber introduced a distinction between interpretation and description (11–14), and in this context the author distinguished among three kinds of representations: descriptions, interpretations, and reproductions. The definition of reproduction is close to the one adopted here: "A reproduction (for instance a quotation, or a scale model) is a representation which is adequate to the extent that it physically resembles that which it represents. The adequacy of a reproduction can never be absolute" (12). The other elements of my classification of qualitative data separate from Sperber's reflection, mixing some of its elements (in a way that Sperber probably wouldn't approve) and adding a new category, that of naturalistic data, which arrives to me through Jonathan Potter's distinction between research-provoked and naturalistic data.

8 This kind of impact on the observed context is also known in methodological literature as the Hawthorne effect and relates to a series of experiments performed in the Hawthorne Works of the Western Electric Company, Chicago, between 1927 and 1933. The experiment that inspired reflection on reactivity was carried out in the Relay Assembly Room where, for 270 weeks, various changes were introduced into work organization to observe their effect on productivity. The productivity grew in a way unrelated to the organizational changes and was interpreted as mainly due to the attention received by the little group of five women workers from the research team. The application of the label "Hawthorne effect" to a piece of qualitative research cannot be done without considering the specificity of the experimental context in which it was proposed. For a critical appraisal of the so-called "Hawthorne effect", see Jones (1992).

9 In a close-up view, open participant observation implies a blend of observational and interactive perturbation. If the social context studied is not too small, i.e., with six or seven participants, it is possible that some people are aware of our role and others not. In my first experience of ethnographic research in the community of *Elfi del Gran Burrone* (Elves of the Great Ravine), a community of 55 people, 36 adults and 19 children (Cardano 1997: 103), although I presented myself as a researcher, were not all aware of my identity. I carried out most of my fieldwork in summer and in that season the community was used to hosting a lot of visitors who came on a sort of pilgrimage to the world of deep ecology. At that time my age was close to that of the multitude of visitors and my appearance – after a few weeks – began to resemble theirs. Near the end of my research, I performed some in-depth interviews with community members, and one of them was surprised by my request to tape-record our talk. She said: "I thought you were one of us, a normal guest of the community!" So, to cut to the chase, my immersion in the Elves of the Great Ravine community was characterized by both observational and interactive perturbation.

10 An excellent essay on this topic is contained in a book – which does not share this chapter's epistemological standpoint – *Choice Welfare and Measurement* by Amartya

On qualitative data analysis 139

Sen (1982). In the chapter entitled "Description as Choice", Sen maintains: "Description isn't just observing and reporting; it involves the exercise – possibly difficult – of selection. . . . In fact, description can be characterized as choosing from the set of possibly *true* statements a subset on grounds of their relevance" (433, italic mine). Replacing "true" with "plausible", the Sen statement perfectly fits in with my perspective.

11 According to Andrea Sormano (2008), I do believe that the transcription of a tape-recorded interview implies the adoption of a specific interpretive model (on communication), but for the purposes of the classification of qualitative data materials we can parenthesize this aspect.

12 The title of the paper is *La spiona, il parassita, l'ortodosso. Tre racconti di osservazione partecipante* that can be translated into English as *The spy, the parasite and the orthodox. Three tales on doing ethnography*. Giovanna, obviously, was the spy; the parasite was a student who carried out covert opportunistic research, working as a barman in a bar; the orthodox was a student of mine, involved in more conventional overt ethnography.

13 Good ethnographies accompany the information on what happened, with the description of the observational relationship between the researcher and the participants (see Altheide and Johnson 1994; Cardano 2014), thus increasing the complexity of this kind of text.

14 Doctor Venice, Daisy, and Carolyn are all invented names.

15 Things are easier in quantitative research where there is a simple rule to establish what statistics can be applied to data, considering how information is represented. The first famous "formula" was introduced by the American psychologist Stanley Smith Stevens, who distinguished four measurement scales: nominal, ordinal, interval, and ratio, each equipped with specific mathematical properties (Stevens 1946).

16 For ethical issues, the sharing of Sub-type 2 of reproductions (see Figure 5.2), covered tape-recordings is out of the question. Data produced through such a deep ethical violation cannot be easily shared.

17 Mills identified the grammar of sociological imagination in cross-classification procedures (Mills 2000: 213, original edition 1959). For reasons that will be clear in a moment, I prefer to use the term categorization proposed by Douglas Hofstadter and Emmanuel Sander (2013) instead of classification.

18 I was in charge of analysing Damanhur ex-members' deconversion, and Nicola Pannofino of the other three new religious movements considered in the study.

19 On the relevance of analogy for the theorizing process see Vaughan (2014).

20 On the role of theory for analogical reasoning, I totally agree with Diane Vaughan who maintains: "In contrast to Glaser and Strauss's (1967) take on grounded theory – that we proceed inductively, always beginning from an objective, neutral theoretical position – in order to let the theory 'emerge' from the data, analogical theorizing assumes that we always have a set of theories and concepts in mind, so must make them explicit in order to reject, reconceptualise, or extend theory" (Vaughan 2014: 66–67).

21 Shadowing is a kind of observation focussed on an individual whom the researcher follows as a shadow for some days or weeks (see Section 2.1).

22 What has been said in the text must not be read as an invitation – particularly to students – to be unsystematic or, worse, careless. Care, orderliness, and methodical attention are important but neither sufficient nor (except for geniuses like Goffman) necessary.

23 In the dependence on the full textual corpus of the matrix, it is possible to recognize an important difference between the matrices in quantitative and qualitative research. In the case of a quantitative cases-by-variables matrix, like the one that represents the answers to a questionnaire, the numerical codes of which it is composed constitute the stenographic and complete representation of respondents' verbal behaviours. [If in the row describing the profile of case n (let us call him Mario), in the interception with column k which contains information on the respondents' education, we see the number 2, we have all the information that we need to measure Mario's education. In the so-colled code-book, that constitutes the accompanying of each questionnaire, for

140   *On qualitative data analysis*

each question we have a (numerical) code that identifies a state on the variable at issue. For the variable education, code 2 has a univocal meaning: "elementary school", and applied to Mario case, this means that Mario has the elementary school licence. Things are different for the qualitative matrices, where the information – less compactly represented – refers to textual contents but without being capable of substituting them, at least in the same way in which a symbol can replace what it designates. In other words, the information in a qualitative matrix cell works as a place card that indicates where the textual passage that underpins the categorization proposed is situated, and anticipates, as a memory aid, some of its contents (see Barbour 2007: 196).

24 The appropriateness of the ideal type as a tool to synthetize the results of an analogical analysis is adumbrated by Diane Vaughan too (Vaughan 2014: 80).

25 The use of the marriage metaphor characterizes the analogical theorizing carried out by Diane Vaughan (2014: 73 ff.).

26 In her book, *Models and Analogies in Science*, Mary Hesse offers some suggestions for the analysis, so to speak, of the "goodness of fit" of a metaphor. Hesse considers the well-known application of the billiard-ball model to represent the kinetic theory of gases (Hesse 1966) and distinguishes three different dimensions of the analogy: the positive, the negative, and the neutral. The distinction was expressed as follows by the author: "When we take a collection of billiard balls in random motion as a model for a gas, we are not asserting that billiard balls are in all respects like gas particles, for billiard balls are red or white, and hard and shiny, and we are not intending to suggest that gas molecules have these properties. We are in fact saying that gas molecules are *analogous* to billiard balls, and the relation of analogy means that there are some properties of billiard balls which are not found in molecules. Let us call those properties we know belong to billiard balls and not to molecules the *negative analogy* of the model. Motion and impact, on the other hand, are just the properties of billiard balls that we do want to ascribe to molecules in our model, and these we can call the *positive analogy.* Now the important thing about this kind of model-thinking in science is that there will generally be some properties of the model about which we do not yet know whether they are positive or negative analogies; these are the interesting properties because, as I shall argue, they allow us to make new predictions. Let us call this third set of properties the *neutral analogy*" (Hesse 1966: 8). Taking some philological liberty, we can say that good metaphors are those that minimize the negative analogy component.

References

Altheide D.L., Johnson J.M. 1994 *Criteria for Assessing Interpretive Validity in Qualitative Research*, in N.K. Denzin and Y.S. Lincoln (eds.), *Handbook of Qualitative Research*, Thousand Oaks and London, Sage Publications, pp. 485–499.

Barbour R. 2007 *Introducing Qualitative Research: A Student's Guide to the Craft of Doing Qualitative Research*, London, Sage Publications.

Berger J., Mohr J. 1982 *Another Way of Telling*, London and New York, Writers and Readers Publishing Cooperative Society Ltd.

Black M. 1962 *Models and Metaphors: Studies in Language and Philosophy*, Ithaca and New York, Cornell University Press.

Blumer H. 1969 *Symbolic Interactionism*, Englewood Cliffs, NJ, Prentice Hall.

Bobbio L., Resta G., Venturini L. 2001 *La spiona, il parassita, l'ortodosso. Tre racconti di osservazione partecipante*, in "Rassegna Italiana di Sociologia", Vol. 42, No. 2, pp. 309–322.

Bury M. 1982 *Chronic Illness as Biographical Disruption*, in "Sociology of Health and Illness", Vol. 4, No. 2, pp. 167–182.

Cardano M. 1997 *Lo specchio, la rosa e il loto. Uno studio sulla sacralizzazione della natura*, Roma, Seam.

On qualitative data analysis 141

———. 2007 '*E poi cominciai a sentire le voci . . .*'. *Narrazioni del male mentale*, in "Rassegna Italiana di Sociologia", Vol. 48, No. 1, pp. 9–56.

———. 2011 *La ricerca qualitativa*, Bologna, Il Mulino.

———. 2014 *Ethnography and Reflexivity*, in "European Quarterly of Political Attitudes and Mentalities–EQPAM", Vol. 3, No. 1, pp. 1–11.

Cardano M., Pannofino N. 2015 *Piccole apostasie. Il congedo dai nuovi movimenti religiosi*, Bologna, Il Mulino.

———. 2018 *Taking Leave of Damanhur: Deconversion from a Magico-Esoteric Community*, in "Social Compass", Vol. 65, No. 3, pp. 433–450.

Conrad P. 2001 *Genetic Optimism: Framing Genes and Mental Illness in the News*, in "Culture, Medicine and Psychiatry", Vol. 25, No. 2, pp. 225–247.

Coser L.A. 1974 *Greedy Institutions: Patterns of Undivided Commitment*, New York, Free Press.

Czarniawska B. 2004 *Narrative in Social Science Research*, London, Sage Publications.

Demaziere D., Dubar C. 1997 *Analyser les entretiens biographiques: L'exemple des récits d'insertion*, Paris, Nathan.

Gadamer H.G. 2004 *Truth and Method*, London and New York, Continuum (original edition 1960).

Geertz C. 1988 *Works and Lives: The Anthropologist as Author*, Stanford, Stanford University Press.

Gergen K.J. 1994 *Realities and Relationship*, Cambridge, MA, Harvard University Press.

Ginzburg C. 2013 *Clues, Myths, and the Historical Method*, Baltimore, The Johns Hopkins University Press (original edition 1978).

Glaser B., Strauss A. 1967 *The Discovery of Grounded Theory*, Chicago, Aldine Press.

Goffman E. 1956 *The Presentation of Self in Everyday Life*, Edinburgh, University of Edinburgh.

Greimas A.J. 1987 *On Meaning: Selected Writings in Semiotic Theory*, Minneapolis, University of Minnesota Press.

Heaton J. 2004 *Reworking Qualitative Data*, London, Thousand Oaks and New Delhi, Sage Publications.

Hesse M. 1966 *Models and Analogies in Science*, Notre Dame, IN, University of Notre Dame Press.

Hofstadter D., Sander E. 2013 *Surfaces and Essences: Analogy as the Fuel and Fire of Thinking*, New York, Basic Books.

Jones S.R.G. 1992 *Was There a Hawthorne Effect?* in "American Journal of Sociology", Vol. 98, No. 3, pp. 451–468.

Kaufmann J.C. 2006 *L'entretien comprénsif*, Paris, Armand Colin.

King N. 2012 *Doing Template Analysis*, in G. Symon and C. Cassell (eds.), *Qualitative Organizational Research*, London, Sage Publications, pp. 426–450.

Latour B. 1993 *Ethnography of a 'High-Tech' Case: About Aramis*, in P. Lemonnier (ed.), *Technological Choices: Transformation in Material Cultures since the Neolithic*, London and New York, Routledge, pp. 372–398.

Miles M.B., Huberman A.M. 1985 *Qualitative Data Analysis: A Sourcebook of New Methods*, Thousand Oaks, CA, Sage Publications.

Miles M.B., Huberman A.M., Saldaña J. 2014 *Qualitative Data Analysis: A Methods Sourcebook*, Third Edition, Los Angeles, London and New Delhi, Sage Publications.

Mills C.W. 2000 *The Sociological Imagination*, Fortieth Anniversary Edition, Oxford and New York, Oxford University Press (original edition 1959).

Plimpton G. 1966 *The Story behind a Nonfiction Novel*, in "The New York Times", January, 16.

142 *On qualitative data analysis*

Potter J. 2002 *Two Kinds of Natural*, in "Discourse Studies", Vol. 4, No. 4, pp. 539–542.

Ramsay G. 2012 *Online Arguments against Al-Qaeda: An Exploratory Analysis*, in "Perspectives on Terrorism", Vol. 6, No. 1, pp. 54–69.

Rapley T. 2004 *Interviews*, in C. Seale, G. Gobo, J.F. Gubrium and D. Silverman (eds.), *Qualitative Research Practice*, London, Sage Publications, pp. 15–33.

Rathje W., Murphy C. 2001 *Rubbish! The Archaeology of Garbage*, Tucson, The University of Arizona Press.

Sen A. 1982 *Choice, Welfare and Measurement*, Cambridge, MA and London, UK, Harvard University Press.

Sormano A. 2008 *Punti di svolta nell'intervista*, in L. Bonica and M. Cardano (eds.), *Punti di svolta. Analisi del mutamento biografico*, Bologna, Il Mulino, pp. 327–352.

Sperber D. 1985 *On Anthropological Knowledge: Three Essays*, Cambridge, Cambridge University Press (original edition 1982).

Stevens S.S. 1946 *On the Theory of Scales of Measurement*, in "Science", Vol. 103, No. 2684, pp. 677–680.

Tilley C. 2001 *Ethnography and Material Culture*, in P. Atkinson, A. Coffey, S. Delamont, J. Lofland and L. Lofland (eds.), *Handbook of Ethnography*, London, Thousand Oaks and New Delhi, Sage Publications, pp. 258–272.

Topolski J. 1977 *Methodology of History*, Dordrecht and Boston, D. Reidel Publishing Company (original edition 1973).

Van der Valk I. 2003 *Right-Wing Parliamentary Discourse on Immigration in France*, in "Discourse & Society", Vol. 14, No. 3, pp. 309–348.

van Eemeren F., Grootendorst R. 2004 *A Systematic Theory of Argumentation: The Pragma-Dialectical Approach*, Cambridge, Cambridge University Press.

Vaughan D. 2014 *Analogy, Cases, and Comparative Social Organization*, in R. Swedberg (ed.), *Theorizing in Social Science the Context of Discovery*, Stanford, Stanford University Press, pp. 61–84.

Weaver A. 1994 *Deconstructing Dirt and Disease: The Case of TB*, in M. Bloor and P. Taraborrelli (eds.), *Qualitative Studies in Health and Medicine*, Aldershot, Avebury, pp. 76–95.

Weber M. 1949 *The Methodology of Social Sciences*, Glencoe, IL, The Free Press (original edition 1904).

Wittgenstein L. 1958 *Philosophical Investigations*, Oxford, Basil Blackwell (first edition 1953).

Wright S.A. 1991 *Reconceptualizing Cult Coercion and Withdrawal: A Comparative Analysis of Divorce and Apostasy*, in "Social Forces", Vol. 70, No. 1, pp. 125–145.

Zadeh L.A. 1965 *Fuzzy Sets*, in "Information and Control", Vol. 8, No. 8, pp. 338–353.

6   The textualization

The arrival stage of any qualitative research is textualization, the process with which we transform the participants' lives in our works (Geertz 1988). Moreover, with textualization, we complete the persuasive argumentation sketched by means of the definition of the research design and progressively elaborated during field-work and analysis. Now we can give the last brush strokes to the arguments that defend the soundness of our research results, considering both the robustness of the methodological path followed and the capacity of our evidence to dialogue with the pertinent theories. The specificity of qualitative research (see Chapter 2), the multivocality of its writing, gives to these arguments a peculiar curvature, in which the defence of the soundness of the research findings and that of the appropriateness of method are backed by both the author's and participants' voices.

In the Introduction I recalled the classic Aristotelian distinction between the means of persuasion – ethos, pathos, and logos – redefined through the extremely context-sensitive proposal by Ricca Edmondson (1984: Chapter 1) as "self-presentation" (for ethos), "sensitisation" (for pathos) and "abstract structure of argument" (for logos). Chapters 4 and 5 focus on the logos dimension. Chapter 4 presents the logical structure of the argument with which to defend the soundness of the research questions, of the case selection and that of the methodological road along which we plan to solve our intellectual puzzles (in Mason's 2002 meaning). Chapter 5 discusses the logic of qualitative data analysis, focussing on the argumentation tools with which we can tackle the heterogeneity of our empirical materials. The following sections elaborate on the two other functions of persuasive arguments, "sensitisation", pursued through the valorization of the multivocality of qualitative data, and "self-presentation", achieved through a reflexive account of the "experience experiment" (Piasere 2002: 27) carried out in the field.

6.1 Multivocality as a "double description"

The multivocality of writing is one of the distinctive features of qualitative research. With very few exceptions, the great majority of the texts which present the results of qualitative research are written through a combination of the researcher's and participants' voices. The participants' voices enter the text principally through the quotations chosen by researchers from their textual corpus.

144 *The textualization*

This kind of writing serves four diverse aims: i) to convince the audience in our scientific community about the soundness of our claims; ii) to evoke in the reader the colours and the emotions of the field, painting them with words ("sensitisation" in Edmondson's 1984 meaning); iii) to give voices to the participants; iv) to expand the sources of the "reflexive account" ("self-presentation", in Edmondson's 1984 meaning). In what follows, I will delve into these four functions in an effort to contrast the scant attention that most of the methodological literature gives them.

The first function – convincing the scientific community of the soundness of our claims by showing them the evidence that underpins these claims – is largely thematized in the methodological literature. As I said before, there are some exceptions to this rule, among which the most relevant is represented by one of the monuments of qualitative research: *Asylum*, by Erving Goffman. However, more recent publications tend to follow the rule of "orchestration" (Bakhtin 2014: 430–431) between the voice of the author and that of participants.[1] Good examples of multivocal writing show that quotations are embedded in the author's argument as either evidence or counter-evidence, imbuing the text with a dialectical dimension, in which the voice of the author can be either reinforced or challenged by those of the participants. A couple of recommendations may be appropriate on this point. The first one suggests that quotations must be long enough to offer the reader an opportunity to test the soundness of the author's arguments against the quotations. The quality of a long quotation is significantly improved when cut-and-paste activities are reduced to a minimum. To decide the right level of editing intervention, we can ask ourselves the critical question: "In the proposed version of the quotation, can the participant recognize her/his point or not?" The second piece of advice goes in the opposite direction, suggesting that researchers avoid the overuse of quotations, asking them to save authors for the task of expressing their points in a more straightforward way. This second recommendation contrasts what can be named as "the lazy way to use quotations".

The second function of multivocal writing, that of evoking the "colours" of the field, "to make readers feel as if they were there, in the field" (Czarniawska 2004: 118), is based on a redefinition of the role of emotions in the nonfictional writing on which further reflection seems appropriate. If in the past – with few exceptions – emotions were considered something to banish from scientific discourse, in recent decades; mainly through the critical contribution of feminist theory, emotions, both of the author (see Behar 1996) and the reader, have gained full citizenship in social sciences. As will be clearer in what follows about the Gregory Bateson's notion of "double description" (Bateson 1979), the combination of an analytical and an emotional register is what can add depth to our text. One of the areas of research to which I have dedicated most of my studies is that of mental health. I have spent many days observing the interaction among patients and medical staff in psychiatric wards, and I have collected and analysed a lot of illness narratives of people afflicted by mental distress. In describing the experience of biographical disruption that accompanies the outset of mental distress, it is possible to be more or less effectual, but nothing can substitute the words of someone who has embodied that experience. Marta was a 32-year-old woman

The textualization 145

who lived (at the time of the interview) with her parents; all three of them were Jehovah's Witnesses. She describes the irruption of mental distress as the invasion of her body by the devil during a night when – contravening the rule of her religious congregation – she went to a disco. These are her words:

> In the disco, I heard voices that told me that if I danced, they would enter me and they would teach me to dance. And I started, I started to dance, and I felt like a puppet in the hands of someone that was making me move, no? However, I . . . what do I know . . . those voices, they everybody said that those voices were a disease, and I thought that [they were] evil spirits. Because we Jehovah's Witnesses believe in the devil, in evil spirits. . . . And then, and then, at night, I felt like my pelvis was moving on its own, as if I was having sexual intercourse with somebody invisible, no? Now I don't want to shock you, but I am really sure that it was the devil who . . . I risked being expelled [she means from the Congregation of Jehovah's Witnesses]!
>
> (Cardano 2010: 260)

This evocation of emotions nurtures one of the most common ways – both for scholars and lay people – to understand "the others" through "resonance". In an intriguing essay on the interpretation of the others, about the translation of their culture into our words, the anthropologist Unni Wikan introduces the notion of resonance (Wikan 1992).

The gist of the essay relates to the necessity to go beyond words in order to understand otherness, being careful to avoid sinking deeply into the "quagmire" of language, getting bogged down in its literal meaning (474). The way proposed is that of resonance understood as the ability to use one's experience "to try to grasp or convey meanings that reside neither in words, 'facts', nor text but are evoked in the meeting of one experiencing subject with another or with a text" (463). It was through his experience of grief because of the sudden and dramatic death of his wife that Renato Rosaldo was able to understand the rage of *Ilongod* head-hunters (465; Rosaldo 1993).[2] The evocation of emotions is – in my view – a way in which it is possible to go beyond words, making possible the experience of resonance for the reader.

The third function performed by the multivocality of qualitative texts relates to the possibility, given to participants, to express – although with different degrees of autonomy – their voices. This issue has been tackled directly in the anthropological community, starting from the 1980s, when the so-called representation crisis emerged in the "Writing Culture" debate (Clifford and Marcus 1986). Representation *in crisis* was that of the native cultures, challenged from the epistemological and ethical points of view. How can an anthropologist plausibly claim to represent *their* culture? What gives anthropologists the right to speak on behalf of natives? This last question is the one relevant to our discussion. Two important antecedents on this aspect, both related to natives' reception of the representation of their culture, deserve to be mentioned. The first is the book by Oscar Lewis, *The Children of Sánchez* (1961), accused by Mexicans of presenting a one-sided

146   *The textualization*

picture of their nation which emphasizes its backwardness. The other antecedent is Nancy Scheper-Hughes's *Saints, Scholars, and Schizophrenics. Mental Illness in Rural Ireland* (1979), which, starting from the title, sheds a sinister light on life in rural Ireland. To give the natives the possibility to say a word on their culture, a new approach – "Dialogical anthropology", as defined by Denis Tedlock (1979, 1987) – was used. This anthropological current maintains that the dialogical structure of the field has to be reproduced in the texts that represent natives' cultures. This idea oriented – almost literally – in two frequently cited works, *Tuhami: Portrait of a Moroccan*, by Vincent Crapanzano, and *Moroccan Dialogues*, by Kevin Dwyer. The structure of these books is very similar. The dialogue between the anthropologists and their key informants is realized through the combination of the author's voice, questioning or commenting, and some long quotations from participants, extracted from transcripts of interviews and/or informal conversations. A short extract from *Tuhami*, the portrait of a Moroccan tile-maker, can give an idea of how the dialogue concept is implemented in these books.

– My mother was still young when my father died. People told her to get married again. She did. Her new husband never accepted me. I left the house. I went to work for a French woman, M.me Jolan. I worked and slept there.
– Why weren't you accepted?
– There were three of us. He could not take care of us all, I was the eldest.
– What did your mother say to this?
– My mother did not have time to say stay or don't stay. I left right away.

There was scorn in Tuhami's voice and gestures. Several months later, he elaborated on his feelings.

– I was angry, I didn't want her to marry. That is why her husband didn't want me around. I was always screaming at him and insulting him – slamming the door in his face.
– Were you angry at your mother?
– No.

(Crapanzano 1980: 39)

If the unfamiliarity with writing of the two key informants is considered – both are illiterate – some doubts can be cast upon the authenticity of their voices. On the whole, the capacity of this kind of textualization to give voice to participants has been questioned by some important scholars of the anthropological debate, starting from Stephen Tyler:

For those would make that dialogue the focus of ethnography are in a sense correct, for dialogue *is* the source of the text, but dialogue rendered as text, which must be the consequence, is no longer dialogue, but a text masquerading as a dialogue, a mere monologue about a dialogue since the informants' appearances in the dialogue are at best mediated through the ethnographer's dominant authorial role. While it is laudable to include the native, his position

The textualization 147

is not thereby improved, for his words are still only instruments of the ethnographer's will.

(Tyler 1987: 65–66, italic in the original)

A less objectivist idea of dialogue as an instrument to give voice to participants guides the "narrative anthropology" approach eloquently expressed by Barbara Tedlock, anthropologist, shamanic healer, and – as she herself means to underline when she signs her books – wife of Denis Tedlock. In her book, *The beautiful and the dangerous*, she orchestrates her voice with those of some Zuni Indians with whom she stayed for a while. Barbara Tedlock does not mean to reproduce in her text the dialogue from the field but, more realistically, to represent her human encounter with the Zuni "as perceived by a situated narrator, who is also present as a character in the story" (1992: xiii–xiv). Her text consists of many voices accompanying the reader on a journey through otherness, without any special pretence to represent their views. In any case, renunciation of any objectivistic claims does not solve the problem of giving them an autonomous voice.

To tackle this issue, we have to move toward the most radical proposal in this field: collaborative ethnography. The contents of this approach are presented by Luke Eric Lassiter in *The Chicago Guide to Collaborative Ethnography*. Lassiter, while recognizing the influence that the metaphor of dialogue has exercised in recent decades, maintains that few scholars have sought to extend it to its next logical step: cooperation between ethnographers and participants in the textualization process (Lassiter 2005: 3). Doing collaborative ethnography means involving the participants – renamed as consultants – in all research steps from design to writing. This approach implies a redefinition of the Model Reader of an ethnographic and – by extension – of a qualitative monograph. In collaborative ethnography we do not write for our "fellow elite in the academy" (6), but for the community to which consultants belong. The text should be comprehensible to that audience, and for this purpose it must be lightened by the absence of technical jargon. To sum up, in the words of Lassiter, collaborative ethnography is "an approach to ethnography that deliberately and explicitly emphasises collaboration at every point in the ethnographic process, without veiling it – from project conceptualisation to fieldwork, and, especially, through the writing process" (16).[3]

The co-writing of a monograph can be achieved through a combination of different strategies based on the formal involvement of consultants in the writing of the text; moving from the assignation of the text's readers and editors role as the principal consultants, to the involvement of a larger group of consultants, organized through focus groups or large community forums (139–146). Adhering strictly to my reasoning about the possibility of giving a voice to participants, indications about the use of quotations are particularly relevant. Lassiter expresses this point clearly:

Because collaborative ethnography rests on an ethical and moral co-commitment between ethnographers and consultants, we must recognize above all that our

148 *The textualization*

> collaborators have as much right to shape and reshape the representation of their speech, expressions, and intended meanings as we do.
>
> (129)

The ethical commitment of Lassiter does not impede his recognizing the difficulties and traps of that approach. Doing collaborative ethnography exposes the researcher to consultants' pressures toward drawing up an apologetic text which celebrates the virtues of the community studied or – more probably – its leading group (147–148). Lassiter is nonetheless aware of the risk: advocates of the collaborative ethnography being stigmatized of "going native" and having serious difficulties in publishing their research where it would matter for their academic careers.

Lassiter contests the argument commonly used to resist the collaborative approach, the pretence of the author to be part of, or at least in tune with, the culture studied. He defines these strategies as "adoption narratives" (106) and calls them nothing but excuses. However, he is forced to admit that to guarantee the success of collaborative ethnography "ethnographers and consultants must first and foremost share a common vision on some level; otherwise, collaboration breaks down" (137). To put it bluntly, researchers are asked to adopt the culture of the community of consultants, risking transforming the purposes of scientific research into outright partisanship (Hammersley 2000), being deprived of the possibility of criticizing the consultants' views, or into something close to social work (Gross and Plattner 2002).

This long digression on dialogical and collaborative ethnography documents how difficult it is to decide to what extent to give voice to participants. Total adherence to this goal, expressed by the collaborative approach, radically modifies the purpose of scientific research which, although fully respecting participants' ethical rights, can be authorized to criticize the values, beliefs, and practices observed. Moreover, the collaborative approach relieves the authors of a responsibility that – in my view – we must assume however heavy it may be, "the burden of authorship" (Geertz 1988: 140; see also Tyler 1987: 66). My basic point is that it is the author who has to orchestrate voices, taking from them – the participants – all possible contributions, but still reproducing their voices in the text in a way that does not ethically damage their images. When it is possible, we can ask the participants to review our quotations (technically "reproductions", see Section 5.1) of their discourses. We can ask for comments on the preliminary version of our works and include them in the printed version.[4] But in any case, I believe that the researcher must accept the main authorship responsibility. According to Barbara Czarniawska, the ethical and political goal of giving them voice must "live side by side with the awareness that we are performing an act of ventriloquism" (Czarniawska 2004: 122). To conclude, the act of giving them a voice is a task which qualitative research can perform, in what can be defined as ethically responsible ventriloquism where the researchers retain their burden of authorship.

The textualization 149

Through the fourth and last function of multivocality, the participants' words can offer a special contribution to the elaboration of reflexive accounts (Altheide and Johnson 1994), constituting a necessary ingredient of the argument with which the soundness of the research results is defended. As I will further elaborate in the next section, the reflexive account is the tool that allows honouring the obligation of accounting for the methodological and practical procedures adopted to analyse data, through the "self-presentation" function of our argument (Edmondson 1984: 16). Their discourses on our research practices can be considered as a source of an enlarged version of reflexivity (Enzo Colombo: personal communication). The way in which obligation accountability is usually honoured is based only on the gaze and the voice of the researcher committed to the production of a reflexive account of his/her experience in the field. Participants' voices can expand the area of reflexivity when the author decides to take advantage of their description – spontaneous or solicited – of the relationship they entertained with him/her.

All the forms of orchestration between the author's voice and the voice of the participants can be framed referring to Gregory Bateson's notion of "double description" (Bateson 1979). Bateson's main point is quite simple: "Two descriptions are better than one" (137). At first glance, this proposition seems nothing more than a banality. In information, more is better than less. But, if we consider this simple statement through the epistemological lens, things change. In the received – positivist – view, a description can be true or false, according to its correspondence with reality. Admitting that two descriptions are better than one implies recognizing that both descriptions cannot be true (if the two descriptions are different and one is true, the other must be false) and, in the best case, a description may be more or less heuristically fecund, more or less able to direct our attention to some relevant aspects of the phenomena studied. This is, by the way, what any Weber ideal type does.[5] Bateson expresses the reason which supports his statement – two descriptions are better than one – by presenting a sequence of arguments from example, among which three best suit my purposes. The first illustration comes from mathematics and shows how the simple combination of two "synonymous languages" can produce an enrichment of our knowledge. The example relates to the mathematical theorem of the square of a binomial: $(a + b)^2 = a^2 + 2ab + b^2$. Bateson observes that this algebraic expression "itself is sufficiently demonstrated by the algorithm of algebraic multiplication" (73). I am not so sure; when I was a schoolboy, I learnt it by heart, to survive a not so brilliant math teacher. I finally fully understood the formula when I read in Bateson's book the geometric representation of the theorem. Let us consider the straight line and imagine that it is composed of two segments, a and b. The square constructed upon the line $\alpha\beta$ can be represented, as shown in Figure 6.1.

The geometrical representation makes what was for me an esoteric formula very clear. In the figure, we can see two squares of different dimensions (being $a \neq b$), a^2 and b^2 and two rectangles of identical dimension, that can be added. So with all my heart I can now pronounce: $(a + b)^2 = a^2 + 2ab + b^2$!

150 *The textualization*

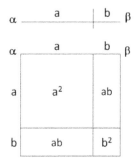

Figure 6.1[6] Double description through the geometrical representation of the binomial square

The second illustration of the magic, if I may, of double description arrives from the field of neurophysiology and relates to the phenomenon of synaptic summation and was presented by Bateson as follows:

> Synaptic summation is the technical term used in neurophysiology for those instances in which some neuron C is fired only by a combination of neurons A and B. A alone is insufficient to fire C, and B alone is insufficient to fire C; but if neurons A and B fire together within a limited period of microseconds, then C is triggered. Notice that the conventional term for this phenomenon, summation, would suggest an adding of information from one source to information from another. What actually happens is not an adding but a forming of a logical product, a process more closely akin to multiplication.
>
> (71–72)

In this last situation, the combination of the two elements brought close together yields an additional piece of information which is even clearer in the example I am about to introduce, that of binocular vision. Our species – the human, not only qualitative researchers – and also many other animals who see the world through two normally identical eyes looking at the same observational object; but this, according to Bateson, can be considered as "a wasteful use of the sense organs" (69). But what makes the difference in observing the world through two eyes instead of one (as Polyphemus learned at his own expense) is the information about depth-of-field. Through binocular vision, we are able "to improve resolution at edges and contrasts; and better able to read when the print is small or the illumination poor. More important, information about depth is created" (69–70). These and some more examples of double description allow Bateson to conclude:

> In principle, extra "depth" in some metaphoric sense is to be expected whenever the information for the two descriptions is differently collected

The textualization 151

or differently coded. . . . The aggregate is greater than the sum of its parts because the combining of the parts is not a simple adding but is of the nature of a multiplication or a fractionation, or the creation of a logical product. A momentary gleam of enlightenment.

(70, 86)

The theme of double description emerges, although not so systematically as in *Mind and Nature*, in one of Bateson's first publications, *Naven*, a book which collects the results of anthropological research carried out on a ritual practiced by the Iatmul, a head-hunting tribe of New Guinea (Bateson 1936). In the first chapter of this ponderous book, entitled *Methods of Presentation*, Bateson maintains that there are two main methods of presenting "the whole of a culture", impressionistic and analytic (1–2). The impressionist method is that used by novelists, among whom he names Charles Montagu Doubty, Jane Austen, and John Galsworthy. All these "sensitive writers" (1) offer a picture of the society that they observe by adding to the simple description of the events narrated a special emotional tone. Considering the continuously reprinted book by Doubty, *Travels in Arabia Deserta* (first published in 1888), Bateson writes:

If we read Arabia Deserta, we are struck by the astonishing way in which every incident is informed with the emotional tone of Arab life. More than this, many of the incidents would be impossible with a different emotional background. Evidently then the emotional background is causally active within a culture, and no functional study can ever be reasonably complete unless it links up the structure and pragmatic working of the culture with its emotional tone or ethos

(2)

The other presentation method developed in "analytic, cognitive terms" (2) finds its most renowned representatives in his masters, Alfred Radcliffe-Brown and Bronisław Malinowki. This is a sober way to describe a culture paying close attention to all or most little details and the cultural premises that give shape to culture being studied. The juxtaposition of these two presentation methods and the absence of a clear expression of preference for one or the other authorizes a reading of this chapter as an invitation to combine the analytic and impressionistic writing styles, in an *ante-litteram* double description.[7]

This last comment orients our returning to writing in qualitative research. The combination of our voice with participants' voices (including images produced by participants), the amalgamation of our theory-laden, analytical representation with the emotional, evocative tone produced by the quotation from the field, is what gives qualitative texts their extra "depth", not to be found in homologous quantitative writing. This extra depth emerges for all the four functions of multivocal writing. In the next paragraph, focussed on reflexivity, particular attention will be paid to the contribution of voices from the field for the establishment of an enlarged version of reflexivity.

152   *The textualization*

6.2 The reflexive account

The definition of the title of this section (incidentally the last in the book) was clouded by an atmosphere of hesitation and perplexity. According to Karen Lumsden, reflexivity has become a buzzword with a lot of divergent meanings (Lumsden 2019). In our community, different versions of reflexivity cohabit with opposite purposes assigned to its complex paraphernalia. Michel Lynch observes how "some research programmes treat reflexivity as a methodological basis for enhancing objectivity, whereas others treat it as a critical weapon for undermining objectivism" (Lynch 2000: 26). Finally, I decided to keep the buzzword in my title as being related to an account of the way in which research has been carried out. In doing so, I deliberately decided to give my discourse a low profile, focussing mainly on textualization aspects without any pretence thoroughness. The discussion will be elaborated in the general frame of the construction of a persuasive argument on the solidity of the research results proposed to the scientific community.

In the first chapter of this volume (Section 1.2), I sketched a comparison between qualitative and quantitative research focussing on both differences and commonalities. Among the commonalities, I identified the shared obligation to account for the methodological path followed in order to gather the information on which the research results are based.[8] On the necessity to honour this obligation, the words of the anthropologist Bronisław Malinowki maintain their freshness.

> No one would dream of making an experimental contribution to physical or chemical science, without giving a detailed account of all the arrangements of the experiments; an exact description of the apparatus used; of the manner in which the observations were conducted; of their number; of the length of time devoted to them, and of the degree of approximation with which each measurement was made. . . . Again, in historical science, no one could expect to be seriously treated if he made any mystery of his sources and spoke of the past as if he knew it by divination.
>
> (Malinowski 1922, reprinted 2002: 2–3)

Malinowski's point is clear: to persuade the scientific community of the robustness of our research results, we have to describe the conditions of the "experience experiment" (Piasere 2002: 27) carried out. According to David Altheide and John Johnson, the description of the conditions that gave us insight into the social phenomena studied is an ethical responsibility (Altheide and Johnson 1994: 489). The contents of this ethical responsibility emerge convincingly in the definition of reflexivity presented by Mats Alvesson and Kaj Sköldberg:[9]

> Reflexivity means thinking about the conditions for what one is doing, investigating the way in which the theoretical, cultural and political context of individual and intellectual involvement affects interaction with whatever is being researched, often in ways difficult to become conscious of.
>
> (Alvesson and Sköldberg 2000: 245)

The textualization 153

This idea of reflexivity contrasts with the metaphor of doing qualitative research as a "mushroom-picking" activity (281). The data we acquired are always embedded in relations with participants in which both the persona of the researcher and those of participants play a decisive role. Producing a reflexive account of our research means describing this observational and human relationship with regard to all aspect that we consider relevant to the qualification of the robustness (or weakness) of our evidence.

Detailed description of the observational relationship allows a preliminary stratification of the acquired information from the "authenticity range" point of view (Topolski 1977: 434, original edition 1973).[10] Let us consider my study of the esoteric community of Damanhur (Cardano 1997). Not being an initiate to the magic doctrine, I was not allowed to enter the underground temple where the magic rituals were performed. Nevertheless, being a guest of a little group of devotees in a farmhouse, I had the opportunity to share with them meals and informal chats. At the end of my stay in Damanhur, I went home with information both about rituals and about the informal relationships among community members. The former was mostly indirect (someone decided to give me a vague idea of what usually happened in the secret spaces of the community) or stolen, through some discreet eavesdropping activities. Most of the information about the informal relationships was of firsthand type and based on repeated participation in the community's daily life. It is quite obvious that the indirect or stolen information suffered from a smaller authenticity range compared with the firsthand ones.

One of the narrative expedients that can be used to describe the relationship between the researcher and the participants with which the study was carried out is that of the natural history of the research. This narrative genre attracted the attention of our scientific community with the publication, by William Foote Whyte, in *Street Corner Society*, of a vast appendix on his research experience (Whyte 1993: 279–373, first publication – with appendix – 1954). Starting from the 1960s, this presentation style gained in popularity, sometimes assuming the form of a reflexive confessional.[11] Due to its pioneering role, it seems appropriate to dedicate some space to the description of William Foote Whyte's natural history, organized into 16 sections totalling just under 100 pages.

The Appendix opens with the researcher's background, so answering the crucial "self-presentation" question: Where is the author coming from?

> I come from a very consistent upper-middle-class background. One grandfather was a doctor; the other, a superintendent of schools. My father was a college professor. My upbringing, therefore was very far removed from the life I have described in Cornerville.
>
> (Whyte 1993: 280)[12]

Whyte candidly confesses his otherness also toward the social context studied from the theoretical point of view, admitting that, before his study, he knew "nothing about the slums" (281). The research – we read – begins thanks to a three-year fellowship that offered Whyte the possibility to study slums. He describes his

154 *The textualization*

preliminary readings and some important intellectual encounters, among which them Conrad Arensbergh, from whom the scholar received an initial smattering of field methods. There follow descriptions of his first disastrous attempts to enter the field, ending with a providential encounter with Ernest Pecci, "Doc" in the book, his key informant and research collaborator. Whyte met Doc at the local settlement houses, marking this encounter as the real start of his research: "In a sense, my study began on the evening of February 4, 1937, when the social worker called me in to meet Doc" (291). Whyte committed himself in a long explanation of his purposes, and Doc's reaction is instructive, an interesting example of what I have already defined as enlarged reflexivity.

> When I was finished, he asked: "Do you want to see the high life or the low life?"
> "I want to see all that I can. I want to get as complete a picture of the community as possible."
> "Well, any nights you want to see anything, I'll take you around. I can take you to the joints – gambling joints – I can take you around to the street corners. Just remember that you're my friend. That's all they need to know. I know these places, and, if I tell them that you are my friend, nobody will bother you. Just tell me what you want to see, and we'll arrange it."
>
> (291)

Whyte then indulges in the description of his host family, the Italian Martinis, introducing an embryo of "adoption narratives" (Lassiter 2005: 106). In the following pages, Whyte's natural history tells us something about methods and his false steps in trying to go native.

> In my interviewing methods I had been instructed not to argue with people or pass moral judgements upon them. This fell in with my own inclinations. However, this attitude did not come out so much in interviewing, for I did little formal interviewing. I sought to show this interested acceptance of the people and the community in my everyday participation.
> At first I concentrated upon fitting into Cornerville. But a little later I had to face the question of how far I was to immerse myself in the life of the district. I bumped into that problem one evening I was walking down the street with the Nortons [a local gang] Trying to enter into the spirit of the small talk, I cut loose with a lot of obscenities and profanity. The walk came to a momentary halt as they all stopped to look at me in surprise. Doc shook his head and said: "Bill, you're not supposed to talk like that. That doesn't sound like you."
>
> (302, 304)

And it is on the side-line of this discourse that his frank expression of an adoption narrative appeared: "My first spring in Cornerville served to establish for me a firm position in the life of the district. I had only been there several weeks when

The textualization 155

Doc said to me: 'You're just as much of a fixture around this street corner as that lamppost'" (306). Whyte tells us about his venture in politics as unpaid secretary of a local politician and as a "repeater", voting four times for a candidate, with some obvious problems of conscience.

> The experience posed problems that transcend expediency. I had been brought up as a respectable, low-abiding, middle-class citizen. When I discovered that I was a repeater, I found my conscience giving me serious trouble. . . . I had to learn that, in order to be accepted by the people in a district, you do not have to do everything just as they do it".
>
> (316–317)

In his long confession, Whyte describes the reformulation of his research project, including that resulting from the arrival of his wife in the field, changing the research from solo to tandem organization: "Now that we were two, we could enter into new types of social activities, and Kathleen could learn to know some of the women as I had become acquainted with the men" (320–321). The natural history closes with a reflection on the impact of Street Corner Society on the people studied, and with some interesting information about the destiny of the "chief characters of the book" (346).[13]

It is quite evident that writing a natural history requires space, which is not always available, particularly when the publication is a concise essay for an international journal rather than a monograph. I believe that the natural history form can help in the pursuit of a reflexive contribution. For what it's worth, I used this tool twice (Cardano 1997: 32–63; Cardano and Pannofino 2015: 321–326), finding in this narrative form a useful methodological expedient.

The description of the relationship between researcher and participants – whatever the form, analytical or narrative – can be written combining our and their voices, so exploiting the fourth function of multivocality (see Section 6.1). This kind of enlarged reflexivity can be pursued through two different forms of participant involvement. The first form, more conventional and easier to apply, sees researchers inserting into their textual corpus the participants' quotations that can shed light on the observational relationship, as was the case of Whyte in his description of his first encounter with Doc (see earlier). In doing so, we have to be aware of performing a kind of "ventriloquism" (Czarniawska 2004: 122) which, however, can contributes to the transparency of the construction of the studied phenomenon's representation. The second, more demanding, form requires the autonomous contribution of participants. The easiest way of doing this is to give participants a little space in our work where they can freely comment on our methodological path and our main results. To this purpose, participants must be informed about the methods and outcomes of our study. They can read a draft of our work, read a synthesis, or be involved in a meeting where both methods and results are discussed. Closer involvement of participants in this enlarged version of reflexivity can be tempted by switching to a collaborative research approach if we are ready to pay for all the costs that full co-authorship incurs (see Section 6.1).

156 *The textualization*

The specific contents of the reflexive account depend on the kind of research experience carried out, but some general remarks may be made. Due to the relevance of the persona of the researcher, it is important to position oneself concerning the context studied. From a certain point of view, readers can detect where authors stand from bibliographical references, writing style, and attitude toward participants. But it may sometimes be appropriate to support the reader's interpretation of these clues with explicit declarations, such as Whyte's confession of his "upper-middle-class background" (Whyte 1993: 280). I felt a similar necessity to declare my attitude toward nature and spirituality when studying of the of the two communities of Damanhur and Elves of the Great Ravine (*Elfi del Gran Burrone*). In my natural history of the research, I wrote:

> I am humanly and intellectually attracted by religious experience and, more generally, by holy experience, but from an irreducibly lay perspective. In this respect, my experience of the two forms of devotion expressed by the Elves and Damanhurians has not changed my initial attitude. The case of my attitude towards nature is different. When I started the research, it was marked by disenchantment barely tempered by a modest ethical sensitivity towards the "rights of the ecosphere". My encounter with Damanhur and above all with the Great Ravine community has radically changed my attitude. This is above all on the ethical level, forcing me to recognize the narrow-mindedness of anthropocentrism, and also, albeit to a lesser extent, on an emotional level, sometimes endowing me with the transitory experience of the enchantment of nature.
>
> (Cardano 1997: 41–42)

The quotation allows me to say that the description of an author becomes more eloquent if it considers its evolution in relation experience of the participants' culture. It is likewise important to describe how the research gained access to the participants, both from the methodological (case selection) and more practical point of views. This means describing the often implicit "contract" through which we obtain their cooperation. Reflecting on the degree and source of their cooperation is another important aspect of the observational relationship that needs to be illustrated. Finally, a clear description of how data are collected, underlying the possible perturbations and biases that characterized our "experience experiment" (Piasere 2002: 27) is compulsory. Our observation is not only "theory-laden" (Hanson 1958) and "trust-laden" (see Section 1.1) but also "practice-laden", and we have to try to observe our practices critically.

To conclude, it seems important to return to Michel Lynch's critical comment on the purpose of reflexivity (see earlier). The purpose of the reflexive account cannot be evaluated with by the measure of objectivity (although this was one of my previous concerns). A reflexive account neither enhances nor erodes the objectivity of our claims. Less pretentiously, it enriches the dialectical dimension of our persuasive argument, facilitating the definition of the plausibility of our research results.

The textualization   157

I can conclude with nothing catchier than inviting you to return to your field research, combining rigour – in a way that does not produce rigour mortis – and abductive creativity.

Notes

1 Goffman wrote *Asylum* (1961) combining his voice mainly with other authoritative ones taken from diaries, autobiographies, novels, film screenplays, and, obviously, from the scientific literature; but only a few pages contain voices of inmates and staff. In a dedicated rereading of the original version, published in 1961, I found only 8 pages out of 390 where participants' voices are reported (Goffman 1961: 152, 153, 154, 161, 292, 293, 302, 311).

2 In Rosaldo's essay, *Grief and a Headhunter's Rage*, we read: "Only after being repositioned through a devastating loss of my own could I better grasp that Ilongot older men mean precisely what they say when they describe the anger in bereavement as the source of their desire to cut off human heads" (Rosaldo 1993: 3).

3 A quintessential expression of this approach is represented by the research project crowned by the publication of *The Other Side of Middleton* (Lassiter, Goodall, Campbell et al. 2004). The title of this book refers to the two famous studies by the Lynd couple in Middletown, discovered to be the city of Muncie in Indiana (Lynd and Lynd 1929, 1937). Muncie had and has proportionally one of the largest African-American communities in the USA, totally ignored in both Lynd's books. To give voice to this substantial portion of Muncie's population, a collaborative ethnography had been projected involving 75 university students and community collaborators involved in the textualization process (Lassiter 2005: 20).

4 I used both these writing devices in my research activity. The book in which I distilled the main results of my PhD thesis closes with a three-page comment written by the leader of one of the communities studied. The comment, entitled "Who are the Elves?", contains an apologetic description of The Elves of the Great Ravine community reproduced verbatim (Cardano 1997: 289–291). I used something close to quotation review in a little book I have written with one of my master's degree students about a small self-help group of Voice-Hearers. These self-help groups are composed of people whom conventional psychiatry define as schizophrenic but who define themselves in a non-stigmatizing way as "voice-hearers". In our book, we carried out eight discursive interviews with members of the group (which numbered ten people). We transcribed the interviews verbatim and then rewrote the histories recounted in first-person narratives ("I was born in Turin, after a ten-month pregnancy, like donkeys. My family comes from a little village near Naples"). We asked the eight participants to check our text and introduce all the changes they wanted with a view to publishion (Cardano and Lepori 2012: 44–75). A most sensitive documentary, *Written by Voice*, was filmed by Elisabetta Angelillo about making the book and the self-help group [available, with English subtitles, at: www.youtube.com/watch?v=XYOPYJfTz5c].

5 Bateson's anti-realist stance emerges clearly a few pages before the quotation. In the previous chapter, we read: "Science sometimes improves hypotheses and sometimes disproves them. But proof would be another matter and perhaps never occurs except in the realms of totally abstract tautology". A few pages after this point, I found a more graphic expression: "Science probes; it does not prove" (Bateson 1979: 27, 30).

6 The figure is adapted from Bateson (1979: 74).

7 In between the publication of *Naven* and *Mind and Nature*, Bateson authored *Balinese Character. A Photographic Analysis,* with his first wife, Margaret Mead, (Bateson, Mead, 1942). The book was presented as an "experimental innovation" (xi) meant to overcome, through extensive use of photographs, the difficulties in translating the *ethos* of Balinese culture into "ordinary English" (xi). In the Introduction, the authors

158 *The textualization*

recalled the opposition between the artistic and analytical presentation styles defined in *Naven*, and explicitly proposed "a new method of stating the intangible relationships among different types of culturally standardized behaviour by placing side by side mutually relevant photographs" (xii). In *Balinese Charater*, the idea of double description became a combination between photographs – just under 800 – and analytical writing. This is an interesting textualization solution, through which – undoubtedly – greater depth is added, albeit without orchestrating the authors' voices with those of the participants. I would like to thank Luigi Gariglio for calling this aspect of Bateson's intellectual production to my attention.

8 As said in Chapter 1, quantitative research honours this obligation at two different times: before the data collection procedures, through the display of pre-arranged operational definitions – and at the end of the methodological itinerary, through illustration of the statistical models utilised.

9 In the text quoted, Alvesson and Sköldberg open the statement with the word "reflection" instead of "reflexivity", but in the note that follows the statement they write: "In this section we will not distinguish between reflection and reflexivity, but see them as synonymous" (Alvesson and Sköldberg 2000: 290).

10 On the notion of authenticity range, see Section 4.2 and 5.1.

11 A review of this narrative genre is offered by Martyn Hammersley (2002, draft).

12 Moving from this premise, from which it seems that no woman has contributed to the author's background, it is not surprising that almost all of the book's chief characters are men.

13 In a successive edition of the Appendix, two other sections were added, entitled "Getting Street Corner Society accepted as a doctoral thesis" and "Revisiting Street Corner Society after fifty years".

References

Altheide D.L., Johnson J.M. 1994 *Criteria for Assessing Interpretive Validity in Qualitative Research*, in N.K. Denzin and Y.S. Lincoln (eds.), *Handbook of Qualitative Research*, Thousand Oaks and London, Sage Publications, pp. 485–499.

Alvesson M., Sköldberg K. 2000 *Reflexive Methodology: New Vistas for Qualitative Research*, London, Sage Publications.

Bakhtin M.M. 2014 *The Dialogical Imagination*, New Delhi, Pinnacle Reading.

Bateson G. 1936 *Naven: A Survey of the Problems Suggested By a Composite Picture of the Culture of a New Guinea Tribe Drawn from Three Points of View*, Cambridge, Cambridge University Press.

———. 1979 *Mind and Nature: A Necessary Unity*, New York, E.P. Dutton.

Bateson G., Mead M. 1942 *Balinese Character: A Photographic Analysis*, New York, Academy of Science.

Behar R. 1996 *The Vulnerable Observer: Anthropology That Breaks Your Heart*, Boston, Beacon Press.

Cardano M. 1997 *Lo specchio, la rosa e il loto. Uno studio sulla sacralizzazione della natura*, Roma, Seam.

———. 2010 *Mental Distress: Strategies of Sense-Making*, in "Health: An Interdisciplinary Journal for the Social Study of Health, Illness and Medicine", Vol. 14, No. 3, pp. 253–271.

Cardano M., Lepori G. 2012 *Udire la voce degli dei. L'esperienza del Gruppo Voci*, Milano, Franco Angeli.

Cardano M., Pannofino N. 2015 *Piccole apostasie. Il congedo dai nuovi movimenti religiosi*, Bologna, Il Mulino.

The textualization   159

Clifford J., Marcus G. (eds.). 1986 *Writing Culture: The Poetics and Politics of Ethnography*, Berkeley, University of California Press.

Crapanzano V. 1980 *Tuhami: Portrait of a Moroccan*, Chicago, University of Chicago Press.

Czarniawska B. 2004 *Narrative in Social Science Research*, London, Sage Publications.

Dwyer K. 1982 *Moroccan Dialogues: Anthropology in Question*, Baltimore, John Hopkins University Press.

Edmondson R. 1984 *Rhetoric in Sociology*, London, The Macmillan Press Ltd.

Geertz C. 1988 *Works and Lives: The Anthropologist as Author*, Stanford, CA, Stanford University Press.

Goffman E. 1961 *Asylums: Essays on the Social Situation of Mental Patients and Other Inmates*, New York, Anchor Books Doubleday & Company, Inc.

Gross D., Plattner S. 2002 *Anthropology as Social Work: Collaborative Models of Anthropological Research*, in "Anthropology News", Vol. 43, No. 8, p. 4.

Hammersley M. 2000 *Taking Sides in Social Research: Essays on Partisanship and Bias*, London and New York, Routledge.

———. 2002 *Guide to Natural Histories of Research*, draft https://martynhammersley.files.wordpress.com/2013/06/natural-histories.doc

Hanson N.R. 1958 *Patterns of Discovery: An Inquiry Into the Conceptual Foundations of Science*, Cambridge, Cambridge University Press.

Lassiter L.E. 2005 *The Chicago Guide to Collaborative Ethnography*, Chicago and London, The University of Chicago Press.

Lassiter L.E., Goodall H., Campbell E., Johnson M.N. (eds.) 2004 *The Other Side of Middletown: Exploring Muncie's African American Community*, Walnut Creek, CA, AltaMira.

Lewis O. 1961 *The Children of Sánchez*, New York, Random House.

Lumsden K. 2019 *Reflexivity: Theory, Method, and Practice*, New York, Routledge.

Lynch M. 2000 *Against Reflexivity as an Academic Virtue and Source of Privileged Knowledge*, in "Theory, Culture & Society", Vol. 17, No. 3, pp. 26–54.

Lynd R.S., Lynd H.M. 1929 *Middletown: A Study in Modern American Culture*, New York, Harcourt Brace & Company.

———. 1937 *Middletown in Transition: A Study in Cultural Conflicts*, New York, Harcourt Brace & Company.

Malinowski B. 2002 *Argonauts of the Western Pacific: An Account of Native Enterprise and Adventure in the Archipelagos of Melanesian New Guinea*, London, Routledge (first edition 1922).

Mason J. 2002 *Qualitative Researching*, Second Edition, London, Sage Publications.

Piasere L. 2002 *L'etnografo imperfetto. Esperienza e cognizione in antropologia*, Roma-Bari, Laterza.

Rosaldo R. 1993 *Culture and Truth: The Remaking of Social Analysis*, Boston, Beacon Press.

Scheper-Hughes N. 1979 *Saints, Scholars, and Schizophrenics: Mental Illness in Rural Ireland*, Berkeley, University of California Press.

Tedlock B. 1992 *The Beautiful and the Dangerous: Encounters with the Zuni Indians*, Albuquerque, University of New Mexico Press.

Tedlock D. 1979 *The Analogical Tradition and the Emergence of a Dialogical Anthropology*, in "Journal of Anthropological Research", Vol. 35, No. 4, pp. 387–400.

———. 1987 *Questions Concerning Dialogical Anthropology*, in "Journal of Anthropological Research", Vol. 43, No. 4, pp. 325–337.

160 *The textualization*

Topolski J. 1977 *Methodology of History*, Dordrecht and Boston, D. Reidel Publishing Company (original edition 1973).

Tyler S.A. 1987 *The Unspeakable: Discourse, Dialogue, and Rhetoric in the Postmodern World*, Madison and Wisconsin, The University of Wisconsin Press.

Whyte W.F. 1993 *Street Corner Society: The Social Structure of an Italian Slum*, Fourth Edition, Chicago, University of Chicago Press (original edition, with Appendix 1955).

Wikan U. 1992 *Beyond the Words: The Power of Resonance*, in "American Ethnologist", Vol. 19, No. 3, pp. 460–482.

Index

Note: page numbers in *italics* indicate figures.

Abbott, Andrew 67, 103–104n12
abduction 48, 60n4
abductive inference 29
abductive reasoning 45–49; creativity of
   49; illustrations of 46–47; specificity of
   48; *see also* theory of argumentation
Abend, Gabriel 21n2
Acceptability of premises 52, 61n9
ad-hominem fallacy 130–131
adoption narratives vs. collaborative
   ethnography 148, 154
Adorno, Theodor 11
a fortiori (with greater reason) argument
   45, 75, 81, 105n30, 106n40, 114
Agnes, Garfinkel study of 94–96, 104n24
Altheide, David 152
Alvesson, Mats 5, 152, 158n9
analogical reasoning 56–59, 61n17, 92,
   105n26, 134, 139n20
Angelillo, Elisabetta 157n4
apple-billiard-ball example 55–57
Arensbergh, Conrad 154
Argumentatiche schemes as pedagogical
   tools 3
argument heuristics 103–104n12
argumentation scheme(s) 54–59; schemes
   for qualitative research 60; *see also*
   theory of argumentation
Aristotle 3, 45, 50, 56, 57, 75, 103n4, 143
artificial intelligence 45, 48
Asylums (Goffman) 23n1, 53, 144, 157n1
Austen, Jane 151
authenticity, range of 4, 5n2, 74, 104n21,
   122
authoritarianism 7, 11
Authoritarianism California F-scale 13
autoethnography 34, 36, 41n13; ethical
   principle of autonomy 69, 102, 107n54

Bagnasco, Arnaldo 103n9
Barbour, Rosaline 16, 65
Basaglia, Franco 126
Bateson, Gregory 2, 4, 34, 144, 149–151,
   157n5, 157–158n7
Becher, Johann Joachim 8
Bechhofer, Frank 105n30
Becker, Howard 23n14
Behaviourist School 8
Benson, Ophelia 30
billiard-ball model 55–57, 61n16,
   140n26
binary logic 17, 18, *18*
Binswanger, Ludwig 126
Black, Max 136
Blumer, Herbert 28
Borges, Jorge Luis 2
Boudon, Raimond 14
Bourricaud, François 14
Bryman, Alan 31

Cameron, William Bruce 30
Camoletto, Raffaella Ferrero 103n11
Cantù, Paola 51
Capote, Truman 121
Carlsson, Christoffer 96
categorization 4; act of 124; procedures
   123, 131; process 124, 126, 130, 132,
   135–136; term 139n17
Charmaz, Kathy 22n13
Coleman, James 67, 95
collaborative ethnography 102n1, 147–148,
   157n3
Collins, Randall 34
Colombo, Enzo 31, 149
community of inquiry 50–51, 53, 61n6, 68,
   95, 98, 101
comparative ethnography 46, 83, 87

162   *Index*

Computer Aided Qualitative Data Analysis
    Software (CAQDAS) 64, 132
conditional plausibility 54, 71, 73–74, 78,
    82, 87, 93–94, 100, 106n33
confidentiality, ethical principle of 69
Conrad, Peter 118
constructive epistemology 19
Conversation Analysis 21n3
Corbin, Juliet 22n13, 102n2
Coser, Lewis 137
Crapanzano, Vincent 146
Creswell, John 20
critical case design 75, *76*, 78–83
critical theory 39n1; Frankfurt School of 26
Czarniawska, Barbara 28, 41n13, 148

Damanhur esoteric community
    99; deconversion study 98, *100*;
    ex-members of community 123, 125,
    139n18; spiritual community of 46, 98,
    153, 156
data analysis 112; phase 64, 101; *see also*
    qualitative data analysis
data collection procedure(s) 13, 14, 158n8;
    context-sensitivity of 2, 28–30, 36,
    58, 124, 135; degree of perturbation in
    32, 118; lack of uniformity in 37, 38;
    deduction 48, 60n4
definition of the situation 9–10
degree of perturbation 32, 117–118, 120
degree of uncertainty 17
Deleuze, Gilles 26
Demazière, Didier 112, 137n1
Denzin, Norman 26, 53–54
Derrida, Jacques 26
Description as a choice (Sen) 138–139n10
details-focalization, qualitative research
    30–31, 71
Dewey, John 103n8
Diagnostic Statistics Manual 117
dialogical anthropology 146
digital data 35
Dimaggio, Paul 83
disguised questionnaire 112, 137n1
double description 2, 4, 158n7; Bateson's
    notion of 144, 149; examples of
    150–151; geometrical representation of
    binomial square 149, *150*; multivocality
    as 143–151
double-hierarchy argument 45, 78–83
Doubty, Charles Montagu 151
Doucet, Andrea 79–82
Douglas, Jack 11, 12, 21–22n5
Doyle, Conan 11

Dubar, Claude 112, 137n1
Durkheim, Émile 9, 13, 21n2
Dwyer, Kevin 146

Eastis, Carla 87–89, 92–94, 106n41
Eco, Umberto 46
Edmondson, Ricca 3, 143
Ellis, Carolyn 41n13
Elves of the Great Ravine 46, 47,
    138–138n9, 156, 157n4
Emmel, Nick 19, 22n11
emotional habitus 72, 73, 104n16
ethnography 22n10; collaborative 102n1,
    147–148, 157n3; dialogical 148;
    see also team ethnography
ethnomethodology 26
evidential paradigm 1, 2, 11, 117
extralinguistic dimension 35, 41n18
extreme-case design *76*, 94–97

Facebook 119
fear of theory 65, 66
feasibility, suitability of method 102
feminist theory 26
Foster, Peter 61n12
Foucault, Michel 26
Frankfurt School 26
Freshwater, Dawn 20
Freud, Sigmund 11
Frohlich, Katherine 41n14
functional magnetic resonance imaging
    (fMRI) 8
fuzzy logic 17, *18*

Gadamer, Hans 2
Galsworthy, John 151
Garfinkel, Harold 40n12, 94, 95, 96;
    breaching experiments 35, 37, 40n12
Gariglio, Luigi 103n11, 137n3
Geertz, Clifford 14, 22n10
generalizability, qualitative researching
    lacking 38–39
Ginzburg, Carlo 11
Glaser, Barney 22n13
Goffman, Erving 12, 23n21, 34, 53, 132,
    144, 157n1
Goldthorpe, John 105n30
Gomm, Roger 61n12
Greimas, Algirdas Julien 126–127
Groarke, Leo 61n9
Grootendorst, Rob 51–52, 131
grounded theory 15–16, 22–23n13, 132;
    analogical reasoning and 139n20;
    naturalization of 64; radical refusal of

theory 65, 102–103n2; sampling 23n15; transparency missing in 104n22
Guattari, Felix 26
Guba, Egon 17, 29, 65–66, 105n26

Hammersley, Martyn 19, 61n12, 158n11
Harper, Douglas 34
Hawthorne Effect 138n8
heap paradox (sorites) 27
Heider, Karl 41n21
Hesse, Mary 140n26
Hitlerjunge Quex (film) 34
Hofstadter, Douglas 4, 123, 124, 139n17
Holmes, Sherlock 11
horror doctrinae 65, 103n4
horro vacui 65
Household Portrait, interview methodology 79
Huberman, Michael 19, 132
Humphreys, Laud 40n12

illness narratives 10, 126–130
impersonality, qualitative researching lacking 37–38
indigenous communities, cases against resource extraction 89–94, *91*
induction 48, 60n4
intellectual puzzle 66, 79, 101, 103n7, 143
interest formula 67
interviews, linguistic dimension 35, 41n18
investigative social research 21–22n5
invisibility 47; issue of 2, 7–9, 13, 117; researcher having 81; visible and invisible 7–13
islands in archipelago, map of qualitative methods *33*

Jacobs, Jerry 65
Jensen, Adolph 104n15
Johnson, John 152
Josephson, John 48–49, 60n3
Josephson, Susan 48–49, 60n3

Kaufmann, Jena-Claude 112
Kehoane, Robert 80
Kennedy, John Fitzgerald 5
King, Gary 80
King, Nigel 4, 124–125
Kirk, Jerome 40n7
knowledge construction version of the argument from example 77–78
knowledge representing version of the argument from example 77, 78, 105n27
Korzybski, Alfred 2

Kosko, Bart 23n19
Krueger, Richard 41n17
Kuhn, Annegret 89–94, *91*, 106n42–44

Lassiter, Luke Eric 147–148
Latour, Bruno 138n4
Laudan, Larry 66
Lavoisier, Antoine-Laurent de 8
le Pen, Jean-Marie 130
Lewis, Oscar 145
Lincoln, Yvonna 17, 26, 29, 53–54, 65–66, 105n26
linguistic dimension, of interviews transcripts 35, 41n18
Lockwood, David 105n30
logic of inference 37, 49, 71
Lumsden, Karen 152
Lynch, Michel 152, 156

Macagno, Fabrizio 2, 56
Maderna, Bruno 46
Madison, Gary Brent 2, 20, 41n22
Malinowski, Bronislaw 34, 151–152
Marshall, Catherine 103n9
Mason, Jennifer 30, 61n13, 61n22
Matthew Effect 84
Maxwell, James Clerk 7
Maxwell, Joseph 19
Mead, Margaret 34, 157n7
Merton, Robert 22n10
method(s): defending suitability of 100–102; map of qualitative *33*, 33–36; principles *vs* orders 20–21
methodological inhibition 19–20
Miles, Matthew 19, 132
Miller, Marc 40n7
Mills, Carl Wright 19–20, 123, 139n17
minimization of harm, ethical principle of 69
Minkowski, Eugène 126
Mixed Method 20
Montesquieu 96, 107n49
morality, thin and thick concepts of 21n2
Morelli, Giovanni 11
Morgan, Mary 60n2
Morse, Janice 15, 23n15, 103n7
most-different-systems design 75, *76*, 83–87, 106–107n47; assumption of linearity in *85*
most-similar-system design 75–76, *76*, 87–94, 106n42, 106–107n47; linearity assumption 107n47
multimodal logic 17; membership of set of adults in *18*

164 *Index*

multivocality, qualitative research 31–36
Murphy, Cullen 118, 120

narrative analysis:; of mental health
  patients 126–130
narrative anthropology 147
Nash, Jeff 40n12
naturalistic generalization 15
negative analogy 140n26
New Religious Movements (NRMs) 97–98,
  100, 107n50, 139n18; classifications of
  99; leave-takers from 114, 137
Newton, Sir Isaac 7
Neyman, Jerzy 104n15

Olbrechts-Tyteca, Lucie 50–51
orchestration 19, 31, 144, 149
orders, principles *vs* 20–21

Pannofino, Nicola 97–98, 117, 139n18
paradigms war 19, 27
paralinguistic dimension in interview
  transcripts 35, 41n18
participatory visual methods 35
passing theory, analogy and abduction
  58, 60
Patton, Michael Quinn 23n16, 30
Pawson, Ray 19
Pecci, Ernest 154
Peirce, Charles Sanders 2, 29, 47, 48, 49,
  50, 58, 59, 103n8
Perelman, Chaïm 50–51
Persian Letters 107n49
persuasion 3–4, 143
Pethes, Nicolas 77
planning phase, methodology 101–102
Platt, Jennifer 96, 105n30, 106n40
plausibility: of argument 93; argument-
  from-analogy 56; conditional 1, 54, 71,
  73–74, 78, 82, 87, 93–94, 100, 106n33;
  relationship of probability and 49, 60n4
positive analogy 140n26
Potter, Jonathan 119
Powell, Walter 83–87
premise acceptability 52, 61n9
principles, orders *vs* 20–21
probability, relationship of plausibility and
  49, 60n4
proleptic argumentation 53–54, 60, 61n11;
  selecting cases by 97–100
Przeworski, Adam 59
psychiatric ward(s) 68, 71–73; British
  halfway community for ex-psychiatric
  patients 78; illness narratives of mental

health patients 126–130; partition of
  property space of nurses in *73*, 104n23;
  team ethnography 71, 113
purposive sample, term 23n16
purposive sampling 71
Putnam, Robert 87–89

qualitative approaches, quantitative and
  13–20
qualitative data analysis: categorization
  process in 123–126, 130; data collection
  phase 112–113; degree of perturbation
  117–118; illness narratives of mental
  health patients 126–130; impact of
  researchers in 118–121; logic of
  123–137; matrix on Doctor Venice's
  psychiatric interviews 132, *133*, 134;
  naturalistic data 119–120, 137n2;
  nature of 113–123; representations 4,
  117, *119*, 120–123, 124, 137n2, 138n8;
  reproductions 4, 117, *119*, 120–123,
  138n7; researcher's agency in action
  portrayal 118–119, *119*; sources of
  heterogeneity in 113–114; studying
  on-line discussion about Al-Qaeda
  130–131; Template Analysis 124–125
qualitative research: argumentation
  schemes for 60; book organization 2–5;
  community of inquiry 50–51, 53, 61n6,
  68, 95, 98, 101; context-sensitivity of
  data collection procedures 2, 28–30,
  36, 58, 124, 135; data collection 12–13;
  details-focalization 30–31; features of
  28–36; in-depth interviews study 114,
  115; lacking generalizability 38–39;
  lacking impersonality 37–38; lacking
  uniformity 38; map of methods *33*,
  33–36; mounting defence of 1–2;
  multivocality of the writing 31–36;
  orchestration between author and
  participants 19, 31, 144, 149; strengths
  of 36–37; weaknesses of 37–39
qualitative research design 64–66; acute
  psychiatric wards 71–73; critical case
  design 75, *76*, 78–83; eloquence of
  context studied 70–100; extreme-case
  design *76*, 94–97; most-different-
  systems design 75, *76*, 83–87; most-
  similar-system design *76*, 87–94;
  most-similar-systems design 75–76;
  phases in 64; relevance of research
  question 66–70, 103n10; selecting cases
  by proleptic argumentation 97–100;
  selection of observational instances 73–74;

Index 165

strategies for obtaining information-rich cases *76*; suitability of method 100–102
quantitative approaches, qualitative and 13–20
quantitative research, standardized questionnaire 114, *115*

Radcliffe-Brown, Alfred 151
Ramsay, Gilbert 130–131
range of authenticity 4, 5n2, 74, 104n21, 122
Rapley, Tim 28–29, 38, 113–114
Rashomon effect 41n21
Rathje, William 118, 120
Reed, Chris 2
reflexive account 4–5
reflexivity 4, 96, 149, 154–156, 158n9; account of 152–157; common sense and 123; definition of 5; expanding area of 149, 151, 155–156; multivocality of writing 31–32; purpose of reflexive account 156; reflection and 158n9
Reichertz, Jo 103n2
reliability 29, 40n7
reproductions 4, 117, *119*, 120–123, 138n7
research question(s): feasibility of 69; flexibility of 69; general principles of 69; originality of 67–69, 103n12; reciprocal adaptations *70*; relevance of 68–69
resource extraction, indigenous organizations against 89–94, *91*
Resta, Giovanna 120
Rhetoric (Aristotle) 3, 45, 56–57, 75
Rosaldo, Renato 145, 157n2
Rosenhan, David 37, 40n12, 107n53
Rossero, Eleonora 103n11
Rossman, Gretchen 103n9
Roth, Julius 123
Ruchatz, Jens 77
Runciman, Walter Garrison 91, 106n44

Saldaña, Johnny 132
sampling: design of properties space for 104n21; gaining eloquent sample 71; prehistory of quantitative strategies 104n15; procedures 16–17, 23n15; qualitative research 22n11; second-stage 16; *see also* data collection procedure(s)
Sander, Emmanuel 4, 123, 124, 139n17
Scheper-Hughes, Nancy 146
Schwandt, Thomas 20
Schwartz, Howard 65
Schwartz-Shea, Peregrine 19, 21n3

Scientific Method 20
Seale, Cleve 19
self-presentation 3, 4, 36, 143, 149, 153
Sen, Amartya 139n10
sensitization 3–4
sensitizing concepts 4, 14, 22n8, 29, 124, 125, 135
shadowing 12, 22n10, 27, *33*, 33–37, 36, 41n13, 112, 119, 131, 137n2, 139n21
Sharp, Victor 78–82
Sivertsson, Fredrik 96
Skinner, Burrhus Frederic 8
Sköldberg, Kaj 5, 152, 158n9
social capital 87–89, 92–93
social control hypothesis 78, 82
social mobilization 90–93
social research, qualitative and quantitative approaches 13–20
society, relevance of research question for *68*
sociological imagination, grammar of 68, 123, 139n17
sociology 9, 30; analysis of deviant practices in 104–105n24; purpose of 21n4; relevance of research question for *68*
Solow, Robert 66
sorites 27, 40n6
Sormano, Andrea 139n11
Sperber, Dan 10, 138n7
Star, Susan Leigh 103n2
Steffens, Lincoln 22n5
Steinhoff, Hans 34
Stevens, Stanley Smith 139n15
Stoller, Robert J. 95
Strauss, Anselm 22n13
straw-man fallacy 93, 106n45–46, 130
Symbolic Interactionism School 9
synaptic summation 150

Tavory, Iddo 66, 103n2, 103n10
team ethnography 38, 67–68; of psychiatric wards 71, 113; solo-ethnography or 101; *see also* ethnography
Tedlock, Barbara 147
Tedlock, Denis 146, 147
Template Analysis 124–125
Testa, Italo 51
Teune, Henry 59
textualization 143; multivocality of writing 143–151
theoretical inference 14
theoretical sampling 71
theoretical saturation procedure 15

166 *Index*

theory of argumentation 45–49, 132; abductive reasoning 45–49; *a fortiori* (with greater reason) argument 45; analogical reasoning 56–59, 61n17, 92, 105n26, 134, 139n20; argumentation schemes 54–59; argument by example 45; argument-from-analogy scheme 55, 61n17, 116–117; critical questions for argument-from-analogy scheme 55–57; double hierarchy argument 45; extended version of argument-from-analogy scheme 57–59, 116; knowledge construction 77; knowledge representing 77, 78; overview of 50–53; proleptic argumentation 53–54, 60, 61n11; relationship between probability and plausibility 49; schemes for qualitative research 60
Theory of argumentation Canadian School 1, 51–52
Thomas, William 9, 40n11
Thomas theorem 10
Thorndike, Edward Lee 8
Tilley, Christopher 113
Tilley, Nicholas 19
Timmermans, Stefan 66, 103n2, 103n10
Tindale, Christopher 61n9
Topolski, Jerzy 5n2, 74, 122
Toulmin, Stephen 50–51, 103n5
transferability, notion of 15, 105n26
theoretical saturation transparency 104n22
Tweety argument, Walton 52–53
Tyler, Stephen 146

uniformity, qualitative researching lacking 38

validity 29, 40n7
Van der Valk, Ineke 130
van Eemeren, Frans 51–52, 131
Vaughan, Diane 76, 139n19, 140n24–25
ventriloquism 148, 155
Verba, Sidney 80
Verheij, Bart 57
videotaping 35, 41n17
Virkki, Tuija 104n16
virtual data 35
visual autoethnography 34
Voice-Hearers 157n4
voluntary associations 87–89, 92

Walton, Douglas 1, 2, 47, 50, 51, 52, 53, 60n3
Watson, John Broadus 8
Weaver, Anna 123
Weber, Max 21n4, 135, 136, 149
Wentzel, Arnold 61n11, 61n21
Whyte, William Foote 153–155
Wikan, Unni 145
Williams, Bernard 21n2
Wisznienski, Wladek 40n11
Wittgenstein family resemblances 2, 27, 32, 39–40n5
Wittgenstein, Ludwig 2, 27, 39n5, 52, 100, 136
wolf metaphor 136
Wright, Stuart 137
Writing Culture, representation crisis in 145
Written by Voice (documentary) 157n4

Yanow, Dvora 19, 21n3

Zadeh, Lofty Askar 17
Znaniecki, Florian 9, 40n11